St. Louis, where he matured as merchant, bank director, corporation executive, land speculator, and progressive farmer. At his death in 1845, he left
a fortune large enough to excite envy
and exaggeration. But he left also the
foundation of what was to become Kansas City, the wagon trail he had blazed
through South Pass to the Far West,
a Jacksonian concept of free enterprise
in the Missouri of his time, and a name
that was not likely to perish even in a
machine age.

The Author

JOHN E. SUNDER, who is a member of
the faculty in history at the University
of Texas, shares some common ground
with Bill Sublette. He is a native of St.
Louis and has followed Sublette's career through all of the available court
records, public documents, and state
and federal archives. The result of his
interest is this first full-scale account of
this mountain man.

The jacket illustration was done by JOE
BEELER of Miami, Oklahoma. His western paintings are now in several private
collections as well as at the Gilcrease
Museum in Tulsa.

Bill Sublette: *Mountain Man*

Bill Sublette

MOUNTAIN
MAN

by John E. Sunder

NORMAN : UNIVERSITY OF OKLAHOMA PRESS

The Library of Congress has catalogued this book as follows:

Sunder, John Edward.
  Bill Sublette, mountain man. [1st ed.] Norman, University
of Oklahoma Press [1959]
  279 p.   illus.   24 cm.
  Includes bibliography.

  1. Sublette, William Lewis, 1799?–1845.

F592.S86S8   923.973   59–7492 ‡
Library of Congress

In Memoriam

Esther Whitley Burch

Preface

ALTHOUGH WILLIAM L. SUBLETTE'S career was one of the most significant to the history of our early nineteenth-century American West, the material pertinent to his life was too scattered for ready use until modern means of transportation and communication facilitated research. After brushing aside a certain amount of frontier mythology which has colored the available information on his life, I have sought to present Bill Sublette in relation to his family, to his Western contemporaries, to his heritage and his time. Explorer, fur trader, politician, merchant, bank director, corporation executive, land speculator, resort proprietor, and progressive farmer, he experienced in his diverse career both the highly civilized and the crudely uncivilized. The development of American geography, politics, business, and agriculture all bear the mark of his accomplishments.

Many individuals and institutions have made the biographer's task an easier one. All of them cannot be thanked in this preface, yet a few must be given the special attention they deserve. Guidance, patience, understanding, and the technique of historical research were the gifts of Professor Ralph P. Bieber, Western historian at Washington University, St. Louis. To the director and staff of the Missouri Historical Society, St. Louis, I express my deepest appreciation and recommend their mine of Western Americana to all devotees of the plains and the mountains. Innumerable bits of valuable information came from the Mercantile Library (St. Louis); the St. Louis Public Library; the State Historical Society of Missouri; the Bancroft Library; the Huntington Library; the Yale University Library (Coe Collection); the Filson Club Library; the Provincial Archives of British Columbia; the state historical societies of Kansas, Kentucky, Nebraska, New Mexico, New York, Oregon, and Pennsylvania; and the records of the federal government preserved in the National Archives. Many officials in charge of state, county, and municipal records in Missouri, Illinois, Kentucky, and California particularly were helpful.

Individual appreciation is due my friends at Washington University and the University of Texas who read all or parts of this manuscript and offered their welcome criticism. Mrs. Norris Davis, Austin, Texas, with funds provided by the University of Texas, produced a praiseworthy final typewritten draft. Last, but certainly not least, my thanks to my traveling companion—my mother—who accompanied me on many of my research jaunts to libraries and into the wilderness.

The errors of fact, interpretation, and topography are mine.

John E. Sunder

Austin, Texas
April 16, 1959

Contents

Illustrations

Maps

List of Abbreviations

To avoid excessive repetition, the following abbreviations have been used in the footnotes for manuscript collections.

AFC MSS: American Fur Company Account Books, 1822–1860, Missouri Historical Society, St. Louis.

Ashley MSS: Ashley, William Henry, Papers, 1811–1840, Missouri Historical Society, St. Louis.

Campbell MSS: Campbell, Robert, Papers, 1825–1879, Missouri Historical Society, St. Louis.

Campbell MSS (Semsrott): Campbell, Robert, Papers, 1832–1842, William H. Semsrott, St. Louis.

CC: County Court.

CCC: County Circuit Court.

Chouteau-Maffitt MSS: Chouteau-Maffitt Collection, 1828–1854, Missouri Historical Society, St. Louis.

Chouteau-Papin MSS: Chouteau-Papin Collection, 1753–1872, Missouri Historical Society, St. Louis.

Chouteau-Walsh MSS: Chouteau-Walsh Collection, 1794–1869, Missouri Historical Society, St. Louis.

Clark MSS, KHi: Clark, William, Papers, 1825–1832, Kansas State Historical Society, Topeka.

Clark MSS, MoSHi: Clark, William, Papers, 1766–1899, Missouri Historical Society, St. Louis.

CPC: County Probate Court.

CRDO: County Recorder of Deeds Office.

DMDI, MSS, MoSHi: Documents on Microfilm from the Records of the Department of the Interior now in the National Archives Relating to the Fur Trade of the Missouri River Area, 1823–1840, Missouri Historical Society, St. Louis.

Draper MSS (or MS): Draper Collection of Kentucky Manuscripts (Microfilms of the Draper Collection in the State Historical Society of Wisconsin), 1775–1845, Filson Club, Louisville.

Ermatinger MSS: Ermatinger, Edward, Letters, 1828–1856, Provincial Historical Society, Victoria, B. C.

Field Diary MSS: Field, M. C., Diary of 1843, Missouri Historical Society, St. Louis.

KHi: Kansas State Historical Society.

Larkin MSS: Larkin, Thomas O., Documents for the History of California. Papers of the Consul of the U. S. in California before the Conquest, Vols. III and IV, 1845–1846, Bancroft Library, Berkeley.

McLeod MSS: McLeod, John, Correspondence, 1812–1844, Provincial Historical Society, Victoria, B. C.

MoSHi: Missouri Historical Society, St. Louis, Missouri.

N. A.: National Archives, Washington, D. C.

PC: Probate Court.

P. Chouteau MSS: P. Chouteau Collections, 1823–1835, Missouri Historical Society, St. Louis.

Private Campbell MSS: Campbell, Papers, In Private hands, St. Louis.

Smith, MSS, KHi: Smith, Jedediah S., Letters, 1827–1831, Kansas State Historical Society, Topeka.

Sublette MSS: Sublette Family Papers, 1819–1860, Missouri Historical Society, St. Louis.

UMWMC: University of Missouri, Western Historical Manuscripts Collection, Columbia, Missouri.

Whitley MSS: Whitley Heirs (Sublette Estate), Papers, 1895–1907, John E. Sunder, Austin, Texas.

Bill Sublette: *Mountain Man*

Lincoln and Pulaski

J USTICE JOSEPH BLEADSOE of Lincoln County completed an entry in his register, smiled, and extended his congratulations to a newly married young couple. His brief civil ceremony united as husband and wife Phillip Allen Sublette and Isabella Whitley. Phillip, age twenty-three or twenty-four, recently had arrived at the county seat of Stanford, Kentucky, near the earlier site of St. Asaph's or Logan's Fort, there to select a livelihood and a wife. Isabella, a few months younger than her adventurous husband, had spent most of her life in Kentucky near Stanford, living at Walnut Flat and on Cedar Creek by the Wilderness Road. Since her older sister Elizabeth had married four years before, to Isabella this November 21, 1797, was not only a happy but a traditionally proper occasion.[1]

The year's harvest was gathered and there was a late autumn crispness in the air, brilliant color in the last leaves, and wisps of smoke rising from scores of homes in and around Stanford. The population of the settlement grew steadily, and throughout the county new families built homes and brought land under culti-

[1] Marriage Licenses, 1797–1800, MSS, Marriage Certificates, 1784–1836, MSS, Index to Marriages No. 1, 1784–1818, p. 270, MSS, Lincoln CC, Stanford, Kentucky; Ednah McAdams, *Kentucky Pioneer and Court Records,* 119.

vation. After General Anthony Wayne's victory at Fallen Timbers and close upon the even more recent Pinckney Treaty with Spain, it was evident that the West of the Ohio Valley, Kentucky, and Tennessee was to be a new Zion for the land-hungry men and women of New England, Virginia, and the Carolinas. Although Spain controlled Louisiana and England only slowly evacuated the Old Northwest, the spirit of immigrants reaching Kentucky and Tennessee, the youngest children of the federal union, was such as to overcome all those temporary difficulties.

Kentucky, between the Green and Cumberland rivers, was rich and well watered. Its soil, said to be "uncommonly favorable to hemp," tobacco, and all fruits, supported fields of wheat, corn, oats, and rye. An enterprising settler could gather wild "pecanes"; hunt quail, grouse, teal, and "summer duck"; and a lucky man might kill an elk in the hilly sections or find a buffalo on the headwaters of Green River or Licking Creek. Perch, trout, and softshelled turtles were proof that nature was as ample in its streams as in its forests.

The land would also support commercial enterprises. Maple sap, brought to perfection by frosty mornings and bright sunshine, could be gathered during a six weeks' period beginning each February. Its marketable by-products—molasses, vinegar, and spirits—provided extra income. Limestone, found everywhere, was calcined easily into excellent lime, and many of the settlers manufactured gunpowder from natural sulphur and nitre deposits. There also was sufficient clay for commercial brick making, and enough stone for millstones, grindstones, and building purposes.

Phillip A. Sublette, groom of the wedding party, had given up the tidewater security of Chesterfield County, Virginia, for the promise of life beyond the Cumberland Gap.[2] Some of his

2 In the Kentucky census of 1810, Phillip was listed as being between twenty-six and forty-five years of age. In the census records for St. Charles County, Missouri, for 1817 and 1819, he was listed as being between the ages of eighteen and forty-five. Isabella Whitley, his wife, was born in 1774. Since her sister stated to Lyman C. Draper that Phillip was older than Isabella, it is almost certain that he was born in 1773 or 1774, and must have been only a few

French Huguenot relatives had settled in Woodford County north of Stanford, and others considered migrating to Kentucky. A few of them had military land grants in the state. Phillip had no such grant, but was reasonably well educated, shrewd, and energetic and did not intend to sustain his family solely from the soil. Instead of going to Stanford, he could have gone to Bardstown, a prominent center of settlement; to Danville, the old political marketplace; to Louisville, which gave "indications of the importance it was ultimately to attain"; or perhaps even to Lexington, the "metropolis of the pioneers." Lexington claimed sixteen hundred inhabitants and outranked all western communities, including Cincinnati and Pittsburgh.

Stanford was not equal to Lexington or Bardstown, but it was centrally located. Lincoln County held inviting agricultural possibilities even a part-time farmer could scarcely overlook. It was located on the dividing line between the bluegrass and mountain areas, and its soil benefited from plentiful rainfall. Prevailing southerly winds blew across the "towering hills and valleys" in the south down upon the lower hills and rolling countryside to the north. Hundreds of those acres belonged to Isabella Whitley's family—a family that together with the Logans and Shelbys formed the more conservative natural aristocracy of the region.

Phillip's marriage to Isabella placed him in close contact with one of Kentucky's most influential men: Colonel William Whitley, his wife's father and his new father-in-law. Colonel Whitley approved of his daughter's marriage to the stranger from Virginia and may have provided the newlyweds a home for their first years of married life, since Phillip neither bought any of the acreage available in Lincoln County at that time nor built a new home for his bride.[3] If he did move into the Whitley home, he found himself in one of the social and political centers of the Transylvania region. Guests, arriving and departing at frequent intervals, imparted a cosmopolitan atmosphere to the inviting family fireside.

months older than his wife. See also *Genealogy and History*, February 15, 1947, for Phillip's approximate place of birth.

[3] Marriage Licenses, 1797–1800, MSS, Lincoln CC.

The tall, two-story, brick Whitley home, one of the most impressive structures in all Kentucky, stood two miles south of Stanford well back from the Wilderness Road atop a low hill. The simple, brick exterior walls contained small windows set high above the ground for better defense against marauding Indians. Over the front entrance were the light-brick initials of Colonel Whitley; over the rear door those of his wife, Esther Fullen Whitley. In this house Phillip courted and won Isabella, and to it following their wedding we may presume they were conducted for a celebration in the large third-floor ballroom frequently used for dances and quilting bees.[4]

The interior of the house contained fascinating architectural and decorative effects. Each of the twenty-three steps on the main stairway was "ornamented with the head of an [hand-carved] eagle, bearing an olive branch in its mouth." On the third floor was a secret hiding place for women and children, originally built as protection against Indians, and a portion of the basement was called the "dungeon." Window glass for the house had been brought in by pack animals from Virginia, and there was said to be a long, narrow escape tunnel from the interior to a small nearby spring.

Colonel and Mrs. Whitley built the house in the late 1780's or early 1790's on their Cedar Creek land grant, after giving up an earlier residence at Walnut Flat, and on an adjoining hill marked off one of the first racetracks in Kentucky. Neighbors referred to their estate as "Sportsman's Hill" and flocked to the races whenever they were scheduled. Barbecues were held on the lawn of the house—one in 1794, in honor of the Colonel's success in an Indian campaign. As a major in the Sixth Militia Regiment he played a prominent role in the Indian actions of his day and won an enviable reputation as a fighter.[5]

---

[4] The Whitley home was built on the left (west) fork of the Wilderness Road, also called "Logan's Trace" [Trail], as it wound its way northward from the Crab Orchard, located eleven and one-half miles south of Stanford.

[5] Lewis Collins, *History of Kentucky*, I, 512; Charles G. Talbert, "William Whitley, 1749–1813," *Filson Club History Quarterly*, Vol. XXV (April, 1951), 102, 105, 107, 110; Draper MS, 9 CC 1–2.

During the frequent absences of the elder Whitley, his wife Esther, a woman reputedly "fully worthy" of him, was in charge of the vast household, slaves, stock, and farmlands. Her greatest responsibility, however, either with or without Colonel Whitley's presence, was the brood of younger Whitleys, of which Isabella was the last one born in Virginia before her parents moved to Kentucky at the time of Lexington and Concord. Eight more brothers and sisters were born before Isabella's marriage: Levisa, Solomon, William, Jr., Andrew, Esther, Mary (Polly), Nancy, and Sally, and one, Ann, in 1802. Such a large family filled the Whitley household with more than its share of activity and provided Phillip prospects of an ever growing group of "in-laws."[6]

Phillip and Isabella resided in Lincoln County nearly three years before they decided to move southward to the territory along the Cumberland River. By that time Isabella's first child was born.[7] As one of the first of the Whitley grandchildren and a boy at that, he was called William Lewis Sublette in honor of his grandfather Whitley and granduncle Lewis Sublette. Exact proof of the place of his birth on September 21, 1799, probably would reveal one of the two large bedchambers on the second floor of the aristocratic Whitley home—a comfortable beginning for a future frontiersman.

The news of William's birth may not have reached his father's family for some time. Phillip's parents, Littleberry and Sarah Burton Sublette, and his brothers had reached Woodford County by 1796. They remained there a short time with Littleberry's brother Lewis before moving south to the Green River. There, on the Green, Littleberry entered a land certificate for two hun-

[6] Family Bible of William Whitley, Jr., Filson Club Library, Louisville, Kentucky; Draper MSS, 9 CC 3–4; 9 CC 5–6; 9 CC 12–13; 9 CC 19; 18 S 184.

[7] Field Diary, Entry of September 21, 1843, MSS; Stella M. Drumm, "William Lewis Sublette," in *Dictionary of American Biography*, XVIII, 189. Miss Drumm gives 1799 as William's date of birth with a question mark. After examination of the Lincoln County census of 1810, the census records of 1817 and 1819 for St. Charles, Missouri, the Benjamin Emmons MSS in the Missouri Historical Society, and the records of the Department of State of the United States, it seems that Miss Drumm's original contention is accurate and should be accepted until more conclusive proof is available.

dred acres on the "South side of Green River," on "Greasy Creek waters of Little Barren," and on the north side of "Jones's Military Survey."[8]

Green River, which flowed through the center of Green County, was noted for the beauty, color, and depth of its water. Geologists believe the stream was once a subterranean one whose ceiling wore away and caved in, bringing the water to the surface. The narrow, peaceful valley was overhung with willows and sycamores and bordered by "low corn bottoms" which beckoned new settlers. Yet the soil of the bottoms was depleted easily, so much so that it was common, in the nineteenth century, to speak of an angular woman as "bony as the hips of a Green River cow."

Littleberry Sublette died in 1800, shortly after bringing most of his family to Green County. His widow Sarah, the mother of Phillip and paternal grandmother of William Lewis Sublette, remarried in 1803 to Jonathan Smith also of Green County. Her children, Phillip's brothers and at least one sister, remained in Green County with their mother and new stepfather until after the War of 1812, when some of them joined the westward migration to Missouri. Two of the boys, Littleberry Sublette, Jr., and Joseph Burton, were apprenticed by their mother as saddlemaker and tanner-currier. Three other children are known to have been of the family: Hill (Hilly), Samuel, and Lenious Bolin. There also may have been two more: Edith and Maston. Not only Isabella, but Phillip Sublette as well, could claim a large family of brothers and sisters.[9]

When young William was scarcely a year old, his parents left the Whitleys and started south to the tiny settlement of Somerset in the new county of Pulaski. Wealth in Pulaski County was based on land, the products of the land, and the services which could be rendered those who lived on or exploited the

---

[8] Surveys—Green County, No. 662, p. 215, MSS, Green CC, Greensburg, Kentucky.

[9] Deed Books 4, pp. 75, 91–92; 6, pp. 136, 138, 143; 7, p. 35; 8, pp. 327–28, MSS, Green CC. Note also Deed Book A, p. 423, MSS, Adair CC, Columbia, Kentucky.

land. Population boomed in the area, and speculation along the fertile Cumberland River, as well as the usual business and political positions to be acquired in a new region, called Phillip with a powerful voice.

The Sublette family made the journey of under fifty miles from Stanford to Somerset before the late spring of 1801, when William was not yet two years old.[10] The road to Somerset passed through high, wooded hills where deer, fox, squirrel, and turkey abounded and where herds of medium-sized, semiwild pigs rooted for food. Isabella, with William in her arms, rode in the wagon. Phillip, assisted by a slave, guided the horses along the bumpy road. A dependable slave and good horses were assets to one's community standing in early nineteenth-century Kentucky. A fine saddle horse was worth over one hundred dollars, and Kentuckians had bred and trained them for years. In early winter it was not unusual to see herds of twenty to thirty being driven from Lexington to Charleston.[11]

Upon reaching Somerset, the family found only a few houses standing on the townsite, but the families living in those already erected were busy at the loom and in the fields. Suffice to say, the Sublettes either moved in with another family or built a temporary shelter of their own until they could construct a house. When the tax assessor made his rounds in May, 1801, they were still without land, although they had added another horse to their possessions. By the following spring of 1802, however, they had purchased "town lotts" upon which they built a home. Meanwhile, the family expanded at a steady pace. A second son Milton Green, later known as the "thunderbolt of the Rockies," was born in 1801, during the family's transition period, followed by Sophronia Fullen in 1805, another daughter, Mary (Polly), in 1806 or 1807, and Andrew Whitley in 1808 or 1809.[12]

[10] Pulaski County Tax List, 1801, MSS, Kentucky Historical Society.

[11] *Ibid.*; Lincoln County Tax Lists, 1799, 1800, MSS, Kentucky Historical Society; François André Michaux, *Travels to the West of the Alleghany Mountains*, in Reuben G. Thwaites (ed.), *Early Western Travels 1748–1846*, III, 234, 243–46.

[12] Pulaski County Tax Lists, 1801, 1802, MSS, Kentucky Historical Society. These dates are approximate and are based upon 1810 census returns for Lincoln

Isabella was busy with toddling William and babe-in-arms Milton in April, 1802, when Phillip, to support his family, opened an "ordinary" at "his dwelling house in the town of Somerset." The location of his house on the main square of the county seat aided his business prospects, since he could draw upon the traveling trade and the flow of courthouse business. A hard-working frontier lot, the people of Kentucky loved "gaming and liquors," and their taverns of logs and stone were an important part of the community—centers for the exchange of gossip and news and the gathering place of impromptu assemblies and entertainers. Public houses were crowded, especially at court time, when lawsuits might momentarily replace horses, crops, and the weather as topics of conversation.[13]

Phillip's family background recommended him to traveling Virginians: he was son-in-law to one of the most noted men of Kentucky, he soon knew the leaders of Pulaski County, and he was to hold several public offices. Isabella, keeping house at the same location, devoted her spare moments to her husband's business. She provided the pleasant atmosphere neighbors and travelers liked to find in a gracious hostess, and her son William spent long hours underfoot, "taking in" the stories of tavern guests and western travelers.

Governmental functions in Kentucky were concentrated largely in the hands of the county court, which in many ways was a limited corporation admitting but few interested, prominent citizens. As a prospective officeholder Phillip was not one to shirk public duty and served on the second committee appointed to plan the town and locate, let out, and superintend public buildings. The same year, 1801, he served as an election clerk and the next year, on the basis of his dependability and evident ambition, was appointed a deputy sheriff and keeper of

County, 1817 and 1819 census returns for St. Charles County, testimony given before the Supreme Court of Missouri, and records in the courthouses of St. Charles County, Missouri, and Pulaski County, Kentucky.

[13] Orders No. 1, 1799–1803, p. 298, and No. 2, 1804–15, p. 1, MSS, Pulaski CC, Somerset, Kentucky. To "keep ordinary" included providing food and drink, but seldom lodging. Lodging was secured at a "tavern."

the county jail. He remained as jailor for two years and, incidentally, was in charge of stray stock—a profitable side line if the owners failed to appear.[14]

Phillip—scarcely thirty—moved up in the ranks. In 1803 he served for a short time as clerk of the Circuit Court of Pulaski and Wayne counties and in the summer took the oath as a Pulaski County justice of the peace. Two years later he was designated a deputy surveyor and on April 1, 1807, crowned his career as a good Jeffersonian Republican: he was appointed federal postmaster at Somerset, which position he held until New Year's Day, 1810—a three-year assignment. Postmaster and tavern keeper was not an unusual combination in that day, and his rapid rise within the county hierarchy was ample proof of the "social institution" that was the county courthouse.[15]

To add to his income and position, Phillip, within a year after he reached Somerset, began to buy lands along the Cumberland in his own name and in the names of his close friends and wife's relatives. In Kentucky, as in Pennsylvania and Virginia, the land was divided, on the basis of tree-coverage, into three classes for tax assessment. Lists of lands to be sold at auction were carried regularly in local newspapers, and anyone with a little reserve capital could purchase hundreds of acres. Low land taxes and his appointment as deputy surveyor helped him secure control of large tracts along most of the important waterways near Somerset. On only one occasion was he taken to court in a land dispute, but his tavern business and slaveholdings brought him into court in twenty-five additional cases. Most of the litigation he won, but the amount of time spent in court was somewhat staggering.[16]

He had good reason to foresee a general rise in land prices. Corn harvests were plentiful, and farmers were converting corn into meal to be sold in New Orleans at four to five dollars per

[14] Orders No. 1, 1799–1803, pp. 104, 244, 276, 298, 315, and No. 2, 1804–15, p. 184, MSS, Pulaski CC.
[15] Orders No. 1, 1799–1803, pp. 184, 399, and No. 2, 1804–15, p. 131, MSS, Pulaski CC; Alma O. Tibbals, *A History of Pulaski County, Kentucky*, 84.
[16] Pulaski County Tax Lists, 1802, 1803–1804, 1806–1809, MSS, Kentucky Historical Society.

ninety-six-pound barrel. There was a growing market for tobacco, hemp, and flax, and grazing lands were needed for milch
cows and for the great herds of horned cattle driven in lots of
two or three hundred eastward to markets in Philadelphia and
Baltimore. Land fit for orchards provided a source of peach
brandy, of which "there was a great consumption," and land
containing salt licks was suited to exploitation by the pork-pack-
ing industry.

William, as the oldest child and "big brother" to the other
children, doubtless knew something of his father's land speculation, although there were many other more interesting projects
for inquisitive young minds and busy hands. Public education was
almost an unknown institution at Somerset, where any education
had to wait until the bare necessities of life were first won. William received little formal schooling—his poor spelling provides
ample proof that he was given little training. He did learn basic
mathematics, however, and wrote legibly. Perhaps his parents
taught him the fundamentals. On the other hand, in his many
free hours, he and the other children could explore the countryside and discover farm animals or the small denizens of the forest
who, then as now, offered unlimited interest for small children,
or they might daub themselves with the red clay of Pulaski
for a rollicking game of "Indians."

In the colder months when activities were confined indoors,
there might be candy pullings. Winter was the season for dances
and whatever games could be improvised for snowy or rainy
weather. At Christmastime there might be visits from the Whitleys
or perhaps from a Sublette traveling in the locality. In the evenings about the fire Phillip could tell them fascinating stories of
land-grabbers and speculators, of surveying trips, of escaped
slaves, of the first days in Somerset, and of how he served the
county years before most of them could remember.[17]

Early in the spring of 1810—in April at the very latest—the
Sublettes packed their belongings and set out to return to Lin-

[17] Tibbals, *op. cit.*, 4. Tax lists for Pulaski County prove that at certain
intervals the Whitleys had land investments there.

coln County.[18] The reason for the move is unknown, but Phillip's legal difficulties and the incorporation of Somerset as a town that year may have played upon his wandering spirit. There is also the possibility that his land speculation was not as profitable as expected or that Isabella was anxious to return to her family. Whatever the reason, they rented or leased their lots, home, and tavern in Somerset and after farewells to the neighbors took a last look at the log houses along Spring Street, at the tannery and wagonmakers, and slowly started northward over the branches of Pitman and Buck creeks. It was "green-up time" in Kentucky when the redbud, dogwood, bloodroot, mountain violets, and spring-flowering anemones turn the countryside into a patch quilt of color. It was also a memorable experience, the season notwithstanding, for the Sublette children, who after the short journey found themselves close to the branches of Cedar Creek in the land of their grandparents.[19]

Lincoln County, generally speaking, offered more of the traditional comforts of life than did Pulaski. There were better educational opportunities, there was a local newspaper, the *Lamp*, begun in 1808, and there was also more extensive religious activity for those so inclined. Colonel Whitley was a Presbyterian as was his wife, but it was said by some that she was really a Baptist, "as were several of her children." Tradition had it that Presbyterian meetings had been held in the Whitley home before a church was built either at Walnut Flat or in Stanford. Later, in 1812, the South District Association of Baptists met in Lincoln, showing the religious importance of the county.[20]

Phillip took up fifty acres of second- or third-rate land along the narrow, winding Dix River, noted locally for its large boul-

[18] Order Book No. 7, 1809–19, p. 40, MSS, Lincoln CC. The Lincoln County tax list for 1810 reported four horses in Phillip's possession, more than enough for transportation purposes from Somerset.

[19] Tibbals, *op. cit.*, 7, 167; Order Book No. 3, 1810–15, pp. 5, 76, 80, 87, 110, 119, MSS, Pulaski CCC. Phillip's town lots in Somerset had decreased in value from $62 in 1803 to $50 in 1808. There is no record that he sold the lots in 1810, when he left for Lincoln County.

[20] Draper MS, 18 S 195; *Minutes of the South District Association of Baptists . . . in Lincoln County, on the third Saturday in August, 1812.*

ders and flat limestone slabs protruding above the surface of its waters. By 1812, he was settled with his family in a house at the Crab Orchard. The little community then comprised a few scattered buildings, not as yet known as a town, approximately two miles southeast of the Whitley house. The Crab Orchard, so called for the immense forest of wild apple trees in its vicinity, had been until quite recently a meeting place for travelers planning to journey east along the Wilderness Road to the Holston River settlements. Between 1788 and 1796, 115 organized groups gathered there for mutual protection against the Indians in their eastward trek. Colonel Whitley, at his Walnut Flat–Cedar Creek location, at times provided supplies to travelers and was active in improving the road.

The Sublette children, now settled at the Crab Orchard, were close enough to make daily visits to their grandparents, young aunts, and uncles. They could participate in holiday festivities at the Whitleys', such as that held on the Fourth of July, 1812, when upwards of one thousand persons gathered about a tall liberty pole erected on the Whitley grounds. They could see the races at Sportsman's Hill, where some of the best horseflesh ran at dawn while the owners and onlookers ate, drank, and wagered. In addition to public celebrations there were also more intimate affairs of family interest: the marriage of William Whitley, Jr., in 1811, and the birth of at least five Whitley grandchildren, including three, Sally, Pinckney, and Solomon Perry, in the Sublette household.[21]

Shortly after the return of the Sublettes to Lincoln County, the aging Colonel dictated his memoirs to Phillip, who acted as his scribe and hence preserved for future generations details of the elder Whitley's life. "Tall, his features strongly marked, hair sandy, light eyes, prominent aquiline nose—somewhat vain," the Colonel "carried in his gun a big charge, and put in 2 bullets." His memoirs complete, he marched off to the War of 1812 as

[21] *Reporter* (Lexington), July 18, 1812; Index to Marriages No. 1, p. 331, MSS, Lincoln CC; Family Bible of William Whitley, Jr., Filson Club Library, Louisville.

a volunteer in Colonel Richard Johnson's Mounted Regiment and was killed, October 5, 1813, in the Battle of the Thames near where Tecumseh fell.[22]

His will was probated that winter, and Isabella's share of his estate was a tract of thirty acres. Those acres, added to her husband's Dix River parcel and holdings in slaves and stock, gave the Sublettes a fair nucleus for farming. Two of the boys, William and Milton, were old enough to be quite useful farm hands. The brunt of labor, however, was never placed upon their shoulders, since Phillip, although a member of "Company & Ridgment 7" of the local militia during the war, had not trudged away to active service.[23]

A few weeks before the outbreak of hostilities, in March, 1812, he opened his second tavern. This one was at his house at the Crab Orchard, where he was to provide "good, wholesome lodging and diet for travellers, and stablage or pasturage for horses," and was forbidden, incidentally, to "permit any unlawful gaming in his house, nor suffer any person to drink more than is necessary, or at any time suffer any scandalous behavior to be practiced. . . ." Prices on basic commodities were high at that time, and he was enjoined to post a current list.[24]

Travelers told their friends of the new inn at the Crab Orchard, and at least one patron left a "Red Morocco Pocket Book" there, for whose owner Phillip advertised in the Lexington *Reporter*. The editor of the paper was a friend of his, and the two men corresponded on subjects as varying as apprenticeship and "copias rock." As might be expected on the basis of previous events in Somerset, Phillip soon found himself a party to cases in the Lincoln County Court, most of them involving the tavern and his land.[25]

[22] Draper MSS, 9 CC 61; 16 CC 294; 17 CC 200; 18 S 195.

[23] Deed Record I, 1817–19, p. 167, MSS, Lincoln CC; Lincoln County Tax Lists, 1810, 1812–15, 1817, MSS, Kentucky Historical Society; Order Book No. 7, 1809–19, p. 43, MSS, Lincoln CC.

[24] P. A. Sublette to the Commonwealth, March, 1812, Tavern Bonds, 1810–17, MSS, Lincoln CC; J. Winston Coleman, Jr., *Stage-Coach Days in the Bluegrass*, 56.

[25] At least three important cases may be noted in the Lincoln County Cir-

Meanwhile, the children grew into adolescence, and their years spent at the Crab Orchard were enjoyable ones. There was a swimming hole in the spring-fed Crab Orchard Lake, fish to be caught in the streams, enough horses to ride, and the usual rural pastimes: corn shuckings and hunting for the boys; apple-peelings and rag-tackings for the girls. The younger children could chase gray squirrels out of the garden patch, and for young and old alike there were always endless household chores and services for travelers at the tavern.

The postwar migration to the Trans-Mississippi West caught the Sublettes in its current scarcely five years after Phillip opened his Crab Orchard business. Late in 1816 or early in 1817, he decided to pull up stakes for a third time and join the trek to Missouri Territory. Eight million acres of bounty lands then were under survey in Missouri and Illinois; the distribution of the Missouri military grants was expected momentarily; and published accounts of the new West, available in newspapers and at bookstores in Kentucky, offered glittering inducements for migration. To a man with an eye for enterprise and profit—and Phillip had just that—Missouri would be hard to overlook.

One of the Whitleys, a cousin Thomas, had settled at Portage des Sioux, St. Charles County, Missouri. He held seventy-one fertile acres in the town's common field and may have written his Kentucky relatives of his good fortune.[26] In contrast, forces then affecting Kentucky's economic life were not uniformly bright. The opening of the Ohio and Mississippi rivers to steamboat traffic was an important factor. When one steamer, the "Enterprise," came up from New Orleans to Louisville in 1816, its twenty-five-day journey fired public imagination. There was soon "lively interest" in new river trade "and . . . prospects of unparalleled . . . prosperity."[27]

cuit Court. *James Stewart* v. *P. A. Sublette*, and *McCutching* v. *P. A. Sublette* appear in Ordinary 1811–12, MSS, and *John Davis* v. *P. A. Sublette* appears in Ordinary 1815, MSS.

[26] The St. Charles County, Missouri, Circuit Court has in its possession a file (No. 6079) which is the case of *Melvin, Clark etc.* v. *LeClaire.* The case mentions in numerous instances a United States land grant to Thomas Whitley in April, 1816. Whitley died in 1820.

The bluegrass area, centered at Lexington, which was the old distribution hub for the region of the state drained by the Kentucky and Licking rivers, began to decline in economic power as Louisville gained. As commercial artery of the bluegrass section, the Wilderness Road experienced an eclipse, and business located near the trail suffered accordingly. Actually, the regional business collapse began in 1818, moved forward quickly, and joined the economic forces precipitating the Panic of 1819 and its subsequent national depression.

Never had there been a greater influx into Missouri than in the predepression years 1816–1818. Like a "mountain torrent" settlers poured across the Mississippi "faster than it was possible to provide corn for breadstuff." Nor was this flood all the flotsam of the Republic; many were respectable people drawn by the magnet of opportunity. Ensnared as he was in the avalanche of favorable reports from the West, in an economic period of trouble descending upon the bluegrass, in the band-wagon psychology of migration, and in his own gypsy-like, opportunistic nature, Phillip prepared to move his family.

He settled some of his pending court cases in Lincoln and Pulaski counties, and Isabella sold her land to her brother Andrew. The sale was on August 4, 1817, and by November 19, the family reached St. Charles, Missouri, after a late summer or early autumn journey. Solomon Whitley, Isabella's oldest brother, seems to have accompanied them westward. He had the same urge to settle beyond the Mississippi. Although he held land in Kentucky, he considered it second in importance to prospects in Missouri and went west to prepare the way for his wife and children.[28]

Phillip, Isabella, Solomon, and the children left the Crab Orchard and its familiar landmarks: the Whitley home and the houses and stores, courthouse and post office of Stanford. They passed Bright's Inn on the trail north of town and headed over-

[27] *Reporter* (Lexington), January 10, 31, 1816, April 23, 1817.

[28] Order Book No. 3, 1810–15, p. 76, Order Book No. 4, 1816–20, pp. 97, 115, 167, 472, and Order Book No. 5, 1820–23, pp. 261–62, 266, 268, 380–81, MSS, Pulaski CCC; Order Book, 1819–20 (*Josiah Evans* v. *P. A. Sublette*), MSS, Lincoln CC; Deed Record I, 1817–19, p. 167, MSS, Lincoln CC.

land to the northwest. The smaller children rode in the wagon with their mother, but William and Milton were old enough to assist their father with the stock. Time has destroyed whatever record they may have left of their journey, but all families moving westward from central Kentucky at that time had the choice of two principal routes: by land all the way through Kentucky, Indiana, and Illinois; or by land to the Ohio River, then by water down its alternating strong and sluggish current to the Mississippi. The land route to Louisville passed through Danville, southwest of the rapid Dix River. Danville contained two hundred homes, six stores, several small factories, and a printing office and was a community rich in memories for Isabella, since the town had sheltered the legislature of 1797 in which her father served.[29]

Beyond Danville were Harrodsburg, Bardstown, and the "village" of Louisville, located on a narrow plain rising above the Ohio River. The broad Ohio was one place to transfer your belongings to a flatboat if you intended to go west by water, or, if you preferred, there were ferry crossings to southern Indiana where the road continued north and west. Land travel the entire distance relieved a family of the "sad monotony" of mosquito-ridden swamps along the lower Ohio and of the currents of the Mississippi, "extremely difficult and dangerous" in places.[30]

The wagon road in Indiana, from Louisville to Vincennes, was crowded with emigrants in 1817, as "caravan after caravan" passed over the high, rolling hills towards the flatter lands of Illinois. There were a few inns along the way, but many of the local settlers looked upon travelers as intruders who could best avoid trouble by keeping on the move. The settlement at Vincennes was scattered over the flood plain of the Wabash in "badly laid out" manner. Half-drunk Indians frequently encamped near the town, adding public disorder to its other problems: swamp fever and growing pains.

To the west were recently settled areas of Illinois and sec-

[29] Edmund E. Dana, *Geographical Sketches of the Western Country*, 97; Collins, *op. cit.*, II, 776.

[30] Dana, *op. cit.*, 101–102; Timothy Flint, *Recollections of the Last Ten Years*, 83–84, 125.

tions of the trail considered too dangerous for individual travel. Through swamps and rich bottoms the trails cut their way via wagon ruts and notches on the trees. Yet, all important trails and roads, whether from Kaskaskia to Illinoistown or Edwardsville, from Shawneetown to Alton, or from Vincennes and points east to Edwardsville and Alton, eventually deposited their tired travelers at the Mississippi River ferry landings.

Before mid-November, 1817, the Sublettes reached the St. Louis–St. Charles area. It was not unusual then for thirty or forty families a day to arrive in that country. Some of them planned to winter in western Illinois; others were determined to move immediately into Missouri. Whether by land or water, the Sublette family's journey of several hundred miles was drawing to a close. They must have been anxious to reach their destination. Eighteen-year-old William may well have been the most anxious, since he was entering manhood and of all the eight children would be the first one most likely to strike out on his own beyond the Father of Waters.

St. Charles on the Missouri

Missouri territory in 1817 included nine counties. Six of them, the most heavily populated, bordered the right bank of the Mississippi north of Louisiana. One branch of scattered Missouri settlements pointed directly westward up the Missouri Valley into the Boon's Lick country, and another budding branch reached northwest to Salt River. St. Louis, the administrative center of the territory, stood astride the main route of east-west immigration. The city's thirty-five hundred to six thousand people congregated in a two-mile area along the river, parallel to which ran the streets, all "verry Narrow and not verry Straight." The old Creole life of St. Louis was changing to assimilate incoming American stock. A rapid cultural evolution was underway, noticeable in religion in a new Presbyterian congregation, in architecture in the substitution of American-style brick buildings for the older garden-enclosed homes of wood and stone, and especially in enlivened commercial enterprise. Beyond the streets on the high ground behind the town were stone forts dating from the Spanish period: remains of an earlier Mississippi Valley empire.[1]

[1] Marie G. Windell (ed.), "The Road West in 1818, the Diary of Henry Vest Bingham," *Missouri Historical Review*, Vol. XL (January, 1946), 182; Prentiss Ingraham (ed.), *Seventy Years on the Frontier*, 17; *The Emigrant's Guide, or Pocket Geography of the Western States and Territories*, 204.

A few miles north of St. Louis near the junction of the Mississippi and Missouri rivers was St. Charles County. Its county seat, St. Charles, was a town nearly as old as St. Louis. Between the two settlements flourished farms and lesser communities. There were old French homesteads, a church, and a convent in the Florissant Valley—a valley of extremely fertile blacklands, richly covered with hazel bushes, prairie plum, and crab apple trees. There was an American settlement at Bonhomme, west-northwest of St. Louis, and, of course, there was the military post, Fort Bellefontaine, on the right-hand side of the Missouri River to the east of St. Charles.

Whenever an overland immigrant party arrived opposite St. Louis or opposite the northeastern tip of St. Charles County, it could select any one of several crowded ferries operating into Missouri, all commanded by men anxious to profit from the "very catchin" Missouri-settlement fever. If an immigrant family crossed directly to St. Charles County, it landed on rich, flat, bottom lands extending inland to the "Mamelles" or river bluffs, on the edge of which was located the town of St. Charles. If, however, an immigrant family crossed to St. Louis and intended to proceed to St. Charles, it was necessary to traverse St. Louis County to a ferry on the Missouri River opposite St. Charles. At that place the river was not as turbulent as it was a short distance downstream. The ferry consisted of two canoes bound together by a two-inch plank, but served its purpose despite dangers of adverse wind and wave.

Phillip, Isabella, and their brood reached St. Charles in 1817, before the colder days of late autumn and early winter. If they journeyed by land, they may have been part of one of the many large companies described by Timothy Flint:

> From the Mamelles I have looked over the subjacent plain quite to the ferry, where the immigrants crossed the Upper Mississippi. I have seen in this extent nine wagons harnessed with from four to six horses. We may allow a hundred cattle, besides hogs, horses, and sheep,

to each wagon; and from three or four to twenty slaves
... the wagons often carrying two to three tons, so
loaded that the mistress and children are strolling care-
lessly along ... the whole group occupies three quarters
of a mile.[2]

The more permanent settlers in St. Charles were mostly
French, but there was a new sprinkling of Anglo-Americans, and
that autumn the immigrant tide was near flood proportion. The
town was "crowded with the refuse of Kentucky," as Flint again
noted and added in disgust: "Fighting, maiming, the most horrid
blaspheming, thieving, & every species of riot & outrage [were]
the order of the day & night." But what could an observer expect
in a sea rough with social and economic change?

Any new family in St. Charles could see at a glance that the
countryside, which supported several "handsome houses with
gardens and orchards," was productive; and that the town might,
from its healthy location, continue to grow and prosper. Certainly
the community then had only six to twelve hundred permanent
residents, many of whom lived on either side of a mile-long
main street wedged between the Missouri River and the bluffs.
Yet there was a flourishing provision trade, and the main street
was part of the crowded Boon's Lick Trail. The *Missouri Ga-*
zette predicted that the town would "undoubtedly become a place
of considerable importance" from the water-borne commerce of
its nearby rivers and from its trade in agricultural commodities
and furs.

Old St. Charles, just as old St. Louis, was being American-
ized. Indian danger, common in the area during the War of 1812,
was no longer an immediate threat, and both a courthouse and a
post office added prestige to the little settlement. In fact, it would
soon become the new state's temporary political center. By June,
1821, the legislature met in quarters on the south side of Main
Street. Nearby was the modest secretary of state's office in the
midst of the town's commercial whirl.

[2] Flint, *op. cit.,* 201.

Living conditions were so crowded in 1817 that the Sublettes temporarily may have had to share quarters with another family, a not uncommon practice. Possibly, if such were the case, they occupied one of the old rambling French homes, so known for their broad, sloping roofs, long verandas, and upright, timbered walls. Although on one occasion there was enough snow on the ground to afford good sleighing, the winter of 1817–18, was not extremely cold, wet, or uncomfortable.[3]

By the following summer they rented or otherwise procured the use of a town house, lot, and stable room for their horses and cattle. There is no conclusive proof that they ever bought land in the town, yet the inventory of Isabella's estate suggestively mentions "1 lot on the Commans."[4] Another inventory, that of her husband's estate, mentions still another tract, reportedly the "unused half of a prempttion Right [bordering the Mississippi River] Laying opposot the mouth of the Illinois River in the Point," in Portage des Sioux Township where Thomas Whitley had settled. The Fourteenth Congress of the United States provided for pre-emption in the area, and distribution was made after January, 1819.[5]

Quite possibly Phillip Sublette secured his pre-emption right from someone else by sale or exchange, a not unusual practice at a time when towns were laid out without regard to population sufficiency, and when "the rage in speculation . . . in lands was at the highest" and "there were people who offered immense tracts of land, the titles to which were contingent, and only in prospect."[6] Exactly when or how the land was acquired is difficult to state, but two parcels in Portage des Sioux Township bear comparison with the tract mentioned, and it is interesting to note that in 1857, Robert Campbell, William L. Sublette's executor,

[3] St. Charles Census Record, 1817, MSS, St. Charles CC, St. Charles, Missouri; James Kennerly to G. C. Sibley, December 19, 1817, Sibley Family Papers, 1803–53, MSS; Lindenwood College, St. Charles, Missouri.

[4] File of Estate of Isabella Sublette, No. 3419, MSS, St. Charles CPC.

[5] File of Estate of Phillip A. Sublette, No. 3420, MSS, St. Charles CPC.

[6] Flint, op. cit., 198–99; James Kennerly to G. C. Sibley, December 19, 1817, Sibley Family Papers, 1803–53, MSS, Lindenwood College.

sold for his estate land in St. Charles County. The sale may have been unrelated to the earlier landholding, but also it may have been the tract Phillip bequeathed to his children.

At the time the Sublettes settled in St. Charles County, business possibilities there were numerous. Trade would prosper as long as immigrants, accompanied by "their flocks and their herds . . . the tinkling of bells, the cloud of dust, the throngs of hogs and cattle," moved freely into and through the region. Phillip's sense of enterprise was sharp, and to wet its edge he took a license from the county court to operate a ferry at his land on the Mississippi.[7] He could receive a steady income from the heavy trans-Mississippi traffic estimated at fifty wagons and four to five hundred passengers per day. William and Milton Sublette were old enough to help him operate and maintain his boat, yet he did not remain in business much over a year. At the time of the Panic of 1819, he relinquished his ferry business and turned to something else.[8]

Quite possibly he first opened his own home as "a matter of private accommodation" to friends in town, but that led, as was usually the case, "to public entertainment," and Phillip found himself once again in the tavern business in partnership this time with a friend, Morgan Swope. They provided their customers the usual refreshments, and the tavern, not unlike the two Phillip operated in Kentucky, became a community gathering place.[9] In St. Charles, tavern keepers had a reputation for "square dealing." Some of them boarded members of the legislature after 1820, and many a later civic leader began his career as a successful tavern owner. Sublette and Swope added a billiard table to their furnishings, one of two in the county, and despite the indignation of neighbors who objected to billiard playing on the Sabbath, utilized it until they were sued in court for the cost of a damaged billiard cloth.[10]

[7] *Missouri Gazette & Public Advertiser* (St. Louis), June 9, 1819; Record Book A–2, 1816–20, p. 236, MSS, St. Charles CCC.

[8] *St. Louis Enquirer*, October 30, 1819.

[9] File of *The State of Missouri* v. *P. A. Sublette and Morgan Swope*, Court Files November Term 1819 to February Term 1821, MSS, St. Charles CCC.

The business might have been an even greater success had the partners bothered to take out a license. In March, 1819, the county authorities dragged them into court and charged them with wrongfully

> *. . . keep[ing] and maintain[ing] a certain common misgoverned & disorderly house and in their said house for their own . . . & gain certain persons of evil name & fame, and of dishonest conversation, to frequent & come together there & on the said other days & times there unlawfully did cause, and procure, and the said persons in their said house at unlawful times, as well in the night as in the day, then and on the said other days & times; there to be & remain drinking, tippling, gambling & misbehaving themselves, unlawfully and willfully did permit, and yet do permit, to the great damage & common nuisance of all the good people of their territory, their inhabiting, resting & passing, to the evil example of others. . . .*[11]

What must Isabella have thought, especially when son William was called into court, along with several other persons, as a witness? But after his father and Swope pleaded not guilty and were released on bond, the circuit attorney dropped the entire indictment.

The case did not appear to harm the Sublette family reputation, and Phillip, never one to shirk his public duty, participated in the life of St. Charles as willingly as he participated in the life of Kentucky. His name was appended to petitions for public projects; he opened, for a short time, a downtown office, possibly even a schoolroom, in the Masonic Hall; he served as both a grand and petit juror; and he appeared before the circuit court from

[10] St. Charles County Tax List, 1819, MSS, St. Charles CC; T. Flint to Rev. Abel Flint, May 4, 1818, Letters of Timothy and Abel Flint, 1817–18, MSS, MoSHi; P. A. Sublette Account Book and Legal Record, 1818–21, MSS, City Hall, St. Charles.

[11] File of *The State of Missouri v. P. A. Sublette and Morgan Swope,* Court Files November Term 1819 to February Term 1821, MSS, St. Charles CCC.

time to time.[12] His political experience in Kentucky recommended him as a likely officeholder in St. Charles. Frederick Bates, secretary of Missouri Territory, who was "exercising the government thereof," in February, 1819, appointed him a justice of the peace for St. Charles Township. He did not take his oath, however, until the following year after settlement of his tavern litigation. Then he took up his duties, fees for which were provided in the territorial fee list, and became an active magistrate. His jurisdiction in criminal cases extended to the entire county, but in civil cases only to his township. When the first state administration under Governor Alexander McNair was elected in August, 1820, he was renominated and subsequently reappointed to a full four-year term.[13]

Uncle Solomon Whitley, who appears to have accompanied the Sublettes westward, having satisfied himself that St. Charles was a suitable homesite, returned to Kentucky, gathered up his wife, six children, and two slaves, and was again in St. Charles by late autumn, 1819. Property values were high, and he speculated in town lots before he settled on one. The lot contained a dwelling house and several other buildings, in one of which he opened a tavern at the "sign of the Eagle."[14] It is evident from his frequent slave and land transactions that he was prosperous in St. Charles—more prosperous than the Sublettes. He served the town whenever requested and was one of the twelve men proposed as trustees of a nonsectarian St. Charles Academy. Active until his death in 1834, he was survived by his wife Margaret Whitley.[15]

[12] Petition of some of the Inhabitants of St. Charles to the Congress of the United States, December 21, 1818, Benjamin Emmons Collection, 1768–1942, MSS, MoSHi; File of Road Petition of July, 1820, Road Papers 1820–29, MSS, St. Charles CC; File of *Daniel Griffith* v. *P. A. Sublette and John Richards*, Court Files March Term 1820 to July Term 1820, MSS, St. Charles CCC.

[13] Deed Record F, pp. 293–94, MSS, St. Charles CRDO; P. A. Sublette Account Book and Legal Record, 1818–1821, MSS, City Hall, St. Charles; *Missourian* (St. Charles), July 29, August 26, 1820; *Acts of the First General Assembly of the State of Missouri . . . 1820*, 6, 9; Deed Record G, p. 27, MSS, St. Charles CRDO.

[14] St. Charles County Tax List, 1819, and St. Charles County Census, 1819, MSS, St. Charles CC; *Missourian* (St. Charles), June 27, 1821.

Another Whitley, Levisa, sister to Isabella Sublette, also spent a few years in St. Charles. In 1818 or 1819, Levisa and her husband, James McKinney, and their children joined their relatives in Missouri. McKinney temporarily hauled wood for customers in St. Charles, but he was more devoted to agriculture. His wife and children, however, were happier there, since they, the Whitleys, and the Sublettes had daily opportunities to visit one another. There were at least nineteen and perhaps as many as twenty-four young first cousins in the three families, and the children provided each other companionship. Nevertheless, two years later McKinney moved his family west to Callaway County, where he settled on land located south of present Kingdom City. This move was fortunate for the McKinney family, since it brought them fertile land and prosperity. James later served as a county judge and became a prominent member of the Ironside Baptist Church.[16]

William, or "Bill" as he was called by family and friends, turned eighteen the year he reached St. Charles. His prominent father and active Uncle Solomon and their careers overshadowed his late adolescence, but he admired both of them, was pleased with their popularity, and lived happily at home. After his father's experimental venture into ferry transportation, William and his younger brothers assisted in the newly opened tavern. William was involved in the suit over the billiard cloth and also may have had a hand in the Whitley tavern. He was at times in his uncle's company and on one occasion was taken into court with him, charged with assault and battery on Joseph W. Garraty, whom they had beaten and abused "in a tumultuous manner." The jury dropped William from the case, but fined Uncle Solomon.[17]

The younger Sublette's single investment in land during his

[15] Record Book A, 1820–35, pp. 78, 100, 116, MSS, City Hall, St. Charles; Wills & Letters of Administration & Letters Testamentary II, 1833–52, p. 22, MSS, St. Charles CPC; Administrators Bonds, 1827–1835, MSS, St. Charles CPC.

[16] *In the Supreme Court of Missouri, October Term 1902*, 56; Missouri Tax List, Callaway County, 1823, MSS, MoSHi.

[17] File of *The State of Missouri* v. *Solomon Whitley and William L. Sublette*, Court Files March Term 1823 to November Term 1823, MSS, St. Charles CCC.

St. Charles years occurred in July, 1820, when he leased two hundred arpents of timberland. He was to improve it and did so by cutting over the trees, which he fashioned into fence rails. They were piled near the Sublette home in a gradually increasing stack and disposed of several years later.[18]

The Sublette home was comfortable, but not lavish. Its furnishings included a small writing desk, spinning wheel, six or seven chairs, delftware, pewter plates, and some books: the first- and last-mentioned items possibly were useful to Phillip as a justice of the peace. Isabella ran the household, aided by her oldest daughter, and if the tavern operated in a portion of the house, as seems likely, the daily chores and frequent visitors must have reminded Isabella of her earlier days at Somerset and the Crab Orchard. William and his brothers cared for the stock, sharpened and repaired tools and utensils, tilled a limited amount of land, and gathered supplementary food supplies from the woods and numerous nearby streams. Family staples, both food and clothing, were purchased in St. Charles from friendly storekeepers. Phillip was widely known in town and counted as friends both business and professional men.

The older Sublette boys grew into "large, fine looking men, of great strength and agility"—desirable physiological traits, since life in St. Charles was not always quiet.[19] Conditions there required the strong right arm of a constable and deputies to keep the peace. William was considered a popular likely prospect, and in the spring of 1820, Osborn Knott, constable of St. Charles Township, appointed him his deputy. Although the new appointee was four months under twenty-one years of age, it was not unusual for the word and letter of the law to be circumvented in such an instance. As one eminent western historian has remarked, "Minors were habitually allowed to vote."[20]

William's duties as a deputy constable were dependent largely upon whatever the constable directed or required. Conse-

[18] Deed Record F, p. 332, MSS, St. Charles CRDO.
[19] LeRoy R. Hafen, "Mountain Men—Andrew W. Sublette," *Colorado Magazine*, Vol. X (September, 1933), 179–80.
[20] Everett Dick, *The Sod-House Frontier, 1854–1890*, 462.

quently, in many instances he was sent to assist his father, who was then a justice of the peace. William collected his father's fees, took men into custody for the court, and served as a witness whenever necessary. In much of his training may be seen his father's directing hand. The young deputy soon was acquainted with the cases in the county court, knew something of legal procedure, and had broadened his circle of friends—need we also add enemies—in the county. He had political ambitions even then. His father was a regular subscriber to the powerful pro-Democratic *Richmond Enquirer*, whose editor was later a fervent supporter of Jackson and Van Buren. William was nourished by his father's sentiments, first voted in a local election in March, 1821, and in the same year experienced jury duty.[21]

Evidently he gave competent and acceptable service as a deputy constable, because on May 21, 1822, he was appointed township constable by the county court. Constable Knott had resigned his St. Charles duties to run for coroner; William took his place. Three months later, on August 5, he defended his office in the county elections, handily defeating John S. Besser and Isaac Taylor, who ran against him. Together they polled only 11 per cent of the 194 votes cast.[22]

There was some delay in his oath-taking, however, until December of that year, possibly occasioned by his preoccupation with the settlement of his parents' estates. Phillip, after a lingering illness, died on Thursday, December 28, 1820, and was buried in the tiny Protestant cemetery near his home. Since he died intestate, without designating an executor, his wife and son William were appointed administrators. William was settling his father's estate, valued finally at only $153.25, when on January 21 or 22, 1822, Isabella died. Prescriptions of calomel, sulphur, elixir, bitters, and bleedings, so common in that day, may have prolonged but could not save her life, and she was interred beside her hus-

---

21 Poll Book for the St. Charles Election of March 16, 1821, Benjamin Emmons Collection, 1768–1942, MSS, MoSHi; Record Book B, 1820–25, p. 172, MSS, St. Charles CCC.

22 *Missourian* (St. Charles), July 18, August 1, 8, 1822.

band.[23] It was not until January, 1823, that William was appointed administrator of his mother's estate. Most of the estate's movable property was auctioned at public sale on March 3, although the family home was not sold until 1827, at a time when William was in St. Louis between trips to the mountains.

He was now the head of a large family of six brothers and sisters. Young Sally, the eighth child, died between 1819 and 1823, and of the remaining children, little Pinckney, apparently contrary to the pattern set by his older brothers, was said to be "delicate," generally in poor health, and in need of regular parental care. Solomon was even younger, but possibly in better health. Milton—if we may believe the available evidence—had entered the fur trade before 1823. Sophronia, Mary (Polly), and Andrew were old enough to care for themselves to a great extent.[24]

The Whitleys and McKinneys did whatever they could to lessen William's burden, since Phillip Sublette's relatives were too scattered to be of much assistance and most of Isabella's family was in Kentucky. Esther Whitley, maternal grandmother to the Sublettes, was nearly seventy and could not be expected to care for Isabella's young surviving children. Levisa and James McKinney, whose children were mature or nearly so, took Sophronia and Mary Sublette into their home. Although the available evidence is quite vague, it appears that young Mary died in their home a few years later. Andrew, Pinckney, and Solomon became joint charges of William and their Uncle Solomon until the spring of 1823, when William saw fit to "seek his fortune" in a trade—the fur trade—which promised a "valuable addition to the commerce of the country."[25]

It is easy to account for his interest in the fur trade, if we realize that his home was located but a few miles from the fur

[23] Files of Estate of Isabella Sublette, No. 3419, and Estate of Phillip A. Sublette, No. 3420, MSS, St. Charles CPC; *Missourian* (St. Charles), January 24, 1822.

[24] St. Charles County Census, 1819, MSS, St. Charles CC; *In the Supreme Court of Missouri, October Term 1902*, 17, 23.

[25] Leopard Buel and Floyd C. Shoemaker (eds.), *The Messages and Proclamations of the Governors of the State of Missouri*, I, 30.

emporium of St. Louis. Fur parties bound for the Upper Missouri and fur-laden boats on their way downriver to St. Louis regularly passed St. Charles. It was known that an Indian agent, representing the federal government, had been sent to open an agency as far west as Council Bluffs. Recently, in 1822, the nonprofit United States Indian factory (trading house) system, after twenty-seven years in operation, had been abolished. Private capital, interested in exploiting the western fur resources without competition from the government, regarded the abolition as a healthy sign. By the autumn of 1822, one thousand men were said to be employed in trade "on the waters of the Missouri."[26]

From his brother in the trade, from travelers, passing fur parties, and business friends, William could learn about the organization of a fur party and of the different types of fur trappers and traders; but beyond those few, simple facts, he relied upon his eyes for information. A keen observer could, however, learn much from the panorama of fur commerce drifting past St. Charles. In July, 1819, several small steamboats, part of a military expedition up the Missouri River, passed the town, and anyone with imagination might have foreseen steam's future use in western fur commerce. Also, the Missouri Fur Company sent boats up and down the river, and in October, 1822, a shipment of its furs valued at fourteen thousand dollars reached St. Louis.[27]

The fur trade was by then the biggest busines of the Upper Missouri, and no enterprise in St. Charles could equal its lucrative, adventurous prospects. The depression subsequent to the Panic of 1819 ended the great era when the town's streets resounded to the footsteps of westward-bound immigrants. The community was becoming one of "handsome street[s and] spacious and neat brick houses," and the legislature pointed to the growing "seriousness and regularity of [its] inhabitants."[28] Moreover, in addition to the sparse economic opportunities in St. Charles, William had other reasons to consider going west. He was unmarried, had

[26] *Edwardsville Spectator*, October 26, 1822.
[27] *Ibid.*, July 24, 1819, October 22, 1822; *St. Louis Enquirer*, July 14, 1819.
[28] Flint, *op. cit.*, 126, 211; *Edwardsville Spectator*, October 26, 1822.

no obligations to a wife and children, his parents had died, and he was completing the administration of their estates. His brothers and sisters were mature or could be placed in the hands of trusted close relatives. His family ties to St. Charles were broken, and he needed only the proper occasion to join a fur party.

The Arikara

ALONG the St. Louis water front, shipping activity was at a bare minimum during the cold, disagreeable winter of 1822–23.[1] River pilots awaited an open channel and melting ice flows before venturing into spring trade, but in the warm counting rooms of the city preparations were under way to send a privately sponsored fur expedition to the waters of the Upper Missouri. The Lieutenant Governor of Missouri, militia General William Henry Ashley, political leader and man of shrewd commercial sense, busily organized his second major trading venture. The previous spring he had sent, under the leadership of his partner, Andrew Henry, a body of trappers and traders to the confluence

[1] Much of the material in this chapter, in addition to the sources cited, is drawn from: Hiram M. Chittenden, *The American Fur Trade of the Far West,* II; Harrison C. Dale, *The Ashley-Smith Explorations and the Discovery of a Central Route to the Pacific, 1822–29; James Clyman, American Frontiersman, 1792–1881* (ed. by Charles L. Camp); Dale Morgan, *Jedediah Smith;* Merrill J. Mattes, "Hiram Scott, Fur Trader," *Nebraska History,* Vol. XXVI (July–September, 1945), 127–62; Addison E. Sheldon (ed.), *Records of Fort Atkinson 1819–1827,* IV; Maurice S. Sullivan, *The Travels of Jedediah Smith: A Documentary Outline, Including the Journal of the Great American Pathfinder;* Frank Triplett, *Conquering the Wilderness;* Clarence A. Vandiveer, *The Fur Trade and Early Western Exploration;* William Waldo, "Recollections of a Septuagenarian," *Glimpses of the Past,* Vol. V (April–June, 1938), 59–94. Triplett is to be used as a source with particular caution.

of the Missouri and Yellowstone rivers. They hunted and were spending the winter in makeshift campsites while they awaited the arrival of Ashley's spring party of 1823.[2]

He equipped two keelboats, the "Rocky Mountains" and "Yellow Stone Packet," and intended to leave St. Louis whenever the river was clear. The boats carried both sails and lengths of towline—frequently an indispensable cord-of-life if the wind died on an upriver journey. Additional power may have been provided by hand-driven side-wheels. A visitor to the river front noted many years later in his reminiscences that in 1822, and perhaps also in 1823, Ashley's keelboats were

> *. . . fitted out with side wheels . . . with shaft crank and fly-wheels and sliding frames erected upon the top deck of the boats, attached to the cranks to move back and forward. They had seats made across the boats under the frames, fore and aft of the shaft, to accommodate men sitting: with round cross pieces as handles for the men to move the frame and propell* [sic] *the boats.*[3]

Many of the men in 1822 and 1823, were hired in reply to advertisements Ashley and Henry placed in local newspapers. There was a considerable difference, however, in the quality of men raised by advertising on those two occasions. The earlier party was notable for its general respectability, youth, and apparent fitness, whereas in 1823, many of the men were from the "grog shops and other sinks of degredation [sic]." James Clyman, Virginian adventurer and ex officio chronicler of the group, referred to "Falstafs [sic] Battallion [sic]" as somewhat "genteel in comparison."[4]

[2] *Missouri Gazette & Public Advertiser* (St. Louis), February 13, 1822; *Missourian* (St. Charles), April 18, 1822; Paul C. Phillips (ed.), *Life in the Rocky Mountains*, 73.
[3] James Haley White Reminiscences, 1822–23, St. Louis Reminiscences Envelope, MSS, MoSHi.
[4] *Missouri Intelligencer* (Franklin), April 30, 1822; *Missouri Republican* (St. Louis), January 15, 1823; *St. Louis Enquirer*, January 25, 1823.

One of the more exceptional men who answered Ashley's call was young Bill Sublette from St. Charles. When we remember that Ashley, in his political position, presided over meetings of the state senate in St. Charles and that many of his men in 1822 were recruited from that town, it is evident that Sublette may have known a considerable amount about Ashley and his enterprise. Through such direct personal contact or lured by the advertisement, William decided to take the Lieutenant Governor's offer of two hundred dollars per year of mountain service. He quickly settled most of the remaining details of his parents' estates, petitioned the City Court of St. Charles to conclude a case in which he was involved, and resigned his position as constable in favor of John S. Besser, who was to take his place until the May term of the county court.[5]

On March 3, in a public auction of his mother's household goods, William sold his bedstead for one dollar and was ready to depart for the West. He took with him a variety of practical experience in law, politics, business, land speculation, and travel. Although he lacked advanced education and had no military training, he knew how to work with people and how to lead men. At the age of twenty-three he stood six feet, two—a tall, "raw-boned brave." His long face—"Jackson-faced" as a friend once said—straight forehead, and slightly hooked nose contrasted sharply with his fair skin and light sandy hair. His blue eyes were "quick"; equal to his "steady . . . hand." In later years he would bear the Indian name "Cut Face" for a scar on his left chin, acquired either in childhood or, as seems more likely, in an Indian scrape. He would be known to some of the red men as "Fate," for reasons now lost to us, and to others as "Straight Walking Cane [Arra-raish]" for his physical bearing.[6] Tradition main-

---

[5] County Court Record, 1821–37, p. 82, MSS, St. Charles CC; File of Recommmendation of J. S. Besser for Constable, 1823, File Box 3-2-2, MSS, St. Charles CC.

[6] File of Estate of Isabella Sublette, No. 3419, MSS, St. Charles CPC; Passport No. 2332, April 9, 1831, Sublette MSS; William Marshall Anderson, *Adventures in the Rocky Mountains in 1834*, reprinted from the *American Turf Register* of 1837, letter of September 29, 1837.

tains that the people of St. Charles outfitted him with a rifle and buckskin suit as their token of esteem and farewell, but there is no adequate proof of the pleasant tale.[7]

He joined Ashley's party either at St. Louis before its departure on March 10, or at St. Charles on the thirteenth, when the boats stopped for last-minute supplies. Each keelboat reportedly carried seventy to one hundred men, but the actual complement was more likely ninety. One unfortunate member was drowned on the very day of departure—a bad omen to a western expedition—and three wagoners, on their way overland from St. Louis to the boats at St. Charles, were killed in the explosion of a large cask of gunpowder. Although Ashley was in command of the entire expedition, he did not join his men until they were ready to leave St. Charles or were slightly above it on the Missouri. He had delayed in St. Louis to arrange for an Indian trading license.[8]

Slowly the boats edged up the river, whose banks were tinged with the faintest green of spring. The French crew members guided the two craft, aided by the hired hunters, who cared for equipment, ventured ashore in search of food, and when necessary helped propel the boats. William had time to meet the other men, a few of whom proved to be "of worth," and to learn trapping techniques. Some of the least desirable *engagés* deserted as the expedition continued upriver and were replaced by much better local recruits. As far as Council Bluffs, at least, there seemed to be no great danger in a trip to the mountains.

They passed the site of Jefferson City, the future Missouri state capital, and on Wednesday, March 25, tied up at Franklin, the largest and most prosperous town west of St. Charles. There they took on supplies from the "law abiding" inhabitants, who

[7] *In the Supreme Court of Missouri, October Term 1902*, p. 31. Miss Stella Drumm in her article on William L. Sublette published in the *Dictionary of American Biography* mentions this story. The only reference which she cites, containing the same story, is Bryan and Rose's *A History of the Pioneer Families of Missouri*. They cite no source for the story, although Bryan was from an old St. Charles family and may have heard the tale from someone living in St. Charles in 1823.

[8] *Missouri Republican* (St. Louis), March 12, 19, 1823.

may have been a bit relieved when Ashley and his motley contingent remained only a day. Franklin was the location of the United States Land Office for Western Missouri and in 1820 contained several warehouses, small-scale industries, and artisans' shops serving the river trade, neighboring farmers, and the town's five hundred to one thousand people. Opposite the town, south of the river on a high bluff, was the settlement of Boonville, then no more than a brick courthouse and twoscore log huts but soon destined, through the river's vagaries, to surpass Franklin.[9]

West of Franklin and Boonville, the Missouri settlements were minute. Chariton, at the mouth of the Chariton River, was a county seat of only thirty homes. Lexington included only a post office and a few improved lots, and Bluffton, seat of justice for Ray County, was a collection of a few log cabins scattered about the community tavern. Gallatin, nearby, was "not in a very thriving condition," and the future town of Liberty, a short distance north of the river, was only a year old. The trading center of Independence, a few miles from the state's western border, was unsurveyed.[10]

Sublette and his fellow hunters went ashore from time to time in search of fresh game, returning from such inland hunts to cook and eat their food on the banks of the Missouri or to add it to the boats' larder. On one such occasion James Clyman said that on the morning after a hunting party returned from a foray, the neighbors in the area protested to Ashley that his men had stolen food from them. A search of the boats revealed nothing, but later, when the sails were unfurled, pigs and poultry fell out "in abundance."

Continuing north-northwest on the Missouri, they soon reached the attractive whitewashed buildings of Fort Atkinson

[9] Jonas Viles, "Old Franklin: A Frontier Town of the Twenties," *Mississippi Valley Historical Review*, Vol. IX (March, 1923), 271–79; *Missouri Intelligencer* (Franklin), December 24, 31, 1822, and January 21, April 1, 1823; Paul Wilhelm, "First Journey to North America in the Years 1822 to 1824," *South Dakota Historical Collections*, XIX (1938), 288.

[10] *Missouri Intelligencer* (Franklin), November 26, December 3, 24, 1822, and January 14, 1823.

and restocked with fresh vegetables. The military post stood on the west bank of the river in the Council Bluffs area. Its stockade was about two hundred yards square with two log houses on each side and three gates. The interior court was a grass-covered square containing a stone powder house. On the northwest side of the fort was an Indian council house, as well as several artillery storehouses. Other buildings housed cabinetmakers, carpenters, a smithy, and a baker, and on the south side of the fort was a grist and sawmill adjoining large corn and wheat fields extending along the river. A handful of Ashley's men decided to remain there with the army; two or three former soldiers joined the fur outfit. While such negotiations were under way, Sublette had an excellent opportunity to acquaint himself with an army post and to hunt in the immediate vicinity.[11]

Above Fort Atkinson on the Upper Missouri the Indian situation changed rapidly in the late spring of 1823. Major Benjamin O'Fallon, Indian agent for the area, writing to the Secretary of War the previous summer, had mentioned that "the harmony so happily existing between us and the Indians in the vicinity of the Council Bluffs" was likely to be alarmed and disturbed by the intrusion of Ashley's trappers. O'Fallon's anxiety was expressed more clearly as open opposition to the Ashley-Henry venture when J. B. C. Lucas, an old and prominent St. Louisian, stated that Ashley had no legal right whatsoever to take a large body of trappers into Indian country. To Lucas, Ashley was clearly "a wrong doer" who disturbed frontier peace.[12]

At least three fur groups had recent skirmishes with the tribes. During the winter a small party of Arikaras had been fired upon by the garrison of the Missouri Fur Company post located some sixty to eighty miles below the Arikara villages on the Upper Missouri. In May, another Missouri Fur Company group, under Jones and Immell, was attacked by Blackfeet on Pryors Fork of the Yellowstone, and almost simultaneously a

---

[11] Wilhelm, *loc. cit.*, 356, 360.
[12] *Letters of Hon. J. B. C. Lucas from 1815 to 1836* (ed. by B. C. Lucas), 292; 18 Cong., 1 sess., *Sen. Doc. No. 1*, pp. 55, 61.

small band of Henry's trappers was attacked near the mouth of Smiths River (Montana).[13]

Although the "wave of [Indian] hostility" was disconcerting, Ashley refused to give up his plans and continued northwest into Indian country. His men poled and pulled their boats upriver, encountering little sign of hostilities until they were approximately four hundred miles beyond Council Bluffs. There, ten miles above the mouth of Rampart River, two important Arikara villages were located on a prairie along the right bank of the Missouri. The villages, containing perhaps six hundred warriors, were three hundred yards apart; and below the lower settlement, where the river in a horseshoe curve sent its channel towards the right bank, was a sand bar and logical landing place. Since the Indians appeared willing to trade horses, which Ashley needed in order to send an overland party to the Yellowstone, he anchored his keelboats in midstream below the lower village and opened negotiations at the nearby sand spit.[14]

Trading was completed on the afternoon of June 1, after which Ashley visited the lodge of a principal chief and was "treated with every appearance of friendship." The following morning before sunrise, however, he and his men were told that a member of their party, Aaron Stephens, had been killed by the Indians and that an open attack was imminent. The assault began shortly thereafter and was directed principally upon the forty Ashley men on the beach. Firing from the cover of picketing below the lower town and from some broken ground, the Arikaras hit two or three trappers and several of their horses. The men on the beach returned the fire, but had few targets since the pickets and the "potatoe [sic] hole" houses in the nearby village gave the Indians excellent cover.[15]

The men on the beach were those selected by Ashley to staff his overland expedition to Henry's post on the Yellowstone and

---

[13] *Missouri Republican* (St. Louis), July 23, 1823.

[14] *Ibid.*, October 8, 1823; "Bradley Manuscript—Book II," *Contributions to the Historical Society of Montana*, Vol. VIII (1917), 133; Broadhead Sketch of the Expedition of 1823, Ashley MSS.

[15] *Missouri Republican* (St. Louis), July 9, 1823.

were the select members of the entire expedition. Jedediah S. Smith, who recently had joined Ashley, bearing messages down-river from Henry's camp, was on the beach and probably in charge of the party, since Ashley was on one of the keelboats. Sublette, with Smith in the midst of the battle, watched his companions fall before the Indian fire and wondered whether his first engagement might be his last. Ashley ordered his boats in to rescue his men, but the boatmen were too panic stricken to execute the order. Instead, two skiffs were sent. One managed to return a few men to the keelboats, but the other was cut adrift. Ashley's rescue efforts were useless, and most of his best men remained on the beach behind a breastwork of dead and dying horses.[16]

Smith, Sublette, and their companions on the beach, according to Ashley at least, were determined not to give way "as long as there appeared the least probability of keeping the ground." They held off the Indians as long as possible, then leaped into the river under a hail of arrows and shot and swam for the boats. Some of the men were swallowed by the river, but Sublette managed to crawl aboard one of the keelboats, exhausted but apparently not wounded. The anchor of the one boat was weighed, the cable of the other cut, and the two floated downstream to the first good stand of timber. To continue upstream past the villages would have been too dangerous, and Ashley knew that many of his more unreliable men might desert the expedition if such were attempted without reinforcements. He added later that, as for the men on the beach, "never did men . . . act with more coolness and bravery."[17]

Twenty-five miles below the villages they rested, waited for survivors who might come in, and counted their dead and wounded. Thirteen men were lost, and of the eleven wounded two would not long survive. Reinforcements were needed badly, and to secure them, Ashley sent a message down-river to solicit aid of O'Fallon and Colonel Henry Leavenworth at Council

[16] Broadhead Sketch of the Expedition of 1823, Ashley MSS; "Jedediah Strong Smith," *Illinois Monthly Magazine*, Vol. XXI (June, 1832), 394. This last source must be used with caution.

[17] *Missouri Republican* (St. Louis), July 9, 1823.

Bluffs. The keelboat "Yellow Stone Packet," loaded with wounded men and surplus goods, carried that message, while another note was dispatched in the care of Smith and a French-Canadian companion to be carried to Henry's men on the Yellowstone. After the departure of the boat and the messengers, Ashley moved his men down-river once again to a new campsite at the mouth of the Cheyenne River. They remained there for six weeks on "scant and frequently no rations." Although there was game in the area, constant Indian danger limited hunting.[18]

The "Yellow Stone Packet" caught the current and was at Fort Atkinson by June 18. Leavenworth and O'Fallon were given Ashley's message and proceeded to act upon the seriousness of the situation. In a letter to his superior, General Henry Atkinson, commander of the Western Department, Leavenworth revealed his intention to use military force in Ashley's behalf, or, as he concluded, "We go to secure the lives and property of our citizens." He readied two hundred men—six companies of his Sixth Regiment—and on June 22 departed for the Upper Missouri. The river, its banks full of spring rain and melted mountain snow, easily carried the Colonel's boats, but the mass of his command, marching near the banks of the river, had to swim or wade waist-deep in flooded tributaries.[19]

Five days out of Fort Atkinson the command was joined by Joshua Pilcher and sixty men of the Missouri Fur Company. They had two boats with them and both would be needed, since one army craft soon was lost in an accident and the "Yellow Stone Packet" barely weathered a storm a few days later. It was with some relief that the reinforcements reached Cedar Fort (Fort Recovery), July 19, on the west bank of the Missouri ten miles above the mouth of White River. A few Yankton and Teton Sioux joined them there in anticipation of a bloody attack upon their enemies, the Arikaras.

Meanwhile, Henry, having received Ashley's message from

[18] Ralph E. Glauert, "The Life and Activities of William Henry Ashley and His Associates, 1822–1826," (A. M. thesis) 40–41.
[19] *Missouri Intelligencer* (Franklin), December 2, 1823.

Smith, left his camp on the Yellowstone and with approximately
fifty men, including Smith, and a small fur catch proceeded down
the Missouri. He and his party sailed past the Arikara villages,
ignoring friendly gestures from the Indians, and joined Ashley's
camp on the Cheyenne River. Sublette and the others were given
more freedom to roam the countryside; Ashley now considered
his position more secure. Nevertheless, he was anxious for help
from Council Bluffs and once again moved his men down-river,
this time to the mouth of Teton (Bad) River. He left them there
and dropped down to Fort Brasseaux (Brazeau) near Fort Recovery to acquire new horses for his proposed overland expedition to the northwest. At Fort Brasseaux he heard of Leavenworth's approach and hurried back to the Teton River camp to
prepare his men for the coming Indian campaign.

By July 30 the military force and its auxiliaries were encamped with Ashley and Henry, and two days of celebration
was under way. Between speeches and feasting the so-called "Missouri Legion" was organized to aid the regular troops. When
temporary ranks were distributed, Sublette was named sergeant
major. The entire party then moved upstream to a point twenty-
five miles below the Arikara villages, where the command left
the boats. It was August 8, one day before the first major Indian
campaign on the Upper Missouri.

Men were sent ahead to scout the approaches to the Indian
camps, followed by Captain Riley with his riflemen, while Ashley
"with two companies of mountaineers" was third in advance.
Sublette, in the third wave, was in an excellent position to watch
much of the impending action. The Arikaras, not expecting to
be attacked by such a formidable force as appeared before their
villages on August 9, had made no general preparations for defense. The Sioux, moving in advance with Pilcher in the first
wave, "made a break" below the villages, dashed forward on
their mounts, and met the Arikaras in a sharp skirmish on a plain
half a mile below the pickets of the towns. The startled Arikaras
fell back to their settlements.

Sublette and his companions were by then on the right flank

by the river; the regulars and riflemen to their left. The entire line moved to within several hundred yards of the towns, where they encamped for the night, while the Sioux withdrew to nearby cornfields and took no further part in the operation. During the evening the artillery was disembarked from the boats and moved up to the advance line, but a general attack was postponed until dawn. Nevertheless, the night was full of "pandemonium" in both camp and villages and not conducive to rest.

In the morning Captain Riley, Lieutenant Bradley, and their men were sent to a hill within one hundred yards of the upper village to annoy the Arikaras with a continuous fire. Meanwhile, a major attack was made on the lower town. Ashley's men again formed the extreme right of the line advancing upon the lower village. Lieutenant Morris, in charge of one of the six-pounders and a howitzer, took his position adjoining them; and the remaining regulars, except for those before the upper town, were deployed to his left. As the infantry advanced, Lieutenant Morris placed a few high artillery shots above the lower town. The Arikaras resisted stoutly, and in the face of their defense Leavenworth ordered an attack upon the upper town. Ashley's men, as a diversion, opened fire from a ravine near the lower village, and Pilcher went to seek further co-operation from the Sioux. They were unwilling, however, to participate in a siege, preferring an open battle or nothing.

By midafternoon it was evident an open attack had failed, and there was the possibility that the cannoneers might run out of shot. Lieutenant Morris was ordered to cease his fire, the upper line was told to disband, and the entire command was pulled back half a mile to the campsite opposite the boats. The Sioux, disgusted with the "disgraceful" turn of events, withdrew with their blankets and horses laden with Arikara corn. Sublette and the other mountaineers had been without provisions for two days and, despite the withdrawal, must have welcomed the chance to forage in the woods and cornfields.

Leavenworth, aboard one of the keelboats in conference with Ashley and Pilcher, decided to resume the offensive the

43

following day. Shortly thereafter a delegation of Arikara chiefs was ushered into the camp and petitioned for peace, since their palisades and homes had been "literally riddled" with cannon and musket shot and they were "all in tears as they said." It was understood that they wished mercy for their families and that they would restore what they could of Ashley's property. They were willing to present Arikara hostages and to promise to behave themselves in the future, but Pilcher was not pleased with professions of peace and smoked the calumet only to humor Leavenworth. After this initial meeting the chiefs departed under warning from Pilcher to beware of his wrath.

The August night passed quietly, and on the following day, the eleventh, several of Leavenworth's men, upon invitation from the Arikara chief Little Soldier, visited the lower village and reported its defenses weaker than expected. Later in the day the promised delegation of chiefs met the white leaders in a new conference, and after the usual formalities and delays drew up a treaty in which they agreed to be kind and civil in the future, to restore Ashley's property, and not to obstruct navigation on the Missouri. Neither Pilcher, who refused to sign the treaty, nor the Sioux, who had retired to the hills to await the outcome of the campaign, were pleased with the arrangement.

The Arikara pledge to restore Ashley's property was fulfilled only partially with the return of three rifles, one horse, and eighteen robes. The upper village refused to return anything, and Lieutenant Morris advised his commander to renew the attack. Leavenworth believed, however, that "the interests of his nation was opposed" to renewed warfare at that time. He and his forces settled down to their first entirely peaceful night's rest only to discover next morning, August 14, that the villages were empty. The Arikaras had fled and could not be located.

Sublette and the others remained in their "stinking disagreeable camp" near the villages for another night, that of August 14–15, and then dropped down-river to a new site near Fort Kiowa. In midmorning on the fifteenth, Leavenworth and his men sailed away for Fort Atkinson, where he resumed command within two weeks. An aged Indian woman was placed in charge of the deserted villages, but the military unit scarcely had sailed away when the towns burst into flame and burned to charred ruins.

The campaign gave the army new knowledge of the Indian country and provided the recruits important experience—experience which cost the government two thousand dollars. Losses in killed and wounded were slight, but repercussions from the campaign were great. The news of the action reached newspaper readers almost immediately, and Pilcher, in several long letters written in anger, attacked Leavenworth for his conduct of the campaign. Leavenworth accused Pilcher's men of burning the villages, and in return Pilcher accused the military leader of placing "impossible barriers" to commerce on the Missouri.[20] Later in the year Ashley would add his voice to the chorus by suggesting that several hundred troops be sent farther up the river to protect trade. He had to defend his expeditions, since such newspapers as the *New York American* maintained that the Indians had every right to "repel the approaches" of his trappers and traders.[21] Certainly the campaign had not been "a disgrace to national arms," nor had Leavenworth been as "vacillating and ineffectual" as some contended. The treaty was nearly worthless, but Leavenworth deserves credit for organizing a relief expedition on a moment's notice, for marching it at his own risk hundreds of miles into Indian country, for waging a precedent-setting campaign on the Upper Missouri, and for chastising the Indians within limits. He entered the battle not to guarantee the economic well-being of Pilcher or Ashley, but to do his duty as a military representative of the American people.

The literary outbursts of Leavenworth and Pilcher were unknown to Sublette and the other Ashley men, who hastened from the battlefield to preparations for the long-delayed northwestern overland expedition. They started downstream from the Arikara villages in company with Leavenworth, but parted at

[20] *Louisville Public Advertiser*, August 6, 1823.
[21] Copy of Letter of W. H. Ashley to the Secretary of War, December 23, 1823, Ashley MSS.

Grand River. At Fort Kiowa, Ashley recouped his supplies and stock of horses and immediately dispatched Henry and at least thirteen others to the Yellowstone. Smith and another party, probably of eleven, which included Sublette, James Clyman, Thomas Fitzpatrick, and Thomas Eddie, set out in late September to cut a trail northwest to avoid the Indian dangers of the Upper Missouri. The trail they used took them away from the normal route of travel. For the first time Sublette was a member of a small trapping party: this was his opportunity to prove himself to his employer and companions.

Summer had ended and "t'was a month ere honking geese would fly Southward before the Great White Hunter's face" when they struck out west from the fort over high, dry, rolling country leading up to the Black Hills.[22] They were guided by a scout furnished from the French Fur Company and their supplies were carried on pack horses borrowed from that same group. Both guide and horses were to leave them in a few days. Time was at a premium, and to conserve it, they traveled quickly to their first encampment on Clay Creek, or White River, so called for sediment "resembling cream" running thick in its water.

On the second day they continued west along the White River Valley, then across a treeless, nearly waterless country, and made their camp that night on a ridge covered with drought-resistant cacti—a warning of arid country ahead. The following afternoon they located a water hole—dry—paused to rest beneath a clump of "scrubby oaks," and set out again, their guide well in advance, searching for water as they proceeded. Two of the men, in most desperate condition, "were buried in the sand with just their head protruding to conserve body moisture"; the others straggled ahead in search of life-giving fluid. About an hour before sunset they located a water hole, to their great relief, fired their guns, plunged in with their horses, and drank their fill of the murky mixture. Smith, about the only one capable of keeping his feet, rode back to the two men buried in the sand to rescue them from their predicament. Thirst was a factor Sublette would

[22] *Collected Poems of John G. Neihardt,* 349.

be forced to cope with in the West, but not something to suc-
cumb to without a struggle. Nor was there time to rest after such
a harrowing experience, since they were still miles from the Teton
River where their guide awaited them.

Early in the morning they broke camp, in a short time
reached the timber-lined banks of the river, and headed upstream,
watching the clear water as it rippled and tumbled over the gravel
river bed. Their destination was an encampment of the "Bois
Brulie tribe" of Sioux, from whom they expected to secure fresh
horses. Fortunately, when they arrived there the Indians proved
friendly. Twenty-seven horses, enough to provide at least two
per man, were obtained, and the guide prepared to return to
Fort Kiowa with the other animals. Sublette was an experienced
horseman, thanks to his earlier years of training, and good horse-
manship was needed in the uninviting country immediately ahead
of him.

As soon as their fresh horses were packed, they proceeded
northwest through dry grass and shrubbery across rolling country. For several days they maintained that general direction, encountering food-giving buffalo and another friendly band of
Sioux. When they crossed the south fork of the Cheyenne River,
a few miles below its issuance from the Black Hills, they noticed
less short grass and cacti; and in attempting to skirt the hills, they
entered a barren, rugged country of gullies and knobs. A light
rain began to fall; the powdery-gray soil became muddy and
"loaded down [their] horses [feet] in great lumps." The area
was, as Clyman suspected, in the advanced stages of erosion
"moveing [sic] to the Missouri River as fast as rain and thawing
of Snow can carry it."

Rapid travel brought them out of the land of narrow ravines
and "cobble mound[s]" into smooth plains leading to the Wyoming Black Hills. The weather, cool and invigorating, was in their
favor—so were the hazelnuts and wild, ripened plums, which they
could pick—and for two days they traversed a rolling, pine-clad
area. At night they rested in excellent little glades of rich soil
and lush grass for their horses. The ascent of the hills, however,

47

was more difficult, through scrub pine and juniper groves covered with purple berries. The descent, also difficult, was through "steep and rocky" ravines whose waters flowed west into Powder River.

Late one evening they inadvertently entered a narrow canyon, without room to turn about in the dark, where they spent a long, tiresome night. Clyman and two others—more fortunate individuals—located a passage leading down a slippery hillside into a small valley. There they killed a stray buffalo and rested in the valley until dawn, when they located the main party and with some "exertion" climbed to the top of a ridge and discovered a long divide. Since their horses were weak from lack of food, they left three men in charge of five of them near the divide, while the others moved ahead to better hunting grounds. They maintained a westerly course, sending Isaac Rose ahead to find the Crow Indians, from whom they could secure fresh horses.

Late in the afternoon of the fifth day after Rose's departure, Smith led his men single file along a brush-covered bottom. Suddenly, a ponderous grizzly appeared on the edge of the thicket and felled Smith with an unexpected attack. He was grievously wounded, but his men did their best to sew up his wounds. Three of the party decided to remain with him, nursing him back to health; the main body continued on to a Cheyenne camp. A few days later Smith and his companions were joined by a Missouri Fur Company party, and proceeded together to the Indian camp, where Smith's group was reunited.

The Cheyennes provided Smith and his men fresh horses and enabled them to return to the trail. They pushed on over a smooth, grassy mountain ridge upon which were located excellent springs and plentiful game; the country below the ridge—immediately adjacent to Powder River—was mountainous and rocky. Rose and a band of Crows, enemies to the Cheyennes, joined Smith, Sublette, and the others in their Powder River camp. The Crows brought fresh horses, but the pack animals were so lively and the Indians so anxious to travel that Rose was sent ahead with them and whatever supplies he could pack. At a slower pace, in the days following, the main party was led by Smith across several high ridges west of Powder River. On all sides were "tolerably high but not generall [*sic*] precipitous" mountains, abounding in game, and the frosty nights and somewhat warmer days attested to the fact that it was well into November. Such weather was ideal for the autumn hunt—a hunt that would be Sublette's first in the Far West. He had a great deal to learn, but his instructors were experienced and could tell him much of traps, snares, and the habits of "king Beaver."

Near the Tongue River they struck the Crow trail which led them along the Owl Creek Mountains to Wind River (the Big Horn). Game grew scarce, the wind howled from the north, carrying light snow with it, and they found themselves in a "barren worthless" location. Near exhaustion, high up Wind River, they reached the Crow camp, where they were to halt for the winter. The valley was "narrow and uneven," but there was plenty of grass, and the Indians, on horse and afoot, took a substantial supply of buffalo in several hunts. Food was not a problem, although wood for fuel was, and the white hunters were forced to move their camp to a nearby location. The clear, cold days and lack of heavy snow in the valley encouraged Sublette and his companions to hunt and visit the Crows. Around his own campfire he experienced the "delights" of mountain cooking and realized the usefulness of pipe, tobacco, awl, and bullet mold on long winter days.

Early in February, 1824, they attempted to cross the mountains at Union Pass, north of the snow-clad Wind River Range, but the drifts were too deep; they were forced back to a more southerly route. Heading for South Pass at the lower end of the Wind River Mountains, they ascended the Popo Agie where, quite accidentally, they stumbled upon an oil spring. Their interest, however, was not that of a later age: food was more important than petroleum, and they were short of supplies. Sublette and Clyman set out to scout for provisions and finally, after nearly a day's search, sighted three buffalo bulls in a clearing. They dismounted from their tired horses and crawled through the powdery snow towards the game. They wounded one of the bulls with their fire, but he charged away to a ravine. Clyman pursued him while Sublette rounded up their mounts, then nearly a mile away, after which he joined his companion. Together they butchered, cooked, and ate their share of the buffalo.

It was dark before they finished, and a strong north wind blew "cold frosty snow" across their camping spot. They ran out of sagebrush and, since there was no wood available, scattered the dying embers of their tiny blaze and "spread down [their] scanty bed and [covered themselves] as close as possible from the wind and snow which found its way through every crevice." After a sleepless night, they realized their situation was desperate. To leave the little shelter of their robes, even to light a fire had timber been available, might mean sudden numbness and death. Finally, after some effort, Clyman took the chance and managed to saddle his horse, but Sublette, nearly overcome with cold, was unable to mount or ride. He lay on the ground wrapped in his blanket, as close as he would ever be to death in the mountains. Clyman found a "coal . . . the size of a grain of corn" and kindled a "handful of sage" into a small, smoky fire, enough to revive Sublette, who kept the blaze going while Clyman saddled the other horse and packed the buffalo meat.

They set out for the nearest timber, four miles distant: Sublette rode the lead horse; Clyman rode the second, urging him along. Within half a mile of timber, Clyman dismounted and led the horses on foot the remainder of the way through foot-deep snow. In the timber he found the remains of an Indian lodge in which he kindled a fire, then "whoped up" his friend's horse, and helped Sublette's nearly lifeless figure to a place where he could rest by the fire, take some cooked buffalo meat, and gradually thaw out. When William was "as active as usual," they rejoined their party and moved along to the Sweetwater.

In camp on the Sweetwater they were buffeted by north winds and again ran low on buffalo. Gusts of wind blew their blankets in every direction and sent clouds of choking smoke and ashes from their fire swirling into their faces. They made them-

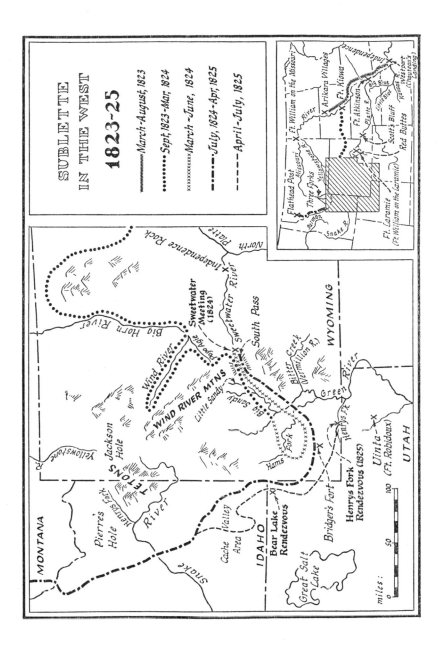

SUBLETTE
IN THE WEST
1823-25

———— March-August, 1823
············ Sept, 1823-Mar, 1824
xxxxxxxxxx March-June, 1824
— · — · — July, 1824-Apr, 1825
— — — — April-July, 1825

Flathead Post
Ft. William on the Missouri
Three Forks
Ft. William on the Missouri
Missouri R.
Yellowstone R.
Arikara Villages
Ft. Kiowa
Independence
Big Blue
Platte R.
Ft. Atkinson
Little Blue
Scott's Bluff
Kansas R.
Westport
(Chouteau's Landing)
Red Buttes
Ft. Laramie
(Ft. William on the Laramie)
Snake R.
Sermon

North Platte
Independence Rock
Sweetwater River
Sweetwater Meeting (1824)
South Pass
Bitter Creek (Vermilion R.)
Big Sandy
Little Sandy
Pope Agie
WIND RIVER MTNS
Wind River
Big Horn River
Green River
Henrys Fk.
Uinta (Ft. Robidoux)
Hams Fork
UTAH
WYOMING
Henrys Fork Rendezvous (1825)
Bridger's Fort
Bear Lake Rendezvous
Cache Valley Area
Great Salt Lake
IDAHO
Snake River
Hemy's Fork
Pierres Hole
TETONS
Jackson Hole
Yellowstone R.
MONTANA

miles:
0   50   100

selves as comfortable as possible in a willow clump while the elements roared, but some of the men who had enough of mountain winters wrapped their robes about them and trudged downstream to a narrow canyon where they found sheltering rocks, shot a mountain sheep, and took it back to the main camp. At first they could not start a fire to cook the animal, but during the night the gusts diminished, a fire was built, and each man arose to eat his fill of mountain ram.

They broke camp as soon as possible and divided into two groups: one to find a better campsite away from the "full sweep from the north wind"; the other, including Sublette, to travel down the Sweetwater about five miles to hunt sheep on the stream cliffs. There they discovered a small aspen grove—their new campsite for two or three weeks—and restocked their packs with a staple diet of wild sheep. When the rams became scarce, they placed a cache of powder, lead, and other articles near their campsite and agreed that if the party separated in the spring hunt, its members would meet there or slightly below on the stream no later than June 1.

The entire party, early in March, left the valley of the Sweetwater bound southwest across bare, wind-swept ridges. On the sixth morning Sublette and Clyman, who were in advance searching for some elusive antelope, came across a fresh buffalo track. They dashed ahead nearly a mile, discovered the animal lying down, and fired at it simultaneously. Sublette reloaded and killed it. The men of the party, without food at least two days in the cold, dry weather, were hungry enough to eat "large slices raw." That night they encamped amidst large clumps of sage, having had a feast of buffalo meat. Their water supply consisted of melted snow, and they were overjoyed soon after to reach the Big Sandy River beyond the "main ridge," where they cut holes in the ice to drink and found a few willows for fuel. While moving down the Sandy, they killed another buffalo and on March 19 reached the Green River, or the Seeds-kee-dee Agie, as many called the stream.

On the Green the party divided. Smith and a half-dozen

men journeyed farther south to hunt, most probably on Blacks Fork of the Green. Another party of four, including Clyman and Fitzpatrick, remained to trap in the upper Green River Valley. Sublette may have been with either group, although on the basis of future association it is most likely that he was with Smith and the larger party. The spring hunt was productive, and by mid-June the two parties were reunited on the Sweetwater. Since the river was high, Fitzpatrick and two others were sent with the furs collected to convey them in skin boats down the Platte.[23] Clyman was believed lost in the wilderness, and the remaining men agreed to stay in the mountains for the duration of the year.

The little meeting of 1824 on the Sweetwater was the forerunner of many important rendezvous. Sublette, completing his first year of western service, was one of the tiny band remaining there for the fall hunt of 1824 and the spring hunt of 1825. He knew that the expedition just completed, despite its initial troubles, was a success and that even greater fur activity could be expected. He had survived at least two serious challenges to his life and, given the opportunity might achieve notable success in his new, dangerous vocation.

[23] *Weekly Reveille* (St. Louis), March 1, 1847.

An Ashley Man

TINY THOUGH the meeting was on the Sweetwater in mid-June, 1824, it was a time for general rejoicing after many dangerous months—a time perhaps for a little gambling, singing, and storytelling mixed with boatbuilding and the more mundane rendezvous duties. Smith, Sublette, and five others prepared to head southwest after the meeting to return to the rich fur area trapped in the spring. Their immediate destination beyond South Pass was the Bear River Divide and Bear River Valley.[1]

Smith successfully led them fivescore miles down Bear River, trapping as they moved, then on to headwaters of the Blackfoot. An Iroquois Indian party met them on the trail, traded with them, and in exchange for companionship and protection led them to the camp of Alexander Ross, the British fur partisan. The Americans cached their furs along the way and proceeded in combined party with the British across Lemhi Pass, on October

---

[1] Much of the material in this chapter, in addition to the sources cited, is drawn from: *The Life and Adventures of James P. Beckwourth, Mountaineer, Scout, Pioneer, and Chief of the Crow Nations of Indians* (ed. by C. G. Leland); J. Cecil Alter, *James Bridger, Trapper, Frontiersman, Scout, and Guide;* Katharine Coman, *Economic Beginnings of the Far West: How We Won the Land Beyond the Mississippi,* I; Dale, *op. cit.;* Phillips (ed.), *op. cit.;* Morgan, *op. cit.;* Glauert, *loc. cit.;* Waldo, *loc. cit.;* Chittenden, *The American Fur Trade,* II; Sheldon (ed.), *op. cit.,* V.

28, and four days later recrossed the divide to the Bitterroot. On November 26, they reached Flathead Post, important way station in the Columbia Department of the Hudson's Bay Company. Winter had started, and Smith and his men busied themselves doing not much of anything while Ross went to work to put a new British party in the field under the leadership of the reliable Peter Skene Ogden.

Sublette had free run of the post, opportunity to observe and learn. Actually, the establishment was not imposing, since it consisted of only a handful of huts. On November 20, however, the Indians, led by the Flathead, began arriving for their winter trade amidst pomp and ceremony alien to most American trading ventures. By December 3, the trade was over and the red men started to leave, but while it lasted, there was a colorful progression of Pend d'Oreille, Kutenai, Spokan, and other Indians. Shortly before Christmas, Ogden's expedition left the post. Smith and his men followed and joined him on the twenty-ninth near Hell Gate.

Ogden was bound for Snake River, despite the cold, snowy weather and the shortage of ready game, and Smith was determined to accompany him into beaver country in order to have an equal chance at the supply whenever spring began. The British-American party used approximately the same route followed the previous fall by Ross and Smith. In mid-January they pushed through Gibbons Pass down to Big Hole River—into Blackfoot country and an area claimed by the United States. By the first week in February they reached the Beaverhead, then crossed Lemhi Pass to the Salmon, but in Lemhi Valley were surrounded by deep snow blocking the trail over the divide. For seven weeks they moved here and there about the valley in search of grass and buffalo.

Smith and his men were tired of waiting and willing to take a chance, so they traded beaver to the British for desperately needed supplies and on March 19 headed out along a route that followed the Little Lost River and took them over the divide. Ogden, unwilling to be outdone by his competitors, followed and

55

on April 7, near the mouth of the Blackfoot on Snake River, caught up with Smith's camp. The next day the Americans secured more supplies from Ogden, and the two groups pushed up the Blackfoot, each trying to gain an advantage, at times in close contact and at other times not. The snow blocked the valley, however, and both of them were forced to turn west to the Portneuf.

When they reached the Bear, Ogden led his men downstream. Smith led his band upriver until he discovered that other Americans had reached and wintered on the river and were by then trapping its lower reaches. Anticipating that they might be Ashley men, he also turned down the Bear. By May 23 he and his men had joined the other American group encamped on the Bear under the leadership of Captain John H. Weber—a group that included Daniel Potts and Jim Bridger from Henry's post on the Big Horn. There were some free trappers with them under Johnson Gardner, and Bridger had a tale to tell of how, during the previous winter, he had reached the Great Salt Lake.

Smith and his followers related their news of British activities and of Ogden's presence in the immediate vicinity. The situation was ripe for international dispute, and friction resulted almost immediately. Early on the twenty-third, Étienne Provost, an independent trader, led his men down Weber River without knowing that Weber and Smith were in the area. He met Ogden's party and was received none too cordially. The same afternoon a group from Weber's camp, consisting of twenty-five Americans and fourteen of Ogden's wayward trappers, reached the scene. Johnson Gardner was in immediate command and had been apprised of the situation by Smith. Gardner took a most belligerent attitude. According to the British, the Americans had "laid . . . plans to decoy [their] trappers and break up [their] expedition." The intent bears better proof, but the fact remains that the Americans encamped one hundred yards from the British and hoisted the Stars and Stripes to proclaim themselves on United States territory. In reality, all of them were trespassing on Mexican soil south of forty-two degrees.

56

In the morning Gardner visited Ogden's tent to ask him if he knew he was in American territory, but Ogden maintained that the area was under joint occupation by provision of the Convention of 1818. Gardner then advised the British leader to remain there at his peril, and departed, in order to visit certain of Ogden's trappers. By evening he had induced a few of them to desert their party, taking their furs with them. Ogden, fearful that his camp might be pillaged at any moment, prepared his remaining forces for attack, but the Americans did not attempt to molest them further, and on the following day the British packed and hurriedly headed west.[2]

The incident in no way improved British-American relations—relations that were constantly beclouded by misunderstandings in the far northwest. British fur posts had been established in opportune locations from the Pacific shore inland as far as the upper reaches of the Columbia and its tributaries. There were several meetings between British and American fur parties in the region—fortunately most of the meetings were peaceful—although there was usually some suspicion. The British regard for Ashley, the "militia general . . . [who had] been a Farmer, a Shopkeeper, a Miner and latterly an Indian Trader," was not heightened by his traffic with deserters from the British fur parties. Ashley's successors, who, according to the British, had "all at once promoted themselves to the . . . title of Captains," would be no more welcome as competitors than the "militia general" himself.[3] On several occasions the Flathead trade of the Hudson's Bay Company was completely or partially lost to American trappers; yet, on the other hand, trappers would at times desert the Americans to take

---

[2] For details on the British fur parties see: *Part of Dispatch from George Simpson . . . to . . . the Hudson's Bay Company . . . 1829 . . .* (ed. by E. E. Rich), *Publications of the Champlain Society, Hudson's Bay Company,* X; Alexander Ross's Journal of the Snake Country Expedition of 1824, MS, Oregon Historical Society; Frederick Merk (ed.), "The Snake Country Expedition Correspondence 1824–1825," *Mississippi Valley Historical Review,* Vol. XXI (June, 1934–March, 1935), 63–67.

[3] Peter Skene Ogden Journal of Proceedings in the Snake Country Commencing in August, 1827, entries of September 28, October 17, 24, 1827, MS, Oregon Historical Society.

their furs to the British. Both Americans and British accused one another of underselling in order to capture the Indian trade, and at least in one instance the Americans intimated that the Hudson's Bay Company encouraged an Indian attack upon an American fur party. Mutual suspicions were exaggerated and intensified by rumors spread amongst the Indians that the United States was to annex shortly the area west of the mountains and that the Indians in the region would do well to cultivate trade with Americans.[4] In 1825, when William Clark as superintendent of Indian Affairs at St. Louis requested advice of the Secretary of War on the subject "in relation to hunting & trapping within & west of the Rocky Mountains," he reflected the prevailing northwestern difficulties and conjured old shadows of the Revolutionary War and the War of 1812.[5]

The furs turned over to Gardner and Smith by Ogden's deserters amounted to seven hundred skins, not an insignificant quantity. Ashley willingly accepted them when he met his lieutenants at the rendezvous that year.[6] After the Arikara disaster of 1823, he had returned home to his duties as lieutenant governor, only to be defeated for governor of Missouri in the election of August, 1824. Shortly after the election, Henry joined him in St. Louis with a "considerable quantity of furs." For reasons of health, finance, or whatever it was, he retired from the partnership.[7] There was talk of Ashley's insolvency, but he put aside any financial fears he might have had and outfitted a new expedition, which he led west in September, 1824. He was at Fort Atkinson on October 21, although it was not until the first week in November that he and his twenty-five men proceeded west

[4] John Work's Journal from July 5, 1826, to September 15, 1826, entry of August 26, 1826, MS, University of Washington; *Daily National Intelligencer* (Washington, D. C.), April 22, 1829, in Ashley MSS.
[5] W. Clark to J. Barbour, October 24, 1825, Clark MSS, MoSHi.
[6] S. W. Foreman to John H. Eaton, May, 1829, Unregistered Letters Received, May, 1829, Records of the Office of the Secretary of War, Record Group No. 107, MSS, N. A.; *Missouri Advocate and St. Louis Enquirer*, October 8, 1825.
[7] *Independent Patriot* (Jackson), September 18, 1824; "Letters of William Carr Lane 1819–1831," *Glimpses of the Past*, Vol. VII (July–September, 1940), 88.

along the Platte to Laramie Fork.[8] By then it was early in the New Year.

West of the Laramie they skirted the Medicine Bow Range and on April 19 reached the Green River, where Ashley divided his men into four groups: three were to trap and travel by land; he was to lead the fourth by water down the Green to Henrys Fork, where the rendezvous was to be held. As he descended the spectacular Green River Valley, Smith and Weber conducted their spring hunts on the waters of Bear River. They found the area particularly rich in beaver and met no immediate British threat, since Ogden had been forced to retire. They continued their activities throughout the pleasant month of June, looking forward to the rendezvous, when they would have much to report to Ashley on their observations of the country. Sublette had spent a most worthwhile year in the mountains and played an increasingly important role in the Ashley enterprise.

The rendezvous was located on the south or right-hand bank of Henrys Fork, a few miles above its junction with Green River, and although there was a small meeting the previous year, this one of July, 1825, was to be the "real prototype" of all rendezvous to follow. Indians, many of whom had never seen manufactured goods, eagerly watched and wondered as Ashley's men gathered on July 1 for a week's meeting. Despite high prices, whiskey was bartered as freely as water, and the firewater lifted the spirits of all present and provided Sublette and his friends a constant stimulus for many sporting events on the river plains. Ashley used the meeting as an opportunity to form a new partnership—this one with Jedediah Smith, his trusted lieutenant—since Andrew Henry had withdrawn. As a result of the new arrange-

[8] Claims of Ashley and Henry for Indian depredations on the Missouri, January 2, 1824; John Dougherty to Lewis Cass, November 6, 1831; Letters Received, 1824–1881, Records of the Office of Indian Affairs, Record Group No. 75, MSS, N. A.; Trading License of W. H. Ashley, 1824, DMDI, MSS, MoSHi; William Ashley to William Carr Lane, October 29, 1824, Ashley MSS; "Diary of James Kennerly 1823–1826," (ed. by Edgar B. Wesley), *Missouri Historical Society Collections*, Vol. VI (October, 1928), 77; James Kennerly to Pierre Chouteau, December 1, 1824, Chouteau-Papin MSS.

ment, Ashley was to remain as business representative of the firm, while Smith would continue to conduct mountain trapping.

Three or four days after the Fourth of July—a date always well celebrated in the mountains—the rendezvous ended, and Ashley, with forty-five to fifty thousand dollars in skins on hand, started for St. Louis. Fifty of his men, including Smith and probably Sublette, accompanied him on horses secured from the British deserters, to convey the fur catch to the Big Horn. En route Ashley, Sublette, and some eighteen or nineteen others reportedly left the main party to recover a cache of forty-five beaver packs which Ashley had left at the junction of Henrys Fork and the Green on his way to the rendezvous. They raised the cache intact and proceeded to return to the main party, but on the way were attacked twice by Indians. In the first attack, at daybreak one morning, sixty Blackfeet attempted to take the camp and failed. They did succeed, however, in frightening off all but two of Ashley's valuable horses and in wounding either Sublette or Beckwith. Immediately an express was sent to the main party to return with new mounts, and while Ashley awaited them, he and his companions fought off a midnight attack of Crows. When they rejoined the main party the following day, it must have been with great relief.[9]

They reached the Big Horn at a logical embarkation point just below the mountains and there built boats to descend the river. Sublette and one half of the party, after a short rest, returned to the mountains, taking the horses with them since all of Ashley's men were to travel down-river by water. On August 19, twelve days after reaching the Big Horn, the Ashley flotilla glided into the Missouri River at the mouth of the Yellowstone. At that place they met a United States military expedition to the Indians, under Atkinson and O'Fallon. The expedition was in temporary quarters at Camp Barbour a short distance below the mouth of the Yellowstone, and Atkinson offered Ashley transportation in his boats if Ashley would wait for the return of the troops to Council Bluffs. Ashley willingly accepted the proposal "to be

[9] *Missouri Intelligencer* (Franklin), October 7, 1825.

sure of a safe passage" and loaded his beaver aboard the keelboat "Buffalo."[10] On the way downstream he reported to O'Fallon, who in turn reported to the Secretary of War, that the trail across the South Pass provided "easy passage across the Rocky Mountains.[11] On Monday afternoon, September 19, the expedition reached Council Bluffs. Ashley continued to St. Louis, arriving on October 4.[12] He immediately purchased twenty thousand dollars worth of merchandise and outfitted a new expedition of 70 men and 160 mules and horses; by October 29, all was ready for the return to the mountains. He had just married Eliza Christy, his second wife, and did not intend personally to lead his new party to the West.[13]

While en route to St. Louis, his trapping parties in the mountains completed the autumn hunt of 1825. After the dispersal of the rendezvous, those trappers not accompanying Ashley to the Big Horn divided into parties to trap on the waters of Green and Bear rivers and their adjoining tributaries. Those men who accompanied Ashley to his embarkation point, before returning to the mountains with his horses, were under Sublette's command and, in fact, all of Ashley's groups remaining in the region might have been "nominally under" his control. Whatever the situation, he led his party back along the Big Horn to the trapping areas around the Green and Bear, where the other groups were active.

The various parties had agreed to gather in winter quarters in Cache Valley. As the days grew cooler and the late summer fields of wild flowers faded, the hunters began to gather at their meeting place. Sublette's party, if we may trust the indefinite

---

[10] Russell Reid and C. G. Gannon (eds.), "Journal of the Atkinson-O'Fallon Expedition," *North Dakota Historical Quarterly*, Vol. IV (1929), 5–8, 42; S. W. Kearny Diary from September 17, 1824, to May 10, 1826, entry of August 20, 1825, MS, MoSHi.

[11] 19 Cong., 1 sess., *House Exec. Doc. No. 117*, pp. 14–15.

[12] *Missouri Advocate and St. Louis Enquirer*, October 29, 1825; *Missouri Intelligencer* (Franklin), October 7, 1825; S. W. Kearny Diary from September 17, 1824 to May 10, 1826, entry of September 19, 1825, MSS, MoSHi; James W. Kingsbury to his parents, October 3, 1825, J. W. Kingsbury Collection, 1791–1911, MSS, MoSHi.

[13] *Missouri Republican* (St. Louis), October 31, 1825; *Missouri Advocate and St. Louis Enquirer*, October 29, 1825.

records, was the last to reach the valley. Whether the delay was due to poor traveling conditions, to a preoccupation with trapping, or to the distance they had to travel is conjectural. Fortunately, they were there before the coldest days of the winter set in—a winter of deep snow and severe winds. The weather necessitated a more comfortable location, and in mid-December the entire camp moved down to the Salt Lake Valley, an area which Provost and his men had traversed and reported "hospitable." Two new camps, including many Indians, were established: one on Weber's River and one on Bear River near its mouth. The Indian women and children, "all strong and healthy as bears," must have given the sites a rather domestic atmosphere.

During the winter Smith brought Ashley's autumn expedition into the mountains.[14] Ashley, in St. Louis, outfitted yet another supply train and by March 8, 1826, was once again on his way west.[15] He and his small party passed through Franklin, Missouri, on the fifteenth and then took the same trail he had used in his midwinter expedition of 1824–25.[16] Grass was plentiful, and they made rapid progress along the Platte, across the Pass, down the Sandys, along the cold, clear Green River to Henrys Fork, where they crossed to the Bear and Cache Valley.

By that time the methods used to move parties through Indian country were well established. In an average supply party of sixty to eighty men, a handful would aid the commander, while the others were divided into "messes" of eight or ten with a suitable man over each mess who was in charge of conduct, supplies, and orders. Normally, each man was mounted on a horse and led two pack mules. Each horse was equipped with two halters, at least one sixteen-foot rein, one saddle, one saddle blanket, one bearskin cover, and one bridle. Each man was given a two-foot wooden stake, having a pointed iron socket at one end

[14] Jedediah Smith to Joel Poinsette, December 16, 1826, MS, Pennsylvania Historical Society, Philadelphia. Copy in possession of Dale Morgan, Berkeley, California.

[15] *Missouri Republican* (St. Louis), March 9, 1826; *Missouri Advocate* and *St. Louis Enquirer*, March 11, 1826.

[16] *Missouri Intelligencer* (Franklin), March 24, 1826.

and an iron band at the other, which was driven into the ground to hold the animals when encamped. All articles of equipment were carefully entered in account books—invaluable records of the era.

At night traveling parties would construct a square camp with one of its sides, whenever possible, bordering a body of water. Each man was assigned a position in camp and required to unload his packs and help erect some type of defensive breast-work. The animals were watered, secured to a stake, and left to graze within the enclosure. At daybreak, especially if there were signs of Indians, two men were sent to scout the region before the main party left the enclosure. If all was well, the horses would be grazed, and the camp would "break" for the day's march. Generally, the messes marched together, the first taking its place behind the leader and so on. Scouts were always sent several miles ahead, as well as short distances to the flanks and rear, and as soon as Indians were sighted, signals were given, and the expedition arranged for a possible attack.

Ashley's party met no grave Indian dangers, descended the Bear, and reached Cache Valley on schedule for the rendezvous of July, 1826.[17] The occasion was, as usual, one of great celebration for all the men: "songs, dancing, shouting, trading, running, jumping, racing, target shooting, yarns and frolic, with all sorts of extravagances." The most important business negotiated involved the transfer of Ashley's fur interests to Smith, Sublette, and David E. Jackson. Ashley had many personal reasons for selling his fur interests. He desired to settle down with his new wife to a more civilized and respectable life. He knew that more and more men were entering the Far West, many as unlicensed trappers, and that such unregulated intercourse caused trouble for the military authorities. It was easy for him to see that in the future there would be ever greater fur competition—possibly also a lessened profit and a diminished beaver supply—and that his St. Louis backers might at any time decide to support some other business venture, especially if the fur returns decreased.

[17] *Arkansas Gazette* (Little Rock), November 28, 1826.

Ashley realized that his profits from the trade of 1824–26 more than repaid his earlier losses and enabled him to build and maintain a mansion in St. Louis.[18] According to the reports of the British traders made to the Hudson's Bay Company, his returns for 1824–26 had "barely covered his losses," and his total gains were "merely a little eclat." Their estimates for his trade of 1824 and 1826 were accurate, but they seem to have overemphasized his debts. Certainly, he had recouped his financial losses, but he could never replace the men lost in his service. Reports of men killed or missing in the fur trade vary in their accuracy, and only an approximate total may be given; yet most reports agree that he lost between twenty-seven and sixty men in the years 1822–26. Possibly, more than all else, he was relieved to abandon the trade because of its human responsibilities.[19]

Ashley had a strong personal attachment to Smith and knew the capacities for leadership of all three of his successors. Doubtless it is correct that Smith was the "real promoter of the new company," but Sublette must have played an important hand in the negotiations. Only Jackson, enigma of the mountain trade, seems to have had little, if anything, to do with the embryonic plans and may have been brought into the agreement at the last minute simply to lessen the financial burden upon Smith and Sublette. Jackson possibly had entered Ashley's service in 1823, but was swallowed up in the trapping business until his sudden reappearance in 1826.

Robert Campbell, witness to the new agreement, was appointed clerk of the company.[20] He was of Scotch-Irish extraction, had reached the United States in 1822, from his home in County Tyrone, and shortly thereafter joined Ashley's force in the West. Since he was not in the best of health, his devoted

18 Mrs. H. R. Clark to M. L. Clark, October 3, 1826, Clark MSS, MoSHi.

19 Report of Joshua Pilcher of Persons Killed in the Fur Trade, November 20, 1831, DMDI, MSS, MoSHi; Report of John Dougherty of Persons Killed in the Fur Trade, October 24, 1831, DMDI, MSS, MoSHi; Tabular Statement of No. of Persons Robbed or Killed, DMDI, MSS, MoSHi; List of Persons Killed in the Fur Trade, Clark, MSS, KHi.

20 W. H. Ashley to T. H. Benton, November 12, 1827, Ashley MSS, MoSHi.

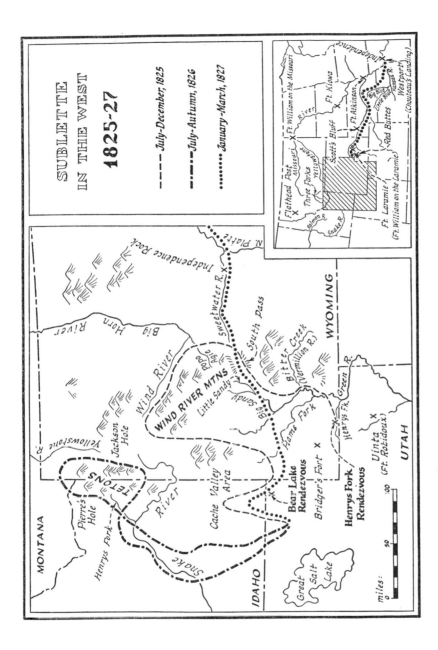

SUBLETTE
IN THE WEST
1825-27

— — — July–December, 1825
— ·· — July–Autumn, 1826
········ January–March, 1827

MONTANA

Pierre's Hole

TETONS

Jackson Hole

Yellowstone R.

Henrys Fork

Snake River

IDAHO

Great Salt Lake

Wind River

WIND RIVER MTNS

Bull Lake

Little Sandy

Big Sandy

Cache Valley Area

Horse Fork

Bear Lake Rendezvous

Bridger's Fort X

Henrys Fork Rendezvous

Henrys Fk.

Green R.

Uinta X (Ft. Robidoux)

UTAH

Big Horn River

Independence Rock

Sweetwater R. X

South Pass

Bitter Creek (Vermillion R.)

WYOMING

N. Platte

miles:
0   50   100

Flathead Post X

Three Forks

Missouri R.

Yellowstone R.

Salmon R.

Snake R.

Ft. William on the Missouri X

Ft. Kiowa X

Scott's Bluff X

Ft. Atkinson X

Red Buttes X

Ft. Laramie (Ft. William on the Laramie) X

Big Blue R.

Little Blue R.

Kansas R.

Independence X

Westport (Chouteau's Landing)

family would never quite become reconciled to his mountain enterprises and would breathe a sigh of relief when he gave up the rigors of the Far West to settle into the commercial life of St. Louis. In the years after 1826, he and Sublette became devoted friends and later established a business partnership. Although Campbell was a "genial hospitable gentleman . . . who was slow to admit strangers to intimacy," over the years he and Sublette forged "a community . . . [of] feelings, wishes, tastes and dangers" of brotherly proportions. They spent as much time together as possible, nursed each other in sickness, and planned for the future in harmony and accord.[21] Obituaries often exaggerate, but the one carried in the *Missouri Republican* in 1879, upon the event of Campbell's death, was exact in noting the "strict integrity of purpose . . . honesty and honorable dealings" of the deceased.

The firm of Smith, Jackson and Sublette was established by formal written agreement drawn up at the rendezvous on July 18, 1826.[22] Ashley transferred his merchandise in the mountains, valued at sixteen thousand dollars, to the three men, but five of the sixteen thousand was due Smith for the dissolution of his earlier partnership with Ashley. Smith, Jackson and Sublette, on their part, agreed to turn over to Ashley whatever beaver they might collect until their debt, due on July 1, 1827, was paid. In return, Ashley was to supply between seven and fifteen thousand dollars in merchandise for the next year, by July 1, 1827, provided that they should notify him of their needs by March 1. He agreed not to supply any other companies or individuals "other than those who may be in his immediate service" during that period, and the partners agreed to pay for their merchandise by October 1, 1828. In addition to the above, Ashley transferred to Smith, Jackson and Sublette, probably by verbal agreement,

[21] "Correspondence of Robert Campbell 1834–1845" (ed. by Stella M. Drumm and Isaac H. Lionberger), *Glimpses of the Past,* Vol. VII (January–June, 1941), 12–13.

[22] File of *Jos. W. Cunningham adms. David Cunningham* v. *Wm. L. Sublette,* Case No. 642, MS, Office of the Clerk of the Supreme Court, Jefferson City, Missouri.

the services of forty-two of his trappers. More specifically, according to Ashley, the arrangement for the transfer and sale of beaver fur was as follows:

> . . . *they promise to pay me in beaver fur delivered in that country at three dollars pr pound or I am to receive the fur, transport the same to St. Louis and have it disposed of on their account, deducting from the amount of sale one dollar twelve & half cents per pound for transportation, and place the net proceeds to their credit in discharge of the debt.*[23]

Once the arrangements were made, Ashley assembled his return party, delivered a farewell address to the camp, and immediately set out to convey the year's beaver catch to St. Louis. He followed the usual route along the Sweetwater and Platte rivers, leading his caravan of over fifty men and "upwards of one hundred horses and mules" to eastern Missouri in about seventy days. They found an abundance of food, water, and good grass along the way, and he stated shortly after his arrival home in late September that wagons could be taken as far as the site of his recent rendezvous. He presented the public with specimens of salt from the Great Salt Lake and willingly gave the newspapers a full account of the Río Colorado of the West and of the importance of his expedition.[24]

[23] Articles of Agreement between Ashley and Smith, Jackson and Sublette, July 18, 1826, Sublette MSS; William Ashley Letter of October 14, 1826, Ashley MSS, MoSHi.
[24] *Arkansas Gazette* (Little Rock), October 17, November 28, 1826; *Missouri Intelligencer* (Franklin), September 28, 1826.

Smith, Jackson and Sublette

THE SHORT Rocky Mountain summer was at least half over when Smith, Jackson and Sublette put into operation their plans to exploit the fur country. Smith, pre-eminently an explorer and discoverer rather than a developer of fur resources, was to lead a band of adventurers into new trapping areas. In the succeeding months he searched for the Buenaventura River, extended geographic knowledge, and secured information on animals and Indian tribes. Jackson was to remain in the mountains trapping and trading, keeping the fur parties about their business. Sublette, best qualified of the three as a businessman, was to supervise fur transportation to St. Louis and attend, with Ashley, to its sale. Sublette's exemplary service under Ashley, from 1823 to 1826, his early business training, his ties to St. Louis, and his inherent shrewdness fitted him for his new position. Ashley's friendship would give him an introduction to the leading business houses of St. Louis and the East, and it would be but a matter of time before the family name of Sublette would be known widely both East and West.

Before the rendezvous of 1826, at Cache Valley, was disbanded, detailed preparations were made for the autumn hunt. David Cunningham and others were employed to serve as free trappers with the understanding that the firm was to receive and pay them for whatever they might catch.[1] Several other old and trusted friends and companions, such as Robert Campbell, Thomas Fitzpatrick, Moses (Black) Harris, Jim Bridger, and Jim Beckwith, who had transferred from Ashley's service, were designated "able lieutenants" in charge of fur brigades. Thirty brigades, reportedly, were organized, but it is more likely that only one-third to one-half that number actually were formed. The rendezvous for 1827 was scheduled at the southern end of Bear Lake in Mexican territory, and about August 15, Smith and fifteen men headed southwest. Their journey would take them overland to Mission San Gabriel, California, where they would be taken into Spanish custody, released, and finally would reach the northwest coast. Their explorations and adventures in the years 1827–28 would be of legendary proportion and would provide many a colorful chapter in the early history of the West.

Meanwhile, Jackson and Sublette led their parties north from the rendezvous into Idaho and Wyoming, where they trapped and traded with the Snakes, Crows, Sioux, and Flatheads. They "kept about one hundred men busy scouring the country for furs; they competed with Ogden's men for the fur of Oregon, they penetrated . . . dangerous [Blackfoot territory] . . . they visited Yellowstone Park and added much to the general knowledge of the country." More specifically, the parties, carrying with them a large amount of merchandise, struck out first for the Snake River country of the Blackfeet and Flatheads. Trapping would not be ideal until the beginning of autumn, but in the interim they expected to trade with the tribes for horses and skins. Along the lower Snake they hunted leisurely, traded, and readied their equipment for the fall hunt; then moved on past the Black Foot Buttes to the upper reaches of the river. From the forks of the Snake their line of march took them to the foot of the Tetons,

---

[1] Much of the material in this chapter, in addition to the sources cited, is drawn from: Alter, *op. cit.;* Chittenden, *The American Fur Trade*, I, II; Dale, *op. cit.;* Beckwourth, *op. cit.;* Morgan, *op. cit.;* Phillips (ed.), *op. cit.;* Sullivan, *op. cit.;* Vandiveer, *op. cit.;* (Mrs.) F. Fuller Victor, *The River of the West.*

across an area rich in buffalo but also, it seems, in lurking Black-feet. Since it was evident the tribesmen were unfriendly, the party moved camp along the Tetons to a place where they could pursue their fall hunt in upper Jackson Hole.[2]

While encamped on the main branch of the Snake in Jackson Hole, they met more Indian dangers and proceeded upriver. After crossing a divide, they reached the headwaters of the Yellowstone at the west thumb of Yellowstone Lake. It was not the first time that the picturesque area was crossed, since John Colter had entered the region as early as 1807, but it was Sublette's first crossing of the present-day national park. They saw paint pots and geysers, but could not delay to admire their surroundings: it was nearly winter, and they wished to head back to Cache Valley. By a "circuitous route" northwest from the Yellowstone, they returned to their old rendezvous site and settled down in log huts to outwait the snow and cold winds. From time to time they foraged for game, but otherwise there were no pressing duties. Sublette supervised provisions and equipment, helped maintain peace and quiet, investigated local Indian activities, and listened to the songs and stories of his men. Some of the trappers probably had wounds to nurse—the usual marks of Indian encounters—but there is no reason to suspect that the season was anything but quiet. As in winters immemorial, the snow fell and the winds blew hard from the west and northwest, driving the flakes before them.

According to the provisions of the Ashley contract, an express had to be sent to St. Louis to notify Ashley on or before March 1, 1827, of the merchandise required by Smith, Jackson and Sublette. Since Sublette was to be entrusted with the firm's business negotiations, it was decided that he would personally carry the message to St. Louis, accompanied by Black Harris, a sturdy, toughened mountaineer. Jackson, in all probability, agreed to remain in charge of the valley camp and to direct the spring hunt of 1827, until Sublette could return to the mountains and

---

[2] Merrill J. Mattes, "Jackson Hole, Crossroads of the Western Fur Trade, 1807–1840," *Pacific Northwest Quarterly*, Vol. XXXVII (April, 1946), 105.

meet him at the rendezvous scheduled at the southern end of Bear Lake.[3]

On New Year's Day, 1827, Sublette and Harris said farewell to their friends and set out on snowshoes for the East, their only traveling companion an Indian pack dog which carried part of their rudimentary camping equipment. By the time they reached Hams Fork, where they expected to find buffalo, their dried-meat supply was short. Their position was rendered doubly dangerous by a lack of water, other than that provided by melted snow or ice, and by the necessity of avoiding Indian bands. At the Sweetwater in mid-January, they found buffalo to replenish their food supply and thankfully bedded down for one sheltered night, at least, "in a hole in Rock Independence." The gray, elephantine mass of rock, always so welcome a landmark to travelers ascending the Sweetwater, was to Sublette and Harris the foreboding sign of hundreds of miles to come. Immediately they pushed ahead through drifted snow, possibly wondering how even sagebrush could exist in such frosty desolation, and at times traveled half the night before they could find a hollow in which to build a small fire upon whose embers they spread their blankets. Arriving at the North Platte, they found themselves without firewood or food, but in the cedar-covered, low, sandy hills around Ash Hollow they discovered evidence of Pawnee Indian activity. Believing it best to avoid the thieving Pawnees, they turned from their trail and three or four days later stumbled into a friendly Indian camp. Big Elk, the chief, cordially received them, tended to their needs, and sent them on their way the following morning.

Continuing down the Platte, they passed Cold Camp Creek and began to meet small Indian bands, with one of whom Sublette traded a hunting knife for a buffalo tongue. The Indian pack dog grew weaker every day: their small supply of sugar, coffee, and dried meat had fallen from his worn pack somewhere along the trail. Near Grand Island they shot a raven for supper, but they were so hungry they could not tell "whether it was good or bad, or how it tasted." Forty or fifty miles beyond, encamped

[3] William Ashley Letter of October 14, 1826, Ashley MSS, MoSHi.

71

in the snow beneath the shelter of three elm trees, they realized they were sick, near starvation, and still two hundred miles from any settlements. In desperation, Harris suggested they kill and eat the faithful Indian dog. Although Sublette, who was quite ill, at first opposed the plan, he consented reluctantly and after some difficulty, because of the darkness and his own weakened condition, helped his companion dispatch the unhappy creature. He was unable to eat until morning, then partook of what they had, helped pack the scraps, and started again. The meat lasted less than two days, after which they ate a little salt and pepper. They were on the verge of exhaustion when, suddenly, a rabbit hopped within firing range and provided them a lifesaving stew.

A few miles from the Big Vermillion they struck an old Kaw Indian trail and found a supply of wild turkeys, several of which they killed, ate, or stored away until they reached the Old Kansas Village, where they drank something more than melted snow. At the village Harris "gave out" with a strained ankle—possibly the result of trudging through many miles of heavy snow. Sublette, realizing that he would have to race against time to reach St. Louis by March 1, bartered a pistol to buy a horse for Harris and hurried on to the east. Nonetheless, although they exerted all their energies, they were unable to reach St. Louis until March 4, three days overdue on the Ashley contract. Sublette had not improved his own health by the grueling midwinter journey and technically had failed to honor his firm's contract agreement—an agreement upon which Smith and Jackson, in the mountains, depended. He had either to arrange something with Ashley, despite the broken date, or to organize on his own, within a month, some type of supply service for his men in the West.[4]

The problem of a supply train to the rendezvous was settled when he learned from Ashley that the contract would be honored despite the delay. Ashley, however, had negotiated with representatives of the French Fur Company, a subsidiary of the grow-

[4] Sublette's Narrative of his Overland Trip of 1827, Field Diary, MS, MoSHi.

ing American Fur Company, and hoped to interest them in new plans he had to send trappers of his own to the mountains. Under a loophole in the contract he had made in 1826 with Smith, Jackson and Sublette, he could have outfitted a trapping group of his own for mountain service, but had pledged not to supply other companies in the West. The French Fur Company hedged and made only a limited agreement with Ashley whereby they invested in part, estimated at up to one-half, of his supply train outfitted for Smith, Jackson and Sublette. As a result, Ashley's supply party was under preparation when Sublette reached St. Louis, but Ashley's new trapping venture had been given up.

As far as is known, Sublette did not resent Ashley's part in the agreement with the Astor interests in the French Fur Company. He knew, however, that John Jacob Astor's hand in the mountains was growing stronger and thereafter would consider Pierre Chouteau, Astor's chief St. Louis representative, as an "opponent." For the present, Sublette was content to know that Smith and Jackson would have supplies at the rendezvous. On March 26, he visited William Clark and took out a trading license for his firm, capitalized at $4,335 under bond of $3,000 posted to cover proposed trading operations at "Camp Defence, on the waters of a river supposed to be the Bonaventura.—Horse Prairie, on Clark's river of the Columbia, and mouth of Lewis's Fork of the Columbia."[5]

Those few short days in March were the first William had spent in St. Louis since the spring of 1823. He had left Missouri a novice in the western trade and returned an entrepreneur, but there was scarcely time to think, much less to examine in any detail the changes made at home. He hurried to St. Charles to see the Whitleys and his old friends. While there he was told family news—news the irregular western message service had not carried to him in the mountains. His sister Sophronia had been married on March 31, 1825, to Grove Cook, a "likable but wild young man" in Callaway County, and it was perhaps at this time that Sublette learned of the death of his other sister who

[5] 20 Cong., 1 sess., *Sen. Doc. No. 96*, pp. 3-4.

had been living with the McKinneys.[6] While in St. Charles, he sold property belonging to his parents' estate and decided to take his brother Pinckney to the mountains.[7] Although he was said to be a "well proportioned, broad shoulder[ed] and straight" young man, Pinckney's health was not good. He would have to be guarded and closely supervised in the West—he was but fourteen or fifteen—yet William believed that the mountain air and sunshine might improve his constitution.[8]

Sublette stayed at one of the downtown hotels or boardinghouses while in St. Louis, but wherever he lodged, he was not far removed from the city's trade. On March 15, the supply train left St. Louis.[9] Ashley accompanied it to the edge of the settlement, where, on account of illness, family obligations, and his determination not to return to the mountains, he turned back to his home. Included in the merchandise carried by the party was the usual inventory: gunpowder, lead, shot, three-point blankets, scarlet and blue cloth, flannel, calico, butcher knives, beaver traps, sugar, coffee, vermilion, and rum. They also carried an artillery piece mounted on a two-mule vehicle—great medicine for the mountain tribes. Sublette caught up with the party after he had secured his license and had stopped at St. Charles to take his brother from his spelling class. Pinckney, more than likely, was happy to go, since he was considerably older than his schoolmates and was at the foot of the class. A school chum remembered, many years later, that Pinckney "could not write" and that he had to do all his letter writing for him.

Possibly Ashley left the expedition when Sublette and his younger brother reached the party, but whatever actually happened, the supply train made good time west along the Platte and Sweetwater to Bear Lake, where the rendezvous started late in June. Smith was there, although the proceeds of his 1827 hunt were still in California. All in all, the three partners had a suc-

[6] Marriage Record A, 1821–36, p. 13, MS, Callaway CRDO, Fulton, Missouri.

[7] Probate Record I, 1827–36, p. 4, MS, St. Charles CPC.

[8] *In the Supreme Court of Missouri, October Term 1902*, pp. 22–23, 239.

[9] *Missouri Republican* (St. Louis), March 8, 1827.

cessful year and turned over seven thousand pounds of beaver in return for which Ashley's agents produced $22,000 in merchandise. The furs, with an estimated eastern market value of $60,000 to $70,000, were transferred to Ashley's agents at $3.00 a pound in the mountains and later purchased by Chouteau at $4.375 a pound.

The Blackfoot Indians appeared during the meeting and caused quite a stir that ended in a small-scale Indian campaign. According to Beckwith, Sublette took a leading part in a desperate battle in which a large number of Blackfeet were killed. After the rendezvous disbanded on July 13, Smith, with eighteen men, set out to return to California. Sublette headed north, Campbell probably south into Utah, and Jackson either south or possibly back to St. Louis with the returning fur caravan, which reached western Missouri by October 1, when either Jackson, or possibly Hiram Scott, acting for the partnership, took over from the Ashley-Chouteau interests the control of the expedition's horses, mules, and miscellaneous supplies. Also transferred were the services of eight mountaineers. The furs were delivered in St. Louis by October 15, but the equipment was reorganized into a new supply train, under the control of the partnership, and taken back to the mountains.[10]

Sublette moved north from Bear Lake after the rendezvous to trade with the Blackfeet, who were then at peace and seemed more friendly. Possibly some Hudson's Bay Company freemen were with him on the way to Flathead Post. He seems to have reached the Snake before winter began and no doubt spent the colder months in that area, since by early spring, 1828, he was north of the Snake plain on the trails to and from the Salmon. It was there he lost one of his fourteen men, shot by an Indian during night guard at their camp on Birch Creek (Cote's Defile). The action was only one of several in that bloody year of 1828. Later, Robert Campbell, on his way to the rendezvous,

[10] Transfer of Property from Ashley to Smith, Jackson and Sublette, October 16, 1827, Ashley MSS, MoSHi; *Arkansas Gazette* (Little Rock), December 4, 1827; *Niles' Weekly Register* (Baltimore), December 1, 1827; Wm. Clark to M. L. Clark, October 23, 1827, Clark MSS, MoSHi.

was attacked, as, late in March, was Samuel Tullock's party. Tullock in the previous December had fallen in with an Ogden group in winter camp at the mouth of Blackfoot River. During the winter he tried to move his group out to Bear River, but did not get under way until March 26. Three or four days later on the Portneuf the Indians attacked, killing young Pinckney Sublette and two others. The news of Pinckney's death must have been a great shock to William since he bore the responsibility of having taken him into the mountains.[11]

That year the rendezvous was held either on Bear Lake or at the Great Salt Lake. The trappers, however, did not expect any Smith, Jackson and Sublette caravan: the winter party already had reached there with goods from Missouri. The only caravan present was one belonging to Joshua Pilcher, late of the Missouri Fur Company, who in partnership with Lucien B. Fontenelle, William Henry Vanderburgh, Charles Bent, and Andrew Drips brought in the remains of an expedition. They started for the mountains late in the summer of 1827 and wintered on the Green, but lost part of their goods to the Indians and were then in rather sorrowful shape. Pilcher, after the rendezvous, explored in the Northwest; Drips and Fontenelle organized a new partnership and entered the American Fur Company.

After the rendezvous, Jackson, who either had stayed in the mountains or had come up with the firm's winter supply train, trapped north into Flathead country. Campbell, Beckwith, and Bridger entered Crow territory, but Sublette again set out for St. Louis, possibly in company with Fontenelle, Vanderburgh, and Bent. Sublette's mule train included seventy-five mounted men plus equipment and furs from the year's hunt. He led them down the Sweetwater past Independence Rock, where he discovered they were being trailed by hostile Indians. As they crossed

---

[11] For reports of Pinckney W. Sublette's death see: Report of John Dougherty of Persons Killed in the Fur Trade, October 24, 1831, Tabular Statement of Persons Killed in the Fur Trade, 1815–31, DMDI, MSS, MoSHi; List of Persons Killed in the Fur Trade, Sublette MSS; Men Killed in the Fur Trade Report, Clark MSS, KHi; Names of Persons Killed Belonging to the Parties of Ashley and Smith, Jackson and Sublette, Smith MSS, KHi.

the North Platte, shortly thereafter, the Indians attacked and several men were killed, a large quantity of furs lost, and at least one man, Hiram Scott, said to be "a clerk employed by Ashley to protect his interests," was wounded seriously. Sublette knew game was scarce—knew that to get his furs to market, he would have to race against time and inclement weather. Accordingly, he ordered his caravan to push on and detailed two men to accompany Scott down-river in a bullboat to the "great bluff [Scott's Bluff]," where, he promised, help would be waiting. Several days later, while Sublette's party descended the Platte below the bluff, they were overtaken by the two men and told that the bullboat had capsized, that all supplies had been lost, and that Scott had died below Laramie Fork.[12]

Sublette did not know the actual story of Scott's death. True, the bullboat had been swamped and lost along with all supplies, but the two men had saved their rifles and had dragged Scott ashore, where they agreed that he was near death and left him to his fate. It was not until the following spring of 1829, when Sublette took another party west, that his hunters found a human skeleton near the great bluff. Upon examination, they decided it was Scott's, and then they knew that though abandoned for dead, he had had enough strength to drag himself to the foot of the bluff which now bears his name. There he died of starvation and exhaustion.

On or shortly before September 26, 1828, Sublette's party reached Lexington, Missouri. James and Robert Aull, well-known merchants in the mountain trade, operated one of their four stores in that town and provided Sublette sums of money to pay his men for their services.[13] While he was there, he planned his party of 1829, and may have spent three full months in central and western Missouri before going farther east. He was definitely in St. Louis by January—one report said he was there shortly

[12] Mattes, "Hiram Scott, Fur Trader," *loc. cit.,* 161.
[13] Cash Book B, September 1, 1828–March 29, 1830, pp. 5-7, MS, Commercial Bank of Lexington, Missouri; "Letters of James and Robert Aull" (ed. by Ralph P. Bieber), *Missouri Historical Society Collections,* Vol. V (June, 1928), 272.

before Christmas—when Ashley wrote Senator Thomas Hart Benton that Sublette was "preparing for an expedition." This would be his first opportunity in five years to spend much time with friends in St. Louis, since his visit of the year before was such a short, hectic one. He told Ashley that his partnership had one hundred men employed in three or four parties operating in territory claimed by the United States west of the Rockies and that losses in men and equipment had been heavy during the last year— very heavy since Pinckney was included in that estimate.[14]

As he prepared his new supply expedition and talked to friends, relatives, and business associates about his forces in the mountains, he must have learned of the increasing attention, on both the state and national levels, given the fur trade and the Far West. There was growing interest in Oregon, and it was estimated that the annual value of the fur trade was $300,000—a sum that "could be increased advantageously under proper regulations, to one million of dollars annually."[15] It was such a valuable enterprise that Governor John Miller of Missouri had recently recognized its importance in his second inaugural address and had spoken of robberies and losses in the trade, of the British traders, and of the necessity to protect American interests. Sublette listened to the many reports and worked towards a departure date of March 1.

Several new men signed on with Smith, Jackson and Sublette to enter the western trade that year. One was George W. Ebberts of Bracken County, Kentucky, who would leave posterity an account of his years in the mountains, and another was Joseph Meek, an eighteen-year-old youth whose brother Stephan had been employed previously by Smith, Jackson and Sublette. Both Ebberts and Meek later became leading Oregonians and Meek a well-known advocate of the Oregon Trail. Two other men, John Hannah and John Gaither, were hired for eighteen

---

[14] W. H. Ashley to T. H. Benton, January 20, 1829, Ashley MSS.

[15] *Daily National Intelligencer* (Washington, D. C.), April 22, 1829; J. W. Taylor to Jane Taylor, December 31, 1828, MSS, University of Washington, Seattle.

months, but both lost their lives in the West and involved Sublette in the settlement of their estates.[16]

Another lad in his late teens, Jesse Applegate, who was a clerk in a St. Louis surveying office, met Sublette at the Green Tree Tavern—a tavern in which the partnership transacted much of its business. It was located on Church Street south of the Catholic church and was a large frame building with a swinging sign in front and a spacious wagon yard in the rear. Benjamin Ayres, the proprietor, was a Kentuckian quite capable of handling the thirsty army officers, traders, farmers, and drovers who frequently clashed in barroom combat. Sublette at times stayed there when he was in town, paying $3.50 a week for room and board.[17] Applegate said that he volunteered his services as clerk to the partnership and that Sublette would have taken him to the mountains but for the opposition of the lad's regular employer. Although the boy was disappointed, Sublette and his friends made it up to him by taking him "to places in the city after the work of the evening was done, where no youth ought to go, and where [he] never would have ventured except under their powerful protection."[18]

Plans for the expedition were completed in mid-March, and on the seventeenth of the month, Sublette, leading a party of fifty-four, left St. Louis for the rendezvous. There was no time to lose, since he was anxious to reach the mountains and doubly anxious to learn the whereabouts of Smith. He placed his party under full discipline and ordered his men up at four in the morning, despite the disagreeable weather encountered. Fortunately, until they reached western Missouri, they found shelter during the nights in corn cribs or under sheds along the way, but food

[16] G. W. Ebbert, "A Trapper's Life in the Rocky Mountains and Oregon from 1829 to 1839," MS, Bancroft Library, Berkeley; E. H. Tobie, "Joseph L. Meek, a Conspicuous Personality, 1829–1834," *Oregon Historical Quarterly*, Vol. XXXIX (June, 1938), 124; File of *William Hannah adm. of John Hannah decd.* v. *Wm. L. Sublette*, File 2, MS; File of *Austin Shelton admr. of John Gaither decd.* v. *Wm. L. Sublette*, File 3, MS, St. Louis CCC.

[17] (Mrs.) Daniel R. Russell, "Early Days in St. Louis from the Memoirs of an Old Citizen," *Missouri Historical Society Collections*, Vol. III (1911), 410; *Pioneer of the Valley of the Mississippi* (Rock-Spring, Illinois), April 24, 1829.

[18] J. Applegate, "Views of Oregon History, 1878," MS, Bancroft Library.

was coarse, and each man had many duties. After a short rest at Independence, they left the tiny town and with pack mules strung out jogged cross-country to the mouth of the Kansas (Kaw) River. From there they followed the usual route northwest to the Platte, at times traveling in a "dead silence" which overtook them and remained for miles.[19]

One morning, near the Platte, a band of several hundred Indians swept down upon the expedition. Sublette ordered his men into immediate battle formation, but told them to hold their fire until his first shot at the yelling, waving, mounted savages. He "was fain to believe it his last battle," since he and his men were so greatly outnumbered. The Indians surprised them by halting within fifty paces of Sublette's line, where the chief dismounted, put his weapons on the ground, and made signs of peace. A conference followed in which the trappers learned that the Indians were peaceful Sioux, Arapahoes, Kiowas, and Cheyennes. Presents were given them, and the expedition proceeded in peace up the North Fork of the Platte to the Sweetwater and along its rapid waters northwest to the head of Wind River east of South Pass and the Green.

About July 1, they arrived at a meeting place on the Popo Agie tributary of the Wind, where a small rendezvous was held. Campbell and some of the other men were there, although neither Smith nor Jackson was present. Sublette opened his packs to sell tobacco at two dollars a pound, whiskey at two dollars a pint, awls at three for fifty cents, *capots* (capotes) at twenty-five dollars, and white blankets at twenty dollars. He restricted his trade to a few days and on July 18, or thereabouts, proceeded to the Snake River area, where he hoped to meet his partners.[20] Campbell was sent east in charge of a small party to convey forty-five packs of fur to St. Louis, and Milton Sublette, who had entered his brother's employ, was sent with a brigade to trap in the Big Horn Basin.

[19] Robert Newell Diary, 1829-43, MS, University of Oregon Division of Archives, Eugene, Oregon.
[20] G. W. Ebbert, *loc. cit.*, Bancroft Library.

The William Whitley home, Sublette's probable birthplace, two miles south of Stanford, Kentucky, on the Wilderness Road

St. Louis water front in 1840, looking north from Walnut Street

Bridger and Meek accompanied William to the upper Snake Valley along a route which carried them up Wind River to Togwotee Pass, over the pass, and along either Spread or Blackrock Creek to their destination at Jackson Hole. Tradition maintains that Sublette named the area in honor of his business associate at that time, but it is more likely that the name had been applied gradually to the valley and lake beneath the Tetons—applied over a period of years during which Jackson frequented the area. The party remained encamped on the shores of Jackson Lake a few days, then headed south, turning sharply west across Teton Pass to the Pierre's Hole region, where Sublette hoped to find Smith, Jackson, and their men. Although there are conflicting stories concerning the meeting with Smith, the most reasonable one seems to be that Jackson's party had proceeded in advance of Sublette's party across the pass, found Smith at Pierre's Hole near the place previously set in 1827 for their meeting, and that shortly thereafter Sublette's group arrived. The rendezvous began in August, most likely on the fifth.

Smith brought packs of otter skins, but his report was not encouraging. He had returned to California after the rendezvous of 1827—a trip which had cost him ten men before he reached Monterey. After securing three hundred pack animals, he had marched from Mission San José into northern California. There on the Umpqua River, in July, 1828, his party of about twenty was attacked by Indians. Only he and three companions had managed to escape to the British post at Fort Vancouver. His losses in men, equipment, horses, and mules was a severe blow. He had spent the winter with the British at Vancouver, and before leaving for the rendezvous in the spring of 1829, he is said to have promised fur-factor Dr. John McLoughlin that he would induce his two partners to cease trapping in the Snake River region. At Pierre's Hole he supposedly told his comrades of his promise and got them to agree to it. Possibly they were quite willing to do so, since several of their parties had lost horses and equipment in that country and had complained of its poverty.[21] Thus, George

[21] Account of Ashley with Smith, Jackson and Sublette, April 6, 1830,

Simpson, of the Hudsons' Bay Company, probably was correct when he wrote the London office in 1829 that "the Flat Head Trade I do not think is likely to be disturbed in future by the Americans, as the exhausted state of the Snake Country, and the great loss of life which has occurred therein, will in all probability breakup their trapping parties."[22]

Early in October the eightscore men gathered at Pierre's Hole began a brief autumn hunt on the nearby waters of Henrys Fork of the Snake. The Blackfeet attacked their encampment early one morning and wounded a few of the trappers, but were driven off to a nearby ravine. After that incident the party moved northeast towards Missouri (Hebgen) Lake and the Madison Fork of the Missouri, crossing a little-known area, yet one rich in beaver. Cold weather made travel difficult, and the Blackfeet harassed them along the way. At night extra guards were posted, and Meek relates that one evening while he was on guard Sublette made the rounds and would have caught him sleeping had not a friend deceived Sublette long enough to awaken Meek.[23]

The entire party left Missouri Lake in November, going northeast over a "rough broken area (the Madison Range)" to the upper reaches of the Gallatin River. Between the Gallatin and the Yellowstone they crossed the Gallatin Range and again were attacked by the Blackfeet, who broke the expedition into several small parties and sent them flying in various directions. They were not reunited until they reached the Sulphur Stinking Fork (Shoshone Branch) of the Big Horn, where Smith and Sublette turned downstream to the Big Horn proper and joined forty men encamped there under the command of Milton Sublette. Before proceeding south to the valley of Wind River—they would

---

Sublette MSS; *Oregon Spectator* (Oregon City), December 24, 1853; Simpson, *op. cit.*, 55, 59–60; Letter of John Work to Edward Ermatinger, March 28, 1829, Letter of William Tod to Edward Ermatinger, July 15, 1829, Ermatinger MSS, Provincial Historical Society, Victoria, B. C.

22 Simpson, *op. cit.*, 50.

23 Robert Newell Diary, 1829–43, MS, University of Oregon Division of Archives.

spend the winter there—they cached their peltries "in the side of a cut bank." A Crow war party met them on the way down-river, and for a few moments a battle seemed certain until the Indians made signs of peace. The uneasy trappers smoked the peace pipe, gave them a few presents, and continued on their way to a favorable winter camping place. Jackson seems to have joined them there with his fur group from Snake country. Shelters were thrown up hastily to ward off the rigors of wind and snow, and they settled down to some semblance of orderly, yet not very enjoyable winter life.[24]

Smith, Jackson and Sublette gave serious consideration during the winter to the prospects of their partnership. The autumn hunt of 1829 had been a trial hunt to decide whether or not a supply expedition should be organized in 1830. They decided that the proceeds justified another year's operations, despite Smith's losses, and that Sublette was to prepare the new party. There is every reason to suspect that this final decision was not reached until the three partners met during the winter. Sublette, instead of returning east after the rendezvous of 1829, had remained in the mountains to see Smith and to aid his partners in the fall hunt. Now that they had decided upon an 1830 expedition, he was determined to return to St. Louis during the winter. After nearly four years of partnership, the firm was barely solvent, and no mistakes could be made. They had lost some forty-four men during those years, and by July, 1830, their losses in horses, mules, furs, traps, and equipment would amount to at least $43,500. Their margin of profit had suffered from the increased cost of trapping and trading, from higher merchandise prices and transportation costs, from regular salary outlays, from business competition, and from the exhaustion of some fur fields. They were still in debt to Ashley for a small amount, since their entire fur return for the years 1826–29, amounted to $87,000, which was simply not enough to cover costs and losses. The common

24 *Ibid.;* Tobie, *loc. cit.,* 126; File of *Jos. W. Cunningham adms. David Cunningham* v. *Wm. L. Sublette,* Case No. 642, MS, Office of the Clerk of the Supreme Court, Jefferson City, Missouri.

belief that "the new firm did not prosper financially, for the heyday of the fur trade was past" was quite possibly true.[25]

The hunt of 1830 was to be the crucial one for the company, and the supply expedition had to be well prepared and well managed. On or shortly after Christmas, 1829, Sublette, accompanied by his old companion Black Harris, started for St. Louis. This time a train of pack dogs, rather than a single wretched animal, carried their supplies. Traveling was much easier than in 1827, and by February 11 they had reached their destination.[26] Immediately Sublette plunged into his duties, met with Ashley, checked on Campbell's fur caravan of the previous autumn, and lost no time in organizing the spring supply train. The beaver Campbell had conveyed to Missouri several months earlier had been loaded on wagons in Lexington and carried to St. Louis under care of the Aull brothers. In St. Louis wagoners had picked up a return shipment of merchandise to western Missouri, thus reducing freight charges to Smith, Jackson and Sublette. Every saving counted, and Sublette now sent a message to the Aull brothers requesting them to meet with their agent in Independence to see if he could secure thirty or forty mules for the 1830 expedition.[27]

It was soon common knowledge that Sublette intended to take ten wagons over the mountains to the rendezvous. Publicly, "the principal men concerned in the enterprise [were] sanguine of the success of the experiment"; privately, they may have had their doubts.[28] Most of the wagons, sturdily built to withstand Indian attacks and capable of carrying heavy merchandise, were purchased from Joseph Murphy, a well-known St. Louis wagonmaker. The Aull brothers may have had something to do with

---

[25] Coman, *op. cit.*, I, 358; Names of Persons Killed Belonging to the Parties of Wm. H. Ashley, Smith, Jackson and Sublette; Amount of Property Lost by the Firm of Smith, Jackson and Sublette . . . July 1826 to July 1830; Accounts of Messrs. Smith, Jackson and Sublette with W. H. Ashley, 1827–28, 1829–30, Sublette MSS.

[26] Jedediah S. Smith to Ralph Smith, December 24, 1829, Smith MSS, KHi.

[27] *St. Louis Beacon*, March 11, 1830.

[28] *Missouri Republican* (St. Louis), April 15, 1830; *Cincinnati Advertiser & Ohio Phoenix*, May 19, 1830.

providing others, but the records are rather vague. By April 10, however, the wagon train was ready. In addition to ten mule-drawn wagons and two one-mule dearborns, Sublette also provided his eighty men twelve head of cattle and one milch cow for their sustenance until they reached buffalo country. He started them west from St. Louis on the tenth, but remained in town to take out a new trading license on the fourteenth and then caught up with them as they moved along Boon's Lick to the western limits of the state.[29]

Leaving the Independence area, he directed his party forty miles along the Santa Fé Trail into Indian country and then turned sharply northwest along the Blue River to the Platte. There he kept to the little-used south bank rather than crossing to the normal route along the north bank, but he did not wish to risk his wagons in fording a stream possibly running high with spring moisture. By keeping to the south bank, he marked out a new trail along the river—a trail to supersede the older north bank route. Grass was plentiful; they met large herds of food-giving buffalo, and consequently averaged fifteen to twenty-five miles each day in crossing the open plains. Except for normal repairs, the wagons were a problem only at steep ravines and creek banks. In those places Sublette sent men in advance to cut the banks into more gradual slopes or in rare instances used ropes to raise or lower his vehicles. Since each wagon weighed eighteen hundred pounds, it was at times a laborious task, and he reported the loss of one man in an earth collapse and noted that another was injured at the same time. Both may have been engaged in hoisting a wagon over an embankment.[30]

His caravan reached the rendezvous, a little below the junc-

[29] Joseph Murphy Account Book, January 1, 1825–January, 1836, MS, MoSHi; E. A. O'Neil Bott, "Joseph Murphy's Contribution to the Development of the West," *Missouri Historical Review*, Vol. XLVII (October, 1952), 25; *Missouri Republican* (St. Louis), April 13, October 19, 1830; *St. Louis Beacon*, March 31, 1831; 21 Cong., 2 sess., *House Exec. Doc. No. 41*, p. 2; Aull Brothers Journal, 1828–30, MS, Commercial Bank of Lexington, Missouri.

[30] *Missouri Republican* (St. Louis), October 19, 1830; *St. Louis Beacon*, March 31, 1831; Mattes, "Hiram Scott, Fur Trader," *loc. cit.*, 160; Draper MS, 12 C 62–6.

tion of the Popo Agie and Wind River, on July 16, and "created a sensation" among the assembled trappers. His men were in good health and fine spirits, having traversed hundreds of miles without Indian troubles, and the meeting was well attended by trappers, the more reckless of whom thought nothing of spending hundreds of dollars a day on alcohol, gambling, Indian women, horses, and trade goods. Both Smith and Jackson were there with a sizable quantity of furs taken in the spring hunt.[31]

The partners, after considering their fur returns and the cost of the expedition, realized they had enough to pay their notes to Ashley and to provide each of them with a small profit. This was their opportunity to escape the mountain trade before conditions grew worse. They decided suddenly and unexpectedly to sell their interests and dissolve their partnership. Perhaps they could follow in Ashley's footsteps: prepare and send annual supply trains to the rendezvous; then trade, carry, and sell beaver caught by others. They were aware that the supply of mountain beaver was diminishing and that there might be a decided decline in market value if a short supply should bring about the substitution of some other material for beaver fur. They were weary of Indian troubles, of cutthroat competition with British fur parties, and of confusion in the Indian administration as reflected in the West. They knew the American Fur Company was broadening its mountain operations by erecting a series of fur posts, the most recently constructed of which was Fort Union. Astor meant business—he meant monopoly at his stone-bastioned, cannon-guarded post at the mouth of the Yellowstone.[32]

The partners also had more personal reasons for wishing to disband their business. Smith and Jackson had seen little of civilization in many years and must have been eager to rest and relax

[31] *St. Louis Beacon,* March 31, 1831; *Missouri Republican* (St. Louis), October 19, 1830; Tobie, *loc. cit.,* 127; Robert Newell Diary, 1829–43, MS, University of Oregon Division of Archives; G. W. Ebbert, *loc. cit.*

[32] Waldo, *loc. cit.,* 86; Chester L. Guthrie and Leo L. Gerald, "Upper Missouri Agency: An Account of the Indian Administration on the Frontier," *Pacific Historical Review,* Vol. X (March, 1941), 50–51; J. McLoughlin to John McLeod, February 1, 1830, McLeod MSS, Provincial Historical Society, Victoria, B. C.; Frank B. Harper, *Fort Union and Its Neighbors,* 5.

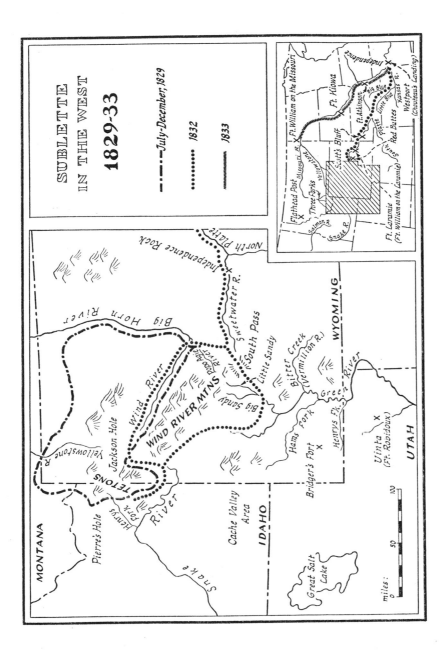

SUBLETTE
IN THE WEST
1829-33

— · — July-December, 1829
· · · · · 1832
———— 1833

MONTANA

Pierre's Hole

Henry's Fork

Snake River

Great Salt Lake

Cache Valley Area

IDAHO

Bridger's Fort X

UTAH

Uinta X
(Ft. Robidoux)

Yellowstone R.

Jackson Hole

TETONS

Wind River

WIND RIVER MTNS

Big Horn River

Popo Agie River

Big Sandy

South Pass

Little Sandy

Sweetwater R.

Independence Rock X

North Platte

Bitter Creek
(Vermillion R.)

Hams Fork

Green Fk. River

WYOMING

miles: 0   50   100

Flathead Post X

Salmon R.

Snake R.

Three Forks

Yellowstone R.

Ft. William on the Missouri X

Scott's Bluff X

Ft. Laramie X
(Ft. William on the Laramie)

Ft. Atkinson

Platte
Little Blue
Big Blue
Kansas R.

Red Buttes

Ft. Kiowa

Westport
(Chouteaus Landing)

Independence X

a while in comfort. Smith's thoughts were "turned homeward" by news brought to him by Sublette that his mother had died. Although he was unmarried, he had taken upon himself the burden of supporting sisters and brothers and had remained in the mountains so long in dangerous explorations only "to help those who stand in need."[33] Both Smith and Jackson were said to be interested in farming ventures, and Sublette shortly after his return to St. Louis began to negotiate for a large tract of land southwest of the city. Their mountain exploits were passing into legend, a new decade was beginning, and the time was propitious for dissolution of their partnership. Moreover, there were five men at the rendezvous willing to buy their interests. On August 1, those five—Fitzpatrick, Bridger, Milton Sublette, Henry Fraeb, and Jean Baptiste Gervais—for a preliminary consideration of $15,532.23, took over the company. They were all experienced mountaineers and "on or about the fourth of August" made final arrangements for an over-all sum of "Sixteen thousand dollars and upwards," to be due Smith, Jackson and Sublette on or before June 15, 1831.[34]

Smith, Jackson and Sublette, with fifty to seventy men, a great number of pack horses and mules, the remaining cattle, and ten wagonloads of peltries, were on their way home late on August 4. Following the course of low passes and green, level valleys skirting the upper, snow-clad reaches of the mountains, they made their way to St. Louis along the same route used by Sublette earlier in the year. Traveling conditions were advantageous, the weather favorable, and the passage was made in comparative safety. By September 10, they were on the Blue River fork of the Kansas, thirty miles from the Pawnee villages, and from there made excellent time to Fort Leavenworth. One mile west of the Missouri line, they passed a Methodist mission recently built—good evidence of encroaching civilization.[35]

[33] Jedediah S. Smith to Ralph Smith, December 24, 1829, Smith MSS, KHi.
[34] John O'Fallon to R. Campbell, June 30, 1831, Campbell MSS, MoSHi; Receipt of W. H. Ashley to W. L. Sublette, January 5, 1833, Sublette MSS; File of Estate of Jedediah S. Smith, File 930, MS, St. Louis PC; Jackson and Sublette Letter of Attorney, August 23, 1831, Sublette MSS.

After leaving Leavenworth, their caravan "created a sensation" on its arrival within the settled area in western Missouri. Homes and towns were going up in many places, and steamboats ran regularly along the river. At Columbia on October 5, the local newspaper noted that the men of the expedition "exhibited great demonstrations of satisfaction, at their approach to their families and homes."[36] Word raced ahead that a large group of "hardy and sun-burnt mountaineers," wagons, and stock was spread out for a considerable distance along the road to St. Louis. The news of their approach created as much excitement amongst the five thousand inhabitants of the city as it had in smaller communities farther west.[37]

Sunday morning, October 10, dawned rainy but mild, with a gentle wind from the southwest. Fortunately, the weather gradually cleared, and when the wagons pulled into St. Louis, the skies were scarcely overcast. Since it was a holiday, citizens gathered along the streets and around the Cathedral and other public buildings to witness the event. The trappers milled about, shook hands, greeted families and friends, and celebrated their reunion with the world they had long ignored. Although many of them were unaware of it, they had participated in a monumental western event. Their wagon caravan was the first to utilize a large portion of the Oregon Trail. Sublette's faith in himself—yes, also in his men—had borne results. He had taken wheeled vehicles west to the Popo Agie and had brought them back to St. Louis. He proved that the overland trail could be crossed by wagon; he had opened the immigrants' road to Oregon.[38]

[35] *Missouri Republican* (St. Louis), October 19, 1830; *St. Louis Beacon*, March 31, 1831; *Missouri Intelligencer and Boon's Lick Advertiser* (Fayette), October 9, 1830; J. S. Smith to Ralph Smith, September 10, 1830, Smith MSS, KHi.

[36] *Missouri Intelligencer and Boon's Lick Advertiser* (Fayette), October 9, 1830.

[37] J. J. Warner, "Reminiscences of Early California From 1831 to 1846," *Annual Publications of the Historical Society of Southern California*, Vol. VII, Parts 2-3 (1907-1908), 176.

[38] *St. Louis Beacon*, March 31, 1831; Diary and Meteorological Record of Genl. Clark, 1826-31, Clark MSS, KHi.

Santa Fé and Pierre's Hole

ALTHOUGH 1830, a year of revolution in Europe, brought William IV to the throne of England for a short seven-year reign and marked, in the United States, the Webster-Hayne debate over nullification, in the American West affairs were more prosaic. The "enterprising, intelligent, and enlightened people" of St. Louis, as one favorably impressed traveler remarked, enjoyed good health and general prosperity. Congressional elections were scheduled for autumn, but Sublette, so long removed from most of the nation's affairs, had ahead of him more business than political problems. Almost immediately after his return, he and his former partners got in touch with Ashley for a general settlement of accounts and on October 13 paid him in full for all charges against them, except for back salaries owed to some employees transferred to their service in 1826. Payments also were made to the estates of three trappers killed in the West. One such payment was completed on October 19, when Smith and Sublette met the administrator of David Cunningham's estate at Ashley's home.[1]

[1] Much of the main narrative of this chapter is based upon the following material: Josiah Gregg, *Commerce of the Prairies,* I; Kate N. B. Powers, "Across the Continent Seventy Years Ago," *Quarterly of the Oregon Historical Society,* Vol. II (March, 1902), 82–106; John B. Wyeth, *Oregon;* F. H. Day, "Sketches of the Early Settlers of California; Isaac J. Sparks," *The Hesperian,* Vol. II

Before the end of October, Smith, Jackson and Sublette drew up a long letter, which they sent to the Secretary of War, giving him an account of their recent expedition and of the feasibility of wagon transport across the mountains to Oregon. They hoped to impress upon him the fact that the British-American Convention of 1818 was "unequal" in its operation and that something constructive should be done to settle the problem of the North-west. But they failed to emphasize that Sublette had driven cattle to and from the mountains, sustaining them on native grasses alone —certainly important news to prospective immigrants and farmers. The three men also agreed to produce "a new, large, and beautiful map . . . of the Rocky Mountains, and the country on both sides, from the States to the Pacific," although it seems that Smith devoted the most time to the project. Samuel Parkman, who had returned with him and was engaged to copy some of his notes, helped draw the map, upon which were placed the routes of their extensive travels, the location of Indian tribes, and other information. Unfortunately the map was never published and may not have survived, despite its great importance.[2]

One series of questions in particular might have been solved by the map: When was the Sublette Cutoff first used, by whom was it used, and after which Sublette was it named? The Cutoff began near the Little Sandy, in present Wyoming, struck the Big Sandy, and continued across thirty-five miles of flat, waterless terrain to meet the Green River. Oregon-bound parties used the route in the 1840's to reach Fort Hall, notably a party under Caleb Greenwood in 1844. In fact, the route often bore Greenwood's name, and his biographer claimed that the trail was called Greenwood's Cutoff until Andrew Sublette, not William Sublette, used the route. Ware, in his 1849 emigrant guide, stated that he had "taken the liberty" to call the route Sublette's Cutoff, thus adding confusion to the previous claim. Also there is reference to a much earlier trail across the same area, beginning near Frémont's

(July, 1859), 193 200; Bernard De Voto, *Across the Wide Missouri;* Warner, *loc. cit.;* Chittenden, *The American Fur Trade,* I, II; Dale, *op. cit.;* Morgan, *op. cit.;* Sullivan, *op. cit.;* Victor, *op. cit.*

[2] *St. Louis Beacon,* March 31, 1821; "Jedediah Strong Smith," *loc. cit.,* 396.

Peak a bit to the north. One of the Sublettes is said to have used it many years before, but it is now entirely obliterated. William had opportunities to use both routes as early as the 1820's, but so many fur parties were active in that area that without the map of 1830–31, or any reliable contemporary account, there is as yet no adequate proof that he was the first to use either route or that the southernmost route bore the Sublette name before Andrew's crossing of 1844.[3]

Smith, now that he was in St. Louis, was rather undecided about what he wanted to do, other than to make his family more comfortable. He told his friends that he had no intention of returning to the mountains, although there were nonmountainous western areas where he could go. Sublette seemed just as undecided while he lodged in St. Louis, visited friends, and possibly rode out to St. Charles to see the Whitleys. Except for a little legal difficulty with Thomas G. Berry, who accused him of taking two slaves and refusing to return them—Negro hire was dear in St. Louis—he evidently passed an enjoyable winter—a winter best spent indoors, since it was the most severe in twenty years.[4]

By mid-February, 1831, all beaver brought in from the previous year's hunt were sold through Ashley. It was "wildly" estimated that the partners had returned with 190 packs valued at $150,000, whereas, when transferred to Ashley, they brought actually $84,500 in the East.[5] He sold a few in St. Louis and Louisville, but disposed of most in New York City and Philadelphia; took a commission of $2,100 plus the cost of shipment and handling; and turned over the residue to the three former part-

[3] John Steele, *The Traveler's Companion Through the Great Interior*, 26; *Gold Rush . . . Journals . . . J. Goldsborough Bruff* (ed. by Georgia W. Read and Ruth Gaines), I, 510; Joseph E. Ware, *The Emigrants' Guide to California*, 26. The term "Sublette (or Soublette) Route" was used in the 1830's to designate the Upper Platte–Sweetwater trail. "Sublette's Cutoff" could have evolved from that term. For an example, see the 1839 map of David Burr (based upon Jedediah Smith's work) in 20 Cong., 1 sess., *Sen. Doc. No. 174*, p. 21.

[4] File of *Thos. G. Berry* v. *Wm. L. Sublette*, File 90, MS, St. Louis CCC, James R. McDearmon to Martha A. McDearmon, January 22, 1821, MS, UM-WMC.

[5] W. H. Ashley to Charles Macatester and Company, January 17, 1831, Simon Gratz Collection, MSS, Pennsylvania Historical Society, Philadelphia.

ners. Out of that they paid their salaries and expenses, taking for themselves a third each of the remaining profits of that "very successful hunt."[6] Smith purchased a house and lot in St. Louis, took in two Negro servants, and was known to be corresponding with Campbell, who was still in Ireland and not too well, about a possible Smith-Campbell business venture. Smith's brothers—Ira, Austin, and Peter—were with him in St. Louis, and another brother, Ralph, had been asked to visit them to celebrate Jed's safe return from the West. Two years before, his family had believed him lost in the West, but now that he was back, their minds were at rest for a while.[7]

Sublette and Jackson, both solvent and with money to invest, considered entering the Santa Fé trade, said by Governor Miller in his address to the legislature and people of Missouri on November 16, 1830, to be "an essential and important branch of the commerce" of the state. Until that very year all wagonloads of merchandise passing through Independence for the West had gone to the Mexican provinces and the commercial Eldorado at Santa Fé, from which place, later each year, they would return laden with Mexican goods. Shrewd western businessmen gave the trade serious thought—thought that now led Sublette and Jackson to form a new partnership, preparatory to a Santa Fé expedition.

Since their venture would take them beyond our southwestern borders, Sublette petitioned Governor Miller for a recommendation for the partnership to the Mexican governors of Santa Fé, Chihuahua, Sonora, and "such other of the Mexican Republics" as he and Jackson might visit. The Governor complied, stating that he had "been acquainted with the reputation of Mr. Sublette for several years . . . that . . . his character and standing is that of a high minded honourable man, fair and generous in all his dealings and punctual in all his contacts & engagements."[8]

[6] Messrs. Smith, Jackson and Sublette in Account with W. H. Ashley, 1830–31, Sublette MSS; John O'Fallon to Robert Campbell, June 30, 1831, Campbell MSS.

[7] Jedediah S. Smith to Ralph Smith, December 24, 1829, September 10, 1830, January 26, February 28, 1831; S. A. Simons to Peter Smith, November 22, 1829; J. S. Smith, Sr., to Peter Smith, February 16, 1830, Smith MSS, KHi.

[8] Santa Fé Trade Recommendation of Governor Miller of Missouri, April 15, 1831, Sublette MSS.

93

Sublette dispatched another letter to the East, asking Ashley to procure him a passport to travel "through some of the Mexican provinces."[9] Ashley willingly co-operated, and the passport, No. 2332, was issued to Sublette on April 9, 1831.[10] He drew up a will, although it was never signed, in which he made bequests to his brothers, to his sister, and to Ashley, who along with Milton Sublette was designated an executor. The will was to provide for the disposal of a female slave Sublette owned, to divide his share of the 1830 hunt, and to supervise the distribution of a large land purchase he had made recently, should he lose his life in the Southwest.[11]

On March 10, he had bought 446 acres of land on the River des Pères, six miles from St. Louis, for three thousand dollars, and a few weeks later, on April 26, his attorney purchased in his name an adjoining tract of 333 acres for four thousand dollars. The two tracts, together more commonly known as the "Sulphur Springs" tract, originally were part of a large grant belonging to Charles Gratiot, a Swiss emigrant who had died in St. Louis in 1817. The total 779 rolling, fertile acres were located in a rough rectangle formed by four modern St. Louis thoroughfares: Kingshighway, on the east; Old Manchester Road (Southwest Avenue), on the south; Tamm Avenue, on the west; and New Manchester Road, on the north. At that time, however, the land was far beyond the city's western limits.[12]

Smith, hearing of Sublette and Jackson's plans, first thought of sending his brothers Austin and Peter along with them to Santa Fé, but then began to think of going himself. The belief that his was a "last minute decision" is probably inaccurate, since in January he asked Ashley to secure him a passport and organized a strong share in the expedition. Perhaps he was weary of a quiet

---

[9] William H. Ashley to the Secretary of State, March 23, 1831, Passport Applications, Records of the Department of State, Record Group No. 59, MSS, N. A.

[10] Passport No. 2332 (blank in part), April 9, 1831, Records of the Department of State, Record Group No. 59, MSS, N. A.

[11] William L. Sublette's Will of 1831, Sublette MSS.

[12] Original (Deed Record) Q, p. 548, R, p. 615, T, p. 355, MSS, St. Louis CRDO; *Missouri Gazette* (St. Louis), May 3, 1817.

life or was pressed by new financial demands, but whatever the case, he plunged into preparations for the party.[13] A possible element of confusion in the plans of all three was the agreement which they may have made in 1830 with the Rocky Mountain Fur Company, as Fitzpatrick, Bridger, Fraeb, Gervais, and Milton Sublette called themselves. Smith, Jackson and Sublette may have promised to send them a shipment of supplies for their mountain rendezvous of 1831. Fitzpatrick left the mountains in March that year, bound for St. Louis to obtain supplies. He either carried a supply order with him or intended to meet a supply train, outfitted by Smith, Jackson and Sublette, on its way west. Possibly he had promised to reach St. Louis by a certain date, as had Sublette in 1827, and having failed to arrive on time was given up as overdue or lost. The year 1831 was not one of close co-ordination in the mountain trade.[14]

The first mule-driven wagons of the Santa Fé party began to leave St. Louis on April 1, although the main body did not depart until the ninth or tenth. At Lexington the wagons halted for about two weeks while last-minute goods were received and arrangements were completed with the Aull brothers. Smith, following Sublette's precedent, drew up a will at Lexington, witnessed by Parkman and Jonathan T. Warner, in which he appointed Ashley executor. Now that he had an estate to consider and was entering dangerous territory, he thought it prudent to anticipate trouble. While still in Lexington or on the road west to Independence, Fitzpatrick caught up with the expedition. They persuaded him to go on to Santa Fé, where they assured him he would be outfitted and sent to the mountains. At Independence they purchased additional stores and after two or three days there moved on to encamp on the left bank of the Blue River, where they made final preparations.[15]

The entire party—eighty-five men—had twenty-three mule-

13 W. L. Sublette to W. H. Ashley, September 24, 1831, Campbell MSS.

14 Robert Newell Diary, 1829-43, MS, University of Oregon Division of Archives.

15 *St. Louis Beacon*, May 12, 1831; Will of Jedediah S. Smith, April 31 [?], 1831, File of Estate of Jedediah S. Smith, File 930, MSS, St. Louis PC.

drawn wagons: ten belonged to Sublette and Jackson and were probably the same ones they had taken west in 1830; two belonged to Smith; one was from the St. Louis firm of Wells and Chadwick; one belonged to Samuel Flournoy of Independence; and another, the joint property of Smith, Jackson and Sublette, carried a small cannon and was "so constructed that it could be readily uncoupled [and the] . . . hind wheels with the piece of artillery mounted thereon drawn out ready for action."[16] They believed that their chances of reaching Santa Fé and there concluding a profitable trade were excellent, since their party was large, well organized, and led by hardened, experienced Mountain Men. As far as they were concerned, they could conquer the wastes between Council Grove and Santa Fé as they had overcome previously the route along the Platte and the rocky fastness of the Wind River Range and the Tetons. Natural difficulties —deep sand, infrequent water holes, sparse grass, choking dust, and sweltering heat—they had met before; and roving Indian bands, out to pillage trading companies, were unlikely to risk losing many warriors in a futile attack on a strong caravan.[17]

They broke camp on May 4 and headed southwest into Indian country. Their wagons, spread out in a long, slowly advancing column, creaked and groaned, but moved smoothly over the grass-covered prairies and rolling hills of present-day eastern Kansas. For the first few days tracks of other wagons, clearly visible in the soil and light dust, guided them along the right trail. East of the Pawnee Branch of the Arkansas they met a band of several hundred Comanche and Gros Ventre Indians who made a fainthearted charge and were driven off when the cannon roared. Then Mr. Minter, clerk to Jackson and Sublette, who "fell behind the company to hunt antelope," was surprised and killed by a party of Pawnees. His death was quite unexpected. Since he was a "favorite . . . endeared to every member of the company," they dearly felt his loss.

Reaching the crossing of the Arkansas, they discovered that

---

[16] Dale, *op. cit.*, contains the quotation, 305.
[17] William Clark to Lewis Cass, November 30, 1831, Clark MSS, KHi.

The Pursuit of the Beaver (detail), from a painting by
Alfred Jacob Miller

"A Blackfoot Indian," a drawing by Charles Bodmer

the river was very low and the area criss-crossed by buffalo tracks which obscured the correct trail and left them bewildered in a "featureless country." Once across the river they headed for the forks of the Cimarron; in front of them stretched fifty miles of gale-driven sand hills and waterless, barren plains. They hoped to strike the Cimarron in a couple of days by making a quick dash across the desert, but the deep sands tugged at their wagon wheels, slowed them to a snail's pace, and exhausted men and mules. All the water holes were dry, their muddy bottoms "deeply cracked by the withering air and the scorching rays of the sun." Two or three days without water left the mules near death and the men nearly maddened from thirst. At that point they decided to make a last desperate effort to find water. They split into search parties to scour the uninviting countryside. As many men as possible spread out, including Smith and Fitzpatrick who headed south, while the wagons under Sublette and Jackson continued along what they believed to be the main trail.

Later the same day, May 27, Smith left Fitzpatrick in a hollow to dig for water and await the caravan. He rode on to the Cimarron, found it dry, and scooped out a hollow in the sand of the river bed, in which a little water began to collect. Fifteen or twenty Comanches suddenly appeared and attacked him on his horse. Although he lost his own life, he killed the chief before falling. Sublette and the others did not learn of his death until later, when some Mexican traders, who had heard the story from the Indians, told them about it. Smith's loss at the age of thirty-two was a shock not only to his family and old mountain companions, but also to his many friends at home, who regarded him as "an intelligent, active, and enterprising citizen." The *Illinois Magazine* declared in an obituary: "gentle and affable . . . he held fast to his integrity. . . . He was kind, obliging, and generous . . . without being connected to any church, he was a Christian."[18]

In the evening after Smith's untimely death, the expedition encamped on the Cimarron several miles from the place where

[18] "Jedediah Strong Smith," *loc. cit.*, 396–97; Austin Smith to Jedediah Smith, Sr., September 24, 1831, Smith MSS, KHi.

he had been attacked. Luckily they found water, but the following morning as they prepared to push ahead, a large war party of fifteen hundred Blackfeet and Gros Ventres bore down upon them. The traders quickly barricaded themselves behind their wagons, threw up improvised ditches, and prepared for the worst, since they were but a handful against hundreds. The tribesmen, however, negotiated with Sublette and passed on with only a menacing attitude. The wagon train hurriedly headed up the Cimarron in the opposite direction and that evening encamped on its banks. To avoid an attack during the dark, gloomy night, they constructed a defense system and tethered the stock inside—preparations well warranted, because a Gros Ventre band surrounded them before dawn. They were frightened off, however, and from there to Santa Fé the tribes in the area kept their distance from the caravan.

At San Miguel, located in the Pecos Valley fifty miles southeast of Santa Fé, the expedition passed through the first sizable Mexican settlement, which was only a cluster of adobe huts. Between that settlement and the capital city, the road climbed over Glorieta Pass northwest along the Pecos. In the valley were corn and wheat fields and scattered adobe homes, and in the distance the irregular outline of Santa Fé. In anticipation the men straightened their hats, sat erect in the saddle, and temporarily forgot desert sand and parching heat. Amidst clouds of dust and the crack of whips, they drove their wagons through the crooked streets to the only architecturally compact part of the city: the square where the Palace of the Governors, a "sprawling pile of native timbers and adobe mud," was located. There they gave official notice of their arrival, met the more important customs officials, and opened trade with local and visiting merchants. Since the day was the Fourth of July, it was one doubly worth celebrating, and it is easy to imagine the scene their arrival must have created.

Perhaps Sublette and Jackson visited the governor before opening trade, but whatever the protocol, they were well received and immediately commenced transactions. Interpreters were always available, and Sublette probably took up temporary residence at an inn in town. He remained there until August 31 or September 1, selling his merchandise in exchange for fifty-five packs of beaver fur and eight hundred buffalo robes. Other traders who reached Santa Fé that summer were not nearly as successful. But after business hours the city compensated all of them with fandangos, dinner parties, and social gatherings of various types. As the capital of a vast province, Santa Fé was capable of providing its visitors with a wide variety of pleasures.[19]

Parkman, rather than Peter or Austin Smith, both along on the expedition, arranged with Jackson and Sublette to dispose of Smith's share in the party. On July 11, Parkman gave Smith's manifest to the Mexican authorities, but since Ashley was executor of Smith's will, final action had to await the expedition's return to the East. In regard to their promise to Fitzpatrick, it was understood that Jackson and Sublette would furnish him two-thirds of his supplies and Smith one-third. Parkman accepted that arrangement, Fitzpatrick was outfitted, and with a few men traveled north to Taos, where he added recruits before starting for the mountain encampment of his partners.[20]

Despite the sizable profit he anticipated, Sublette was not "pleased with the country or the business" at Santa Fé and believed the year to be one of "hard luck."[21] Jackson wanted to dissolve their partnership in order to go to Southern California in the mule-trading business with Parkman, Peter Smith, and David Waldo, an old friend. Sublette agreed to the dissolution, made on or shortly before August 23, and sold to Jackson whatever goods he had on hand. Jackson immediately entered into an agreement with Waldo, and Sublette appointed Waldo his legal agent in New Mexico to receive from the Rocky Mountain Fur Company its 1830 note payable in beaver at $4.25 a pound to the old Smith, Jackson and Sublette account. On August 29, Jack-

[19] W. L. Sublette to W. H. Ashley, September 24, 1831, Campbell MSS.
[20] Inventory of the Trade Goods of Jedediah S. Smith, July 11, 1831, MS, Museum and Historical Society of New Mexico, Santa Fé; Jedediah S. Smith Account against the Rocky Mountain Fur Company, July, 1831, Sublette MSS.
[21] W. L. Sublette to W. H. Ashley, September 24, 1831, Campbell MSS.

42913

son left for California with ten companions. They reached their destination by way of the Presidio of Tucson and the Gila and Colorado rivers, completed a trade in horses and mules, and returned with them to Santa Fé by the same route, arriving there in the summer of 1832.[22]

Sublette was on his way home by September 1, traveling with his wagons as part of a much larger caravan. Austin Smith accompanied him, and by September 24, having followed in general the same route they used going west, they reached Walnut Creek, near the Arkansas, with the loss of only a few animals. At the creek, Sublette sent an express ahead to Ashley to inform him of the fur he had on hand and to request that he make $3,500 available to him at New Franklin, Missouri. Two or three days march beyond Walnut Creek, the caravan split into smaller units, each seeking the route most convenient. Sublette's animals were weak, causing him to travel slowly, and he did not reach Independence until about October 13, nor Lexington until the sixteenth. At that place he made contact with the Aull brothers and engaged Austin Smith to hurry ahead with part of the furs in order to reach St. Louis before the market was flooded with skins. He then proceeded to St. Louis as quickly as possible, passing through Arrow Rock, New Franklin, and Columbia. He stopped at Echerts' hostelry in St. Charles, probably on the night of October 28–29, and ferried his goods across the Missouri the following day.[23]

On the thirtieth he was in St. Louis, where his most immediate duty was to see that his fur and buffalo hides were processed and packed properly. He bought casks and nails and set five men to work washing and packing the skins—a job they completed in four or five days, after which the casks, numbering sixteen, were stored in Ashley's warehouse and then hauled to the levee to be shipped east for sale under Ashley's auspices. While that was under way, Sublette and his brother Andrew, who might have

[22] Jackson and Sublette Letter of Attorney, August 23, 1831, Sublette MSS.
[23] W. L. Sublette to W. H. Ashley, October 16, 1831, Campbell MSS; Jackson and Sublette in Account with William L. Sublette, 1831, Sublette MSS.

been in Santa Fé with him, roomed at E. Town's place—the City Hotel—located on the edge of St. Louis. Sublette spent many weeks discussing business conditions and accounts with Ashley and others. In mid-November he purchased mules, horses, and miscellaneous materials from the Smith estate; in December he hired from it a "negro man Bill."[24]

During the autumn Ashley ran against Robert W. Wells for a seat in the United States House of Representatives vacated by the death of the Honorable Spencer Pettis. He ran on a platform favoring internal improvements at the expense of the federal government, rechartering of the United States Bank, a judicious protective tariff, and the re-election of President Jackson—a platform for a Jackson man "against Jackson measures." Sublette, who had learned of the campaign while returning from Santa Fé, had written from Lexington, October 16, "I dont think there is the least doubt but you will get a majority in [Lafayette and Jackson] counties." Ashley won the election as Sublette expected, but by a narrow margin, and entered the House to become a popular member noted for elegant entertaining. He was the spokesman, among other interests, for the Rocky Mountain Fur Company in opposition to Astor's gigantic organization.[25]

Sublette spent the winter in St. Louis, cared for his new farm, and prepared the supply expedition he had promised the Rocky Mountain Fur Company he would lead to the rendezvous of 1832, on the "Teton Fork of the Columbia River." He placed his mules and horses, for winter care and feeding, in the hands of various friends. Most of the stock went to his brother-in-law Grove Cook in mule-raising Callaway County. Cook had performed such services for him since 1829. Prospects looked bright

[24] File of Estate of Jedediah S. Smith, File 930, MSS. St. Louis PC; Jackson and Sublette in Account with William H. Ashley, March 29–April 20, 1831, November 7, 1831–October 25, 1832, and April 29–September 3, 1831; Promissory Note of Jackson and Sublette to William H. Ashley, November 7, 1831, Sublette MSS.

[25] Edward Dobyns to J. G. Hickman, July 15, 1876, Dobyns Papers, 1867–76, MS, MoSHi; *Arkansas Gazette* (Little Rock), November 23, 1831; *St. Louis Beacon*, September 22, 1831; W. L. Sublette to W. H. Ashley, October 16, 1831, Campbell MSS.

for the supply expedition of 1832, Campbell was back in St. Louis, and Fitzpatrick came down from the mountains. There was a hustle and bustle in the city's commerce as hundreds of men bound west poured in during the spring; and close upon their heels, but going in the opposite direction, large troop detachments from Jefferson Barracks moved out to the Black Hawk War. The central market place was filled with a jabber of French, English, and Indian dialects; the billiard rooms, taverns, hotels, and small industries were doing good business; and substantial citizens were busy erecting costly homes about the town. The prices of corn, bacon, flour, and other commodities were high—higher than Sublette expected, and he had to ask financial assistance of Ashley and a friend, Robert Wash, in order to outfit his party.[26]

Capable men were not difficult to hire, since many free trappers resented the American Fur Company and willingly joined its opposition. Sublette easily gathered together fifty men, including his brother Andrew, by then an experienced mountaineer and crack shot; and possibly William B. Almond, a Virginian who had served as clerk in the Aull brothers store at Lexington, named a son after Sublette, and years later became a territorial judge in California. Five of the fifty men were under Campbell's jurisdiction and four under Fitzpatrick's, both of whom intended to accompany the caravan. By mid-May, 1831, Sublette had paid $1,126.70 in wages to his hired men and arranged with Ashley for payments to many of their dependents. On April 25, he was granted a two-year trading license by William Clark and also received a special "passport" to carry up to 450 gallons of whiskey "for the special use of his boatmen." This was "an unmitigated sham," as one observer noted later, since Sublette intended to travel by land and had no boatmen. But the Indians wanted hard

[26] Jackson and Sublette in Account with William L. Sublette, 1831–33; Messrs. Smith, Jackson and Sublette in Account with W. H. Ashley, 1829; W. L. Sublette to W. H. Ashley, 1832; Articles of Agreement between the Rocky Mountain Fur Company and William L. Sublette, July 25, 1831; Sublette MSS; Austin Raines to Robert Campbell, January 24, 1832; W. L. Sublette to W. H. Ashley, May 12, 1832; Campbell MSS (Semsrott); W. L. Sublette to W. H. Ashley, April 1, 19, 20, 1832, Sublette MSS; A. Richey to A. D. Borradaile, February 26, 1832, Missouri History Envelope, MSS, MoSHi.

liquor, despite the law prohibiting its sale, barter, or gift to the tribes, and Sublette realized the situation.[27]

Shortly after April 25, he left St. Louis for Independence. His mules and horses had not all wintered well—in fact, he had to purchase some replacements—but he had 165 in good condition. A few supplies were to be shipped from St. Louis, probably by water, to his camp in western Missouri, but were delayed by heavy rains. The rains also flooded creeks and rivers along the trail and severely hampered his journey to Independence. Spring was in the air, though it be wet; the grass along the trail grew high; and he moved his party slowly, but surely, west over rolling prairies, along wooded river bottoms, and past the endless miles of limestone bluffs marking the course of the Lower Missouri. Despite the weather, the trail was well traveled that spring as trappers, traders, "wagons, pack-horses, droves of mules, &c" moved west. By May 12, Sublette's party was settled near Independence. Although behind schedule, William took time to visit Samuel C. Owens, who operated a large mercantile company on the town square. Owens lent him a wagon to carry some excess supplies for four or five days until his lame mules were strong enough to assume their burdens.[28]

Near Sublette's camp were several easterners — probably twenty-five in all—who intended to start upon an expedition into the western wilderness under the leadership of Nathaniel Wyeth. Wyeth had gathered his company from the Boston–Baltimore area for the avowed purpose of opening "a fur trade" near the Columbia River and in St. Louis had met Scottish-born Kenneth McKenzie, a former Hudson's Bay man, now of the American Fur Company. McKenzie had given Wyeth and his followers river transportation up the Missouri to Independence, where Wyeth immediately petitioned to join Sublette's party, since he was "the best guide of the country." Sublette was hospitable, believed their plans no threat to his own western prospects, and agreed to

[27] Trading License of William L. Sublette, 1832, Sublette MSS; W. L. Sublette to W. H. Ashley, May 12, 1832, Campbell MSS (Semsrott).

[28] W. L. Sublette to W. H. Ashley, May 12, 1832, Campbell MSS (Semsrott); *Missouri Intelligencer and Boon's Lick Advertiser* (Fayette), April 7, 1832.

take them under his guidance to the mountains in a spirit, not of jealousy or rivalry, but of friendship, assistance, and respect. He was to be in full command, with the understanding that Wyeth's group was to carry its share of trail duties; and to start in good order, he suggested that they purchase sheep and oxen to sustain them on the first part of the trip. Their equipment, although basically sufficient, was not complete in every detail, and since none of them had traveled in the West, they took his suggestions. Many of them were college graduates, "men of theory, not of practice," but most also had ability and courage and were willing to learn the hard way how to shoot, ride, and endure.[29]

The combined party leaving Independence on May 13, numbered about eighty-six men plus three hundred head of stock. In double-file military order they pushed west, and each day at sundown the stragglers were ordered by Sublette to "catch up." They camped in a hollow square, within which they made their beds by spreading their blankets and using their saddles for pillows. During the night, guard was changed every four hours until dawn, when ordered again by Sublette to "turn out." Under such strict discipline they proceeded west rapidly up the Santa Fé Trail for two days, then northwest to the Kansas River Agency. Favorable weather and a plentiful food supply enabled them to reach the Little Blue River by May 21, where they camped for the night and crossed early next morning. Nearby they found a nearly deserted Indian village whose occupants lived in skin-covered tipis and tended small plots of corn and pumpkins—friendly people, perfectly harmless.[30]

From the source of the Blue a twenty-five-mile march carried them across a dry, barren prairie to the Platte near Grand Island. Firewood, as usual, was scarce in that country, the last of the sheep and oxen were killed for food, supplies ran short, and three of Wyeth's men deserted in disgust. The Platte splashed along "foul and muddy," warm enough for a tepid bath and too poor to

[29] W. L. Sublette to W. H. Ashley, May 12, 1832, Campbell MSS (Semsrott).

[30] *Missouri Intelligencer and Boon's Lick Advertiser* (Fayette), October 20, 1832.

drink, although some tried and quickly fell ill with diarrhea. Herds of buffalo thundered by, however, and the hunters replenished their dwindling food supplies. Two men of Wyeth's party admitted that "but for Sublette's guidance" they would have perished, and according to one: "Sublet . . . knew every step of the way. . . . To me it seems that we must have perished for want of sustenance . . . had we been by ourselves . . . but for him we should probably never have reached the American Alps."

For twenty-seven days they ascended the Platte: the main branch, south fork, and north fork. Timber remained scarce and food again was low, causing sickness and weakness, but on June 12 they reached Laramie Fork, where they found willows for firewood and plenty of cool, rapid, drinkable water. There they stumbled upon an encampment of twenty trappers, who agreed to join the expedition. Fitzpatrick, mounted on one of the fastest horses, dashed ahead to survey the Indian situation, promising to meet Sublette's party again near the rendezvous. The main party continued its march beyond Laramie Fork into Wyoming's Black Hills, a region plentiful in rattlesnakes, bears, and rugged red sandstone escarpments. The snow-topped Laramie Range provided a scenic backdrop and probably was responsible for the inclement weather they met. It took them four days to cross a spur of those hills, during which time the sick members of the party suffered from exposure to the heavy, violent rainstorms. But finally, on June 18, they struck the flower-lined banks of the Platte "where it comes from the south," probably near the Red Buttes southwest of the present town of Casper. They crossed the stream in a hastily built bullboat, turned slightly north, then southwest across a rough, hilly plain covered with sage, greasebush, and wormwood. Bare granite rocks, sand, and sandstone gave the country a bleak appearance. The snow-capped mountains were always in view, there was frost every night for weeks, and frequently they encamped beside snowbanks.[31]

31 *Adventures of Zenas Leonard Fur Trader and Trapper, 1831–1836* (ed. by W. F. Wagner), 92–93; *The Rocky Mountain Letters of Robert Campbell* . . . , Letter of July 18, 1832.

Early on the twenty-third they reached the Sweetwater and pitched camp beneath the shadow of Independence Rock. Smoke from their buffalo-chip fires drove away some of the bothersome mosquitoes, but a more immediate problem was how best to cross the river. Sublette ordered his men to fashion a new bullboat, but Wyeth, some of whose men were still recovering from mountain fatigue, despite Sublette's admonitions, began to construct a raft, which, when completed, was loaded with traps, casks of powder, an anvil, vise, and certain other goods. One of his men swam across the river, carrying in his mouth the raft's rope, which he tied to a tree on the opposite bank. Sublette assured Wyeth the rope would not control the float, but Wyeth persisted and allowed the raft to be drawn into the water, where it entangled itself in the branches of a partially submerged tree, tipped, and lost nearly all its valuable and irreplaceable cargo. Sublette's supplies were ferried over safely in the bullboat. Fortunately Wyeth could rely on William's equipment. With each ensuing day Sublette became more and more "under Providence, the instrument of [Wyeth's] preservation."

The following day, as they marched up the south bank of the Sweetwater, they met another party of trappers, whom they first mistook for fast-approaching Indians. After an exchange of greetings, they moved along first through a region rich in game, then through an area lacking the usual edible wildlife but filled with quicksand, grizzly bears, snakes, violent winds, hot weather, and at least one day of heavy rain. In the highlands they waded through snowdrifts; in the lower places they struggled across sandy prairies. Still, they kept up their average rate of fifteen to twenty-five miles per day to the South Pass—and buffalo by "hundred thousands"—on June 29. Beyond the Pass they traveled northwest close to the foot of the Wind River Range, and on July 2–3, during a chilly night in camp, were attacked by three hundred screaming, shooting Indians out on a horse-stealing raid. The skirmish lasted almost an hour before the warriors withdrew with five of Sublette's horses, leaving others dead. There were no trapper casualties, but the Indians lost three and had eight or ten wounded.[32]

In the morning the expedition headed up the valley of the Green, north and west to a place convenient for crossing to the Snake (Lewis's Fork of the Columbia). They encountered fresh Indian signs, increasing their fear of ambush, although the only warriors met were peaceful Flatheads, one of whom joined them as a guide and took them through Hoback River Canyon to the Snake directly south of the Three Tetons. The day was July 4, which occasion they toasted with water from the "upper waters of the Columbia," and then plunged into the half-mile-wide river to reach its opposite bank. Daytime temperatures in July often reach a pleasant eighty degrees in that country—conducive to swimming—but the nights were freezing, and they quickly headed for camp. In the morning they found abundant wild strawberries and improved vegetation upstream—vegetation badly needed by their weak horses.

Below the Three Tetons they spent a "pleasant and serene" day in camp, waiting for scouts to locate Fitzpatrick. Sublette visited Wyeth in his tent to inquire after the health of his company and probably was responsible for Wyeth's decision to cache some of his equipment in order to provide mounts for his ill and weary followers. Since Fitzpatrick was not to be found, the camp broke next day, and the party climbed over Teton Pass along thickly timbered mountain slopes covered with snow. Footing was difficult and the horses slipped, some of them rolling over and over down the rocky slopes; others were bruised and lamed by the sharp, snow-hidden stones. Under a dreary sky Sublette, with part of the company well in advance, reached the summit and encamped to await the sick men, who could hardly keep up with the experienced mountaineers. That night a snowstorm struck, and in the morning they dug out from under its white blanket to descend twelve miles to the valley of Pierre's Hole, through which flowed the Teton River on its way to the Colum-

[32] W. L. Sublette to W. H. Ashley, September 21, 1832, Sublette MSS.

bia. The valley extended north to south twenty miles; in average width, about two. To the east were the towering, frequently mist-shrouded Tetons; to the west, high, rolling prairie hills. Many other streams, in addition to the Teton, watered the valley and provided abundant pasture for a rendezvous.

Sublette's party reached the valley on July 6, according to one of its chroniclers, two days ahead of schedule, and encamped in two locations: Sublette and his band in one camp, where they prepared their trade goods; Wyeth's company nearby at another site designated by Sublette. Hundreds of other trappers and Indians were scattered about the valley—testimony to the importance of the year's meeting—but Fitzpatrick still was unaccounted for. He soon appeared, however, ragged and weary, having been chased by Indians and detained, and the cloud of gloom lifted from the meeting. After "a few days with plenty to eat and good water to drink," as well as other liquid refreshments, the trappers forgot their troubles. Although the Indian belles were said to be bashful, they dressed up in their shells, feathers, beads, and skin frocks for the benefit of any interested trapper and prospective husband.[33]

Trade was carried on in a mixture of dialects, and Sublette had the advantage of having arrived with the first supply caravan. Lucien Fontenelle came in from Fort Union with goods for Vanderburgh and Drips from the American Fur Company, but the Rocky Mountain Fur Company did not wish to trade with Fontenelle. Sublette knew how to handle Indians as well as trappers and so staged a parade for his tribal friends, after which the Flathead chief, to prove his people were well meaning and companionable, mounted his horse and lectured his followers on morals and honesty. Meanwhile, the members of Wyeth's party divided into two groups: one group intended to return to St. Louis with Sublette, since they "had been dissatisfied for some time"; the other group, including Wyeth and eleven others, resolved to proceed

[33] *Missouri Intelligencer and Boon's Lick Advertiser* (Fayette), October 20, 1832; Robert Newell Diary, 1829–43, MS, University of Oregon Division of Archives; George Nidever, Life and Adventures of George Nidever, a Pioneer of California Since 1834, MSS, Bancroft Library.

to the Columbia in company with a party belonging to Milton Sublette. This second group, on July 17, set out southwest from the rendezvous to a campsite eight miles down the valley.

As Wyeth and Milton Sublette broke camp on the eighteenth, they noticed two groups of Blackfeet, numbering in all about 250 to 300, moving on foot and horseback across the plain. Antoine Godin, a trapper, and a Flathead chief, both of whom had personal reasons for hating the Blackfeet, rode out to meet a Blackfoot chief who approached them with a peace pipe. Godin and the Flathead—Campbell called them "two halfbreeds"—killed the chief, seized his scarlet blanket, and rode back to camp amidst a "hail of bullets." The Blackfeet, who evidently had accidentally stumbled into the valley, took shelter in a nearby thicket. Milton Sublette hastily sent an express rider up the valley to the main camp, requesting assistance of his brother. William received the message and with Campbell quickly gathered their more experienced followers into a rather disorganized mass, "since you do not marshal your forces in Indian conflict," and dashed down the valley, their Flathead—Nez Percé allies trailing along. As they rode, Sublette and Campbell made verbal wills to each other, certain they were "entering on a perilous engagement, in which one, or both of us might fall."[34]

At Milton's camp the assembled force held a council, elected William leader, and decided to attack the Blackfeet in the willow swamp a mile away. Some of the mountaineers protested the foolishness of a frontal assault, but Sublette said they would have to fight them there or somewhere else and that they should show a bold face at the beginning of the trapping season or lose the trade for the coming year. Twenty of the trappers and an equal number of Indian allies followed Sublette and Campbell into the thicket to within about fifteen feet of where the Blackfeet had hastily thrown up a fort of timbers, lodge skins, and trenches in the shape of a half-moon with its opening at the rear, toward the river. Completely covered as they fired between the logs, the

34 W. L. Sublette to W. H. Ashley, September 21, 1832, Sublette MSS; *The Rocky Mountain Letters of Robert Campbell*, Letter of July 18, 1832.

Blackfeet resisted stoutly. Sublette, Campbell, a free trapper named Sinclair, and four others crawled up to the edge of the fort. Sinclair, while pulling back a bush to peer at the fort, was shot and had to be sent back to his brother's care. Then another trapper, Mr. Phelps, was hit in the thigh, and a third in the head. An Indian peeped out and was shot by Sublette, but as William reloaded, he in turn was hit in the left arm—the bullet "fracturing the bone, and passing out under the shoulder blade"—and possibly also in the breast. He continued to press the attack, though losing blood, and had to be carried to safety by Campbell, who dressed his wound at a creek and had him taken to camp on a litter.[35]

Certainly a frontal attack had failed, and another group led by Milton Sublette along the creek had not won its point either. They decided to burn out the Blackfeet. Dry wood was placed about the fort, but just as it was to be lighted, news came that an even larger Indian war party was in the area. The story was a hoax, yet the fight was discontinued and the torches never applied. By then it was evening, and the trappers gathered in Milton Sublette's camp to await dawn. Some of the men were angry over failure to take the fort, but little could be done in total darkness. The wounded were carried to the main camp, and when calculations were made, it was estimated the trappers had lost three to seven killed. The dead were buried promptly in a horse corral on the plain near the woods. In the morning a small detachment was sent to the thicket and reported the Blackfeet had fled under cover of darkness, leaving behind their baggage and at least twenty-five dead horses, but "bearing with them their wounded on litters." It is estimated they lost at least twenty-six killed, while the allied Indians probably had lost seven.

Following the battle the rendezvous continued, during which time Sublette cared for his wounds with the professional assistance of Wyeth's physician and drew up some new business agreements. The most important one, made on July 25, stipulated that he was to carry to market some 11,246 pounds of fur for the Rocky Mountain Fur Company, for which he was to receive

[35] Nidever, *loc. cit.*, MS, Bancroft Library.

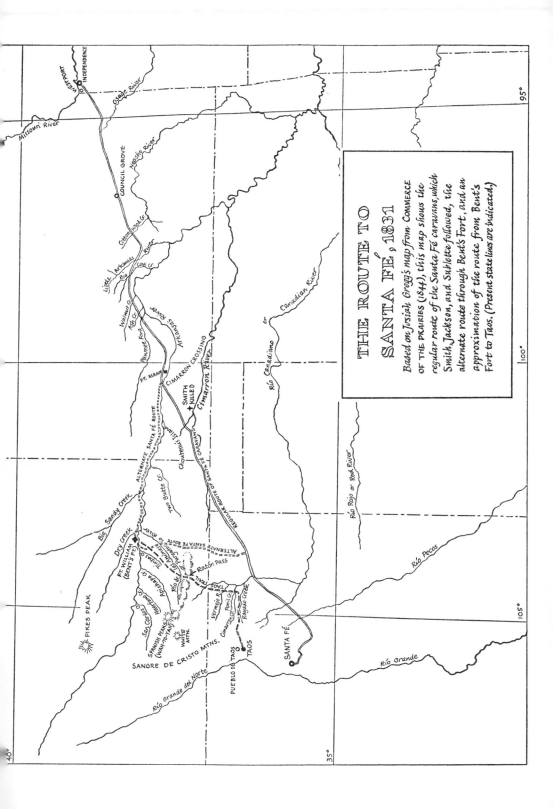

THE ROUTE TO
SANTA FÉ, 1831

Based on Josiah Gregg's map from COMMERCE OF THE PRAIRIES (1844), this map shows the regular route of the Santa Fé caravans, which Smith, Jackson, and Sublette followed, the alternate route through Bent's Fort, and an approximation of the route from Bent's Fort to Taos. (Present state lines are indicated.)

fifty cents a pound as his sales commission. Other agreements were made the same day for the payment of debts owed by the company to the former partnership of Smith, Jackson and Sublette and to Jackson and Sublette. He transferred to the Rocky Mountain Fur Company the services of five of his men and promised to convey a herd of company horses to St. Louis, where he was to inform Ashley, for the company, that the western country was "much . . . infested by intruders and bad men." Sublette also negotiated two small notes with representatives of Fontenelle and Drips, and by July 30, was ready to leave for home. Milton Sublette and Wyeth had resumed their journey on the twenty-fourth, Bridger and Fitzpatrick prepared to head north to the headwaters of the Missouri, and the year's meeting was nearly over.[36]

Sublette and Campbell, with 169 packs of beaver and perhaps sixty men, crossed Teton Pass to the east. Instead of using Hoback Canyon, as they had on their outgoing trip, they crossed the Snake, ascended the Gros Ventre River, and went over Union Pass. A small party of trappers had left the rendezvous earlier and had been attacked by Blackfeet near Hoback Canyon, and Sublette did not want to risk his party in that area. Nevertheless, near Union Pass they encountered a large Blackfoot band, but the Indians did not attack and the caravan was "suffered . . . to pass unmolested." East of the pass they ascended Wind River, then Beaver or Longs Creek, to the Sweetwater. In that region they met a second Blackfoot party, but after a hasty conference between Sublette and the chief, the two groups rode off in opposite directions—the Indians twenty-five pounds of tobacco to the good for the parley.[37]

From there the trappers proceeded in peace, raised fur caches

[36] Articles of Agreement between the Rocky Mountain Fur Company and William L. Sublette, July 25, 1832; Sublette–Rocky Mountain Fur Company Agreement concerning the Transfer of Five Employees, July 25, 1832; Instructions of Thomas Fitzpatrick to William L. Sublette, 1832, Sublette MSS; Fontenelle-Drips and Company to P. Chouteau, July 27, 1832, Chouteau-Maffitt MSS.

[37] W. L. Sublette to W. H. Ashley, September 21, 1832, Sublette MSS; *Missouri Intelligencer and Boon's Lick Advertiser* (Fayette), September 29, October 20, 1832.

along the Sweetwater and Platte, and reached Independence on or shortly before September 18. They were all in good health, and according to Washington Irving, who met them in western Missouri, "their long cavalcade stretched in single file for nearly half a mile. Sublette still wore his arm in a sling. The mountaineers . . . looked like banditti returning with plunder. On the top of some of the packs were perched several half-breed children . . . of the trappers.[38] The ill-kept company marched into Lexington on the twenty-first. Sublette wrote a lengthy letter to Ashley almost immediately and conferred with the Aull brothers on important business matters. In Columbia, on the twenty-seventh, he stopped to borrow money to pay his expenses to St. Louis and on October 3, led his party into the city.[39]

[38] Washington Irving, *The Adventures of Captain Bonneville, U. S. A.,* 277.
[39] *Missouri Intelligencer and Boon's Lick Advertiser* (Fayette), September 29, October 20, 1832; W. L. Sublette to W. H. Ashley, September 21, 1832; Note of W. L. Sublette to James and Robert Aull, September 22, 1832, Sublette MSS; *St. Louis Beacon,* October 4, 1832.

The Upper Missouri

St. LOUIS barely had recovered from a late summer cholera epidemic when Sublette arrived from the mountains. Business conditions were somewhat unsettled. The powerful *Missouri Republican* declared in a statement only partially true that he had "determined to discontinue his mountain excursions, and locate himself in the immediate vicinity."[1] He did take up part-time residence at his farm, but he had no immediate intention of relinquishing his mountain interests. His days that autumn were spent in the city or at his farm while he settled outstanding accounts for the Rocky Mountain Fur Company. In their name he paid over $9,700 in bills by late November. Brother Andrew directed preparation of the year's beaver catch, a portion of which was sold in St. Louis, although most skins were transferred to Ashley's agents for eastern sale. Allison and Anderson, a Louisville firm, took at least one shipment, and some furs were sent to New Orleans for transshipment east, but the bulk went directly to Frederick A. Tracy and Company in New York City. Sublette realized the importance of Ashley's friendship, and it is difficult to imagine how he could have conducted his business at that time without his close Congressional confidant. While Sublette was in the West in 1832, Ashley bought trade goods for him on

[1] *Missouri Republican* (St. Louis), October 16, 1832.

114

the eastern market, and would continue to do so for some time. By January, 1833, Sublette had sold two-thirds of his fur return, most of it beaver at $4.25 a pound or better—a favorable price in light of the growing market competition.[2]

Campbell had returned with Sublette from the mountains to the quiet and solitude of Sulphur Springs, where they worked on final details of a partnership agreement, destined to be a long lived, powerful, intimate, and profitable fur-trading commitment. Considering the frequent reports, circulating for years, that the trade was declining, it may seem strange that Sublette should have formed a new partnership. But to him the trade was still promising. He knew beaver would be scarce in some areas, yet there remained a few more years of profitable business in the trade. He was still a young man, thirty-three, and had no other promising vocation readily at hand. His private fortune was not large enough to cover his growing expenses at the farm or to permit him to settle there supported by its produce. Until he had substantial proof on his balance sheets that the fur trade was dying, he had to accept an investment risk. In 1832, silk hats were already on the London market, but it would be half a dozen years more before they would undermine thoroughly the vast hat market for beaver fur.

As Sublette's close friend of many years, Campbell was a man of proved business ability and a logical choice as partner. Five years Sublette's junior, he had participated in the 1832 expedition as a free associate. Recently he had saved William's life at the Battle of Pierre's Hole. His brother, Hugh Campbell, was a respected Philadelphia merchant who had valuable eastern business contacts. Robert had accumulated enough capital to invest in a partnership, and his name was a credit to the fur trade—a name respected by both white trader and Indian. Sublette had learned from experience that partnerships had good and bad points, but that in the fur trade the good probably outnumbered

[2] Notes of Rocky Mountain Fur Company due Robert Campbell, W. H. Ashley and Various Employees, September–November, 1832, Sublette MSS; The Rocky Mountain Fur Company in Account with William L. Sublette, 1832–33, Sublette MSS.

the bad. A partnership meant a division of labor and of capital risk and, incidentally, would also permit one partner to remain in St. Louis or the East while the other operated in the West.

Sublette intended to enter stiff competition with the growing colossus of the western fur trade: the American Fur Company. He looked forward to heated intercompany competition—perhaps the most heated to date—since he intended to contest Astor's control of the Upper Missouri. The American Fur Company was noted for underselling its opposition or threatening to do so; it lobbied freely in Washington, D. C., was interested in the tariff, and returned an annual fur profit estimated at $200,000. Granted its trade goods were usually of the best quality, but as a company it seldom pioneered new areas, preferring to encroach upon regions opened by other groups. Recently it had moved into the mountains, taking trade from the Rocky Mountain Fur Company and causing considerable anxiety. To contest the giant called for more than the energy of one man—possibly for more than the energy of two—but Sublette and Campbell were willing to try. Their familiarity with market conditions, their eastern supply associates, and above all else their western experience encouraged them.

Their final partnership agreement would not be completed until December 20, but they decided before then to make their expedition of 1833 a large, well-provisioned one. On December 1 or 2, they left St. Louis via steamboat on an eastern business trip and hoped to establish credit with several eastern firms, since they needed supplies on credit for future operations. Also, they expected to see the Ashleys and to visit Hugh Campbell and his family. Their boat steamed down the Mississippi past the limestone cliffs at Herculaneum and the thriving town of Ste Genevieve on the western bank of the river, veering sharply to port at Cairo to ascend the Ohio towards Louisville. Although they were running against the Ohio's current, they, nonetheless, arrived at Louisville by December 5. There, evidently, they took dinner with the merchants Allison and Anderson; then retired to their quarters aboard the steamboat anchored on the levee, amidst a "motley scene—huts—steamboats—carriages—heaps of iron—of lead—leather & C."[3]

They spent the next five days on the river, moving slowly upstream through the cold, wintry December days. Having transferred their luggage to another boat at Louisville, they churned on to Wheeling, past Madison, Indiana, and "a mere village . . . of no great pretensions": Cincinnati. Late on the tenth they docked at Wheeling—a flourishing town but not an attractive one. It lay on a narrow strip of land below the river bluffs; its two main streets, parallel with the river, were lined with buildings crowded one upon the other and gray with the soot of soft coal. They spent the night at a local hotel and in the morning boarded a stage and rumbled away over the National Road through Uniontown, Cumberland, and Hagerstown to Frederick, Maryland. Campbell, because of his recent eastern trips, was familiar with the countryside and probably served as ex officio guide, but this was Sublette's first trip east of Louisville and his first view of the Ohio Valley since 1817.[4]

After two days on the road they reached Frederick and purchased two tickets on that marvel of the age, the Baltimore and Ohio Railroad, which ran between Point of Rocks east to Baltimore, a distance of seventy-three miles. The B&O was then the longest track in the country and consisted of a flat, iron rail riveted to granite blocks placed along the right-of-way. The cars, designed to resemble stagecoaches, swayed and bumped along at anything but an even pace over their irregular route. The scenery along the way was eye-catching, and the experience of a railroad ride in 1832 was a rare one reserved for the most courageous travelers. Later on the thirteenth they reached Baltimore safely— a bit shaken perhaps—left the train at the ticket office, and checked into the fashionable "Tavern Beltzhoover."[5]

[3] Sublette-Campbell Partnership Agreement, December 20, 1832, Sublette MSS; Sublette and Campbell to W. H. Ashley, December 24, 1832, Campbell MSS (Semsrott).
[4] Sublette's Small Account Book, 1832–33, Sublette MSS; Charles F. Hoffman, *A Winter in the West*, 45–48.
[5] *Baltimore Republican & Commercial Advertiser*, December 13, 1832.

A dark blue stagecoach of the Phoenix line, Beltzhoover and Company, sped them, the next morning, from Baltimore through the rolling farmlands of Maryland to Washington. Late in the afternoon the stage dashed into the capital city, and Sublette and Campbell signed the register at Jesse Brown's Indian Queen Hotel, just six blocks west of the Capitol, a favorite meeting place for politicians and businessmen. They planned to ask Ashley about the sale of beaver from the 1832 hunt and believed he would be willing to give them letters of introduction to certain eastern firms. They remained in town until the twentieth, during which time Ashley agreed to their plans and thereby sealed their partnership with his blessing. Two copies of the final agreement, dated that day, were drawn up and provided, among other things, that "The firm shall transact business under the name and style [?] of Sublette and Campbell and shall continue three years after first of January next. . . . The expenses shall be mutually furnished by the parties, each furnishing three thousand dollars in Cash." Then, with Ashley's letters of introduction in hand, they checked out of the Indian Queen, said farewell to the wonders of the federal city, and took the stage back to Baltimore.[6]

They were there early in the morning of the twenty-first, but stopped for only a few hours' rest before proceeding to Philadelphia. Sublette disliked stage travel—it made him ill—and so they took a steamboat from Baltimore north to the head of Chesapeake Bay. At Frenchtown on the Susquehanna they transferred to the recently opened Newcastle-Frenchtown Railroad, which ran east to the Delaware River—a fifty-minute trip. At Newcastle on the Delaware they took a second steamboat upriver thirty or thirty-five miles to Philadelphia, where they arrived late the same day, after many hours of travel, and took quarters at the Congress Hall Hotel.[7]

They intended to see three Philadelphia firms: Siter, Price and Company; Ferguson, Jones and Company; and Gill, Campbell

[6] *Globe* (District of Columbia), December 14, 1832; Sublette and Campbell to W. H. Ashley, December 24, 1832, Campbell MSS (Semsrott).
[7] W. L. Sublette to Robert Campbell, February 3, 1833, Campbell MSS.

and Company. All three, when approached, were co-operative, but certain goods were difficult if not impossible to buy in Philadelphia. White three-point Mackinaw blankets were "not to be found in the city," fusils (light flintlock muskets) were unavailable, scalping-knives were scarce, beads were not readily purchasable, and gunpowder was usually sold for cash. They decided to order what dry goods they could, on credit of forty days to eighteen months in some instances, and to complete their order in New York City. Meanwhile, they spent a delightful Christmas with the Hugh Campbells.[8]

Sublette had to content himself with another stage ride, this time to New York City, where he and Campbell arrived on the evening of the thirtieth and rented quarters in the well-known City Hotel. Before leaving Philadelphia, they had arranged to have their purchases shipped to Riddle, Forsythe and Company in Pittsburgh. Ashley was authorized to purchase for them, either at Pittsburgh or Louisville, two keelboats, "Rigg Complette," of eighteen to twenty tons each, to be ready at Pittsburgh by February 20, when river commerce normally opened. The partners planned to send both a water and a land expedition to the West that year, and Pittsburgh was to be the initial outfitting point before final preparations were made in St. Louis.[9]

Much depended upon their success with New York City's business houses. Wolfe, Spies and Clark, prominent Pearl Street hardware dealers, granted them credit with the understanding that Ashley would back them, and during New Year's week they purchased three to four thousand dollars' worth of equipment at that store. They also interviewed Frederick A. Tracy, Ashley's broker, and learned that he had a ready market for their 1832 fur catch; but another dealer, John C. Halsey, on Water Street had not been as successful with his small portion of the shipment. Sublette immediately arranged to have Tracy sell the remaining

[8] Sublette and Campbell to W. H. Ashley, December 24, 1832, Campbell MSS (Semsrott); W. L. Sublette to Robert Campbell, January 11, February 3, 1833, Campbell MSS.

[9] Sublette and Campbell to W. H. Ashley, December 31, 1832; W. L. Sublette to W. H. Ashley, December 28, 1832; Campbell MSS (Semsrott).

furs, since he wanted his account settled by the time he left for the West.[10]

They planned to leave New York City no later than January 6 or 8—an impossible deadline. Sublette's fur negotiations dragged on for several days. He was discouraged by the market price on beaver of $3.50 a pound and also by the shortage of scalping-knives and guns. Campbell decided not to wait, but returned to Philadelphia between the eighth and eleventh of the month. Sublette visited a number of other New York City merchants and in a spare moment dropped in to see the operator of the Lyceum of Natural History, possibly to exchange information on the West. By January 15, he had completed all arrangements in New York City, including one to bring Riddle, Forsythe and Company of Pittsburgh into the sale of his remaining furs, and took a steamboat to the Jersey shore and then a stage to Philadelphia.[11] Already a week behind schedule, he still had arrangements to make and was homesick for the West: "the land that flows with Milk & Honey which I long to see."[12]

He checked in at the Congress Hall Hotel—Campbell had gone on to Pittsburgh—and spent his evenings at Hugh Campbell's home. Several pleasant young ladies, especially one named "Cate," were there to welcome him. In such merry company he could not forego telling them that he and Robert were ". . . lords of the Western Country. . . . Both devilesh clever fellows and candidates fer matrimony But it was necessary we should make one trip to the mountains first & then we wisht [*sic*] to settle our selves." The girls were awed, but he had to leave for Baltimore and Washington. He used the same steamboat-railroad route which he and Campbell had followed in December, stopped over-night in Baltimore, and the next morning, January 29, continued by stage to Washington. His visit, however, was a short one, until

[10] Sublette and Campbell to W. H. Ashley, December 31, 1832; W. L. Sublette to W. H. Ashley, January 4, 8, 1833, Campbell MSS (Semsrott).

[11] W. L. Sublette to Robert Campbell, January 11, 1833, Campbell MSS (Semsrott); W. L. Sublette to Robert Campbell, February 3, 1833; Allison and Anderson to W. H. Ashley, January 28, 1833, Campbell MSS.

[12] W. L. Sublette to Robert Campbell, February 3, 1833, Campbell MSS.

February 5, and, like the previous one, was devoted principally to talks with Ashley. His old friend advised him to purchase more scarlet and blue cloth. Sublette told him that he had decided to use larger keelboats, if possible, and to take only one up the Missouri as far as the mouth of the Yellowstone. While in the capital, he examined the Indian liquor laws and concluded that wine could be taken legally into Indian country.

His business affairs were not as orderly as he would have liked, and he found it necessary to return once again to New York City. Leaving Washington, he took the stage back to Baltimore, remained there until the morning of February 8, and then boarded a boat for the head of Chesapeake Bay. Unfortunately, there was heavy ice in the channel, and he was forced to land and transfer to a stage to Philadelphia, arriving at three o'clock on a bleak, uninviting morning, February 9. He made contact with Siter, Price and Company to make final arrangements; arrived in New York City by the evening of the twelfth; supervised the shipping of his goods to St. Louis, although he could not close his account with Tracy; and on the sixteenth took a boat from Manhattan Island to Perth Amboy, New Jersey. The Camden and Amboy Railroad had opened recently, and he took advantage of it to avoid the stage travel he so hated. From Camden he crossed to Philadelphia, spent the night, and the following morning was on his way via stage for Pittsburgh. The journey west must have been tiring, since the roads were never in the best condition during late February's days of alternate frosts and thaws.[13]

On the twentieth he rolled into Pittsburgh, the triangular city near "... the tall cliffs of the Monongahela, blackened by the numerous furnaces that smoke along their base, and pierced in various points with ... deep coal-shafts." The steeples of the city rose above dense smoke clouds, but Sublette paid little attention to the atmosphere because he had a great deal to do. He found accommodations at Griffiths Hotel in the very center of the city and promptly visited Jacob Forsythe and Robert M. Riddle. De-

<hr/>

[13] W. L. Sublette to W. H. Ashley, February 9, 1833; W. L. Sublette to Robert Campbell, February 22, 1833, Campbell MSS (Semsrott).

spite a shortage of available keelboats, they had found two, each of twenty-five tons, but the cost was well above Sublette's estimate. Moreover, the craft had scarcely any rigging. Still, he needed them and so improvised rigging and had his goods, including fifty kegs of powder, loaded aboard. The two keelboats were attached by towlines to the steamer "John Nelson," upon which Sublette took passage, and at sundown, February 22, the strange flotilla moved down the Ohio, bound for Louisville. There he bought two thousand pounds of tobacco and a quantity of alcohol, switched his towlines to the steamboat "Chieftain," since the "John Nelson" had gone immediately to St. Louis, and on the twenty-eighth was again on his way.[14]

In the nation's capital President Jackson celebrated his second inaugural. It was an important political event to many westerners, although, to Sublette, March 4 was more memorable for something else: he was home at last, and his keelboats were safely in port. He had been "up to his knees in Business" while in the East, but now he could shift more of the burden to Campbell's trusty shoulders. Tracy notified him that all his beaver, less one hogshead, had been sold, certainly good news. Also, he was told that David E. Jackson was again in St. Louis. He had arrived several days earlier. Sublette expected him, but not until later in the month or possibly even in April. On March 20, in Campbell's presence, they met and settled most of their outstanding old accounts. Jackson's future plans were in doubt, but they did not include the fur trade.[15]

Sublette spent most of the spring in St. Louis, seldom venturing to his farm because his time was precious and final prepara-

[14] Riddle, Forsythe & Company to W. H. Ashley, January 10, February 20, 1833, Campbell MSS; W. L. Sublette to Robert Campbell, February 22, 1833, Campbell MSS (Semsrott); *Missouri Republican* (St. Louis), February 19, March 12, 1833.

[15] W. L. Sublette to Robert Campbell, February 22, 1833, Campbell MSS (Semsrott); Frederick A. Tracy to Jackson and Sublette, February 27, 1833; Jackson and Sublette in Account with Frederick A. Tracy, 1833–34, Sublette MSS; W. L. Sublette to W. H. Ashley, February 9, 1833, Campbell MSS (Semsrott); David E. Jackson's Receipt for Accounts Settled, March 20, 1833, Sublette MSS.

tions were under way for the expedition. He and Campbell probably stayed at E. Town's comfortable thirty-six-room City Hotel, frequented by them in the past. There was a bar and dining room at hand, and they could meet with friends there and remain in close contact with their business. The two keelboats were docked on the water front, where men rigged them amidst a flourishing spring river trade. Upon performance of the boats would depend the success of their Upper Missouri operations. If the craft were to be lost through mishandling, there would be no ready replacements on the Upper Missouri, where American Fur Company boats dominated the traffic. The new, growing market for buffalo robes required spacious transportation, and the partners knew they would need boats to carry their produce down-river to St. Louis from the posts they hoped to build on the Upper Missouri in competition with Forts Pierre, Union, and Clark, belonging to the Astor group.[16]

Twenty-five men, ten of whom were Germans neither well qualified nor experienced in the Indian trade, were hired for the expedition and agreed to serve until July 1 or November 1, 1834, "as the said Sublette & Campbell may require." At least one of the men, and possibly more, deserted before that time, but of the others, one was the young Charles Larpenteur, who would leave an excellent record of service and a vivid personal account of the fur trade on the Upper Missouri during the 1830's and 40's.[17] Two other men, not in any way part of the expedition, yet interested in it, passed through St. Louis that spring. One was the eminent traveler Prince Maximilian of Wied, who visited in the city for several days before ascending the Missouri aboard the American Fur Company steamboat "Yellowstone." The other was Sir William Drummond Stewart, on his way west for the first time, who was described by an unfriendly critic as "a man with strong prejudices and equally strong appetites." Sir William was a Scottish nobleman on half-pay from the British Army. Although not

[16] Joseph Murphy Account Book, January 7, 1836–December 17, 1840, p. 22, MS, MoSHi; *Missouri Republican* (St. Louis), March 5, 1833.

[17] 23 Cong., 2 sess., *Sen. Doc. No. 69*, pp. 3–4; Elliott Coues (ed.), *Forty Years a Fur Trader on the Upper Missouri*, I, 8–9, 11.

over five feet, nine, he cut a commanding figure on the plains and in the mountains. He met Maximilian, probably also met Sublette and Campbell—he would later be one of Sublette's most intimate friends—and traveled by steamboat to western Missouri, where he struck out later for the Northwest.

Sublette and Campbell received their trading license on April 15, permitting them to trade for a year and a half at thirty-three places in the Indian country. They knew that British traders and American Fur Company factors used large quantities of liquor in Indian trade and that the red men expected "firewater" in exchange for part of their furs. Despite the federal government's Indian liquor-control regulations, recently redrafted in 1832, they knew that "liquor [they] must have or [they] might as well give up" in the Indian country. Some traders evaded the law by sending their liquor a short distance over the Santa Fé Trail; then sending it cross-country to their boats on the Missouri. Others, such as Kenneth McKenzie of the American Fur Company, had cargoes of liquor confiscated when they attempted to smuggle them up the Missouri. To solve the problem, McKenzie soon opened a distillery at Fort Union. He drew his corn supplies from a farm at the mouth of the Iowa River, but when the government finally heard of his project, the news nearly ruined his outfit and did end his usefulness to his company. Sublette and Campbell had one hundred kegs of alcohol which they intended to take into Indian country one way or another. Once in the West it could be watered down as occasion demanded or mixed with red pepper and tobacco, much-used adulterants, for trading purposes.[18]

More particularly, their over-all plan for 1833 was as follows: Campbell was to leave St. Louis first with an overland party and was to encamp at Lexington. Meanwhile, Sublette was to send the

[18] 23 Cong., 2 sess., *Sen. Doc. No. 69*, pp. 3–4; 23 Cong., 1 sess., *House Exec. Doc. No. 45*, pp. 3–4; William Clark to E. Herring, August 17, 1833, Letters Received, 1824–41, Records of the Office of Indian Affairs, Record Group No. 75, MSS, N. A.; Henry L. Ellsworth to E. Herring, November 8, 1833, Indians Envelope, MSS, MoSHi; W. L. Sublette to Robert Campbell, February 22, 1833, Campbell MSS (Semsrott).

two keelboats upstream to meet Campbell between Lexington and Liberty Landing. Campbell would get additional last-minute supplies from the boats and would leave immediately for the West as leader of the land expedition to the rendezvous. Sublette was to take passage on a steamboat from St. Louis to Lexington, where he would send one keelboat back to St. Louis. The other keelboat under his command would be towed by the steamer upriver to the last settlements, at which point Sublette would direct his boatmen to propel the keelboat to the mouth of the Yellowstone. The overland party under Campbell was outfitted with three mules per man, two of which were pack animals loaded with guns, powder, lead, blankets, clothing, beaver traps, and hidden quantities of liquor. Bedding for the men on the expedition was not plentiful, but Sublette and Campbell provided a better than average food supply, supplemented with wild game.

Having agreed upon the general outline of the expedition, the partners began to implement their plan early in April. On the ninth, Campbell and four others set out for Lexington and there on the eighteenth or twentieth joined an encamped party including the adventurous Edmund Christy of St. Louis; Dr. Benjamin Harrison, the "wild" son of former President William Henry Harrison; and Stewart, who had passed through St. Louis earlier in the spring. They and their associates intended to accompany Campbell to the rendezvous as "tourists." Sublette, during that time, arranged last-minute details in St. Louis; placed the "store," or rather the small warehouse in which he and Campbell transacted business and kept supplies, in competent hands, possibly in Andrew's; and left between the sixteenth and nineteenth on the steamer "Otto," bound for Lexington and Liberty. He did not reach Campbell's camp, five miles beyond Lexington, however, until the twenty-eighth. Apparently, he was delayed because he had to meet the Aull brothers in Lexington on business matters.[19]

19 W. L. Sublette in Account with W. H. Ashley, April, 1833; W. L. Sublette to W. H. Ashley, April 16, 1833; W. H. Ashley to W. L. Sublette, April 19, 1833; W. L. Sublette to Frederick A. Tracy and Company, May 4, 1833, Sublette MSS; Joseph Aull to Robert Campbell, February 22, 1833, Aull Brothers Letter Book III, February 21, 1833–December 19, 1835, MSS, Commercial Bank

By that time Campbell's party had grown to forty or forty-five men and was ready to leave the settlements. Sublette transferred supplies to them from the keelboats, and by May 7, they were on their way. They passed the Kansas Agency four days later, followed the regular overland trail across Kansas to the Platte, and made fair time. Their good progress was a bit surprising because their mules were balky, and they drove along their own food supply: cattle and a herd of twenty sheep.

At Lexington, Sublette ordered the one keelboat to return to St. Louis and directed Captain James Hill of the "Otto," about May 12, to start up the Missouri with the other keelboat in tow. Near the mouth of the Kansas River they stopped to investigate and to transfer some crewmen to the American Fur Company steamboat "Yellowstone," hove to with a case of cholera aboard. At Bellevue, on May 28, they landed long enough to talk to the men in charge and possibly also to add fresh supplies. News of Sublette's project had reached the traders along the Upper Missouri, and William Laidlaw, American Fur Company agent at Fort Pierre, was most unhappy to see him on July 17.[20] Later some of Laidlaw's confidence returned, but for the moment he anticipated serious trouble, since Sublette intended to erect an opposition fur post, with an agent, as close as possible to every American Fur Company post on the Upper Missouri and its tributaries. He had already selected a party to start a post near Fort Pierre. The battle for control of the Upper Missouri was on, and the free traders wished the contestants "good luck" in their quarrels—quarrels which might destroy both giants. Such ferocious competition added to the declining beaver supply drove up fur prices to new highs three times above the old market price.[21]

Sublette did not tarry at Fort Pierre, but directed his keel-

of Lexington, Missouri; Hiram Martin Chittenden, *History of Early Steamboat Navigation on the Missouri River*, I, 36.

[20] William Laidlaw to Pierre Chouteau, August 29, 1833, U. M. O. Letter Book B, 1832–35, P. Chouteau MSS; Letter of September 1, 1833, Private Campbell MSS; C. E. DeLand and D. Robinson, "Fort Tecumseh and Fort Pierre Letter Books," *South Dakota Historical Collections*, Vol. IX (1918), 167.

boat to the mouth of the Yellowstone. He reached the river junction on or a day or two before August 29, and settled down to wait for Campbell. Robert reached Green River between July 15 and 24, and there met at rendezvous three hundred white trappers and several Snake Indians. It was a boisterous gathering, highly competitive and extravagant. Fontenelle came overland with supplies from the American Fur Company at Fort Pierre, but Campbell had beat him to the meeting and secured some fur which otherwise would have gone to Fontenelle and Drips. Fontenelle claimed that both Campbell and the free trader Captain B. L. E. Bonneville, on leave from the army and then encamped with his group in the valley, had large supplies of liquor on hand to distribute to the trappers and Indians. He charged also that Campbell "made much of a boast about" his trading prowess and "spread the report . . . that I would not be out for six weeks after him." Another report circulated that Campbell planned to sell out to the Rocky Mountain Fur Company—an interesting but highly improbable action.[22]

Campbell, Stewart, Fitzpatrick, Wyeth, and Milton Sublette—Wyeth and Milton were on their way east with new plans afoot—left the rendezvous July 24, fell in with Bonneville near the Big Horn, and in company moved to a navigable point on that river. While the men were building bullboats to carry the furs down-river, Milton and Fitzpatrick, as two members of the Rocky Mountain Fur Company, made a final agreement with Wyeth whereby he agreed to furnish them three thousand dollars in goods to be delivered to them at or before July 1, 1834, "within two hundred miles of the Trois Tetons." Wyeth was to be paid

[21] Those Sublette and Campbell posts positively identifiable are: Fort William on the Upper Missouri; the small post near Fort Jackson, sixty miles above Fort Union; a Mandan trading house near old Lisa's Fort; the tiny post on White River near Fort Kiowa; the trading group at Crow Camp on Wind River; and, as mentioned in the text, the post a little below Fort Tecumseh and Fort Pierre.

[22] Note of W. L. Sublette to W. H. Ashley, August 28, 1833, Sublette MSS; Letter of September 12, 1833, Private Campbell MSS; Fontenelle to William Laidlaw, July 31, 1833, Chouteau-Walsh MSS.

upon delivery of the goods in 1834, and Milton was to accompany him eastward to oversee procurement.[23]

The various groups then broke camp and struck out for the Missouri, but Fitzpatrick wandered away into Crow territory to hunt, fell afoul of a Crow war party he maintained was inspired by the American Fur Company, and lost almost everything he had. Campbell, Wyeth, Milton Sublette, and the other trappers had an easier time. They quickly floated down the Big Horn in their bullboats loaded with furs and equipment and, except for the capsizing of one boat, made an uneventful descent of the Big Horn and Yellowstone to the Missouri. The stock, taken by a land party, followed the river banks and reached the Missouri a little later.

The bullboats landed at Sublette's camp on the north side of the Missouri two miles below the Yellowstone on August 30. Available shelter at that place was the most primitive—willows cut along the river bank and fashioned into crude cabins—but satisfactory, however, until a post could be built. So far Sublette and Campbell had carried out their plans successfully, and their fur returns were good, although construction of a post at the mouth of the Yellowstone had only begun.[24]

Fort William, as the post was called in Sublette's honor, was built at the site of later-day Fort Buford, about the same distance —one and one-half miles by land or three miles by water—below the mouth of the Yellowstone as Fort Union was above that stream. Three hundred paces from a brush-cleared bank of the Missouri, the 130x150-foot Fort William was constructed in a beautiful location, commanding a view of both rivers as well as the country surrounding each to a considerable distance. Sublette was ill and, according to his partner, "at the point of death," possibly from respiratory trouble, and Campbell was largely in charge of construction. Eight cabins plus various storehouses and a stock-

[23] Wyeth-Fitzpatrick-M. Sublette Agreement, August 14, 1833, Sublette MSS.

[24] Letter of September 12, 1833, Private Campbell MSS.

Robert Campbell,
friend and business partner

Dr. William Beaumont,
Sublette's physician
and friend

St. Louis Branch of the Bank of the State of Missouri

ade, with a single well-guarded entrance, were erected. Since they had a "heavy outfit" of supplies, storage space was needed.[25]

Sublette left for St. Louis in mid-September, before construction was complete, taking his keelboat downstream before the ice closed in. The outside of the fort, except for the icehouse and a storeroom, was finished by mid-November. The interior was unfinished, but the men moved in, happy to escape the approaching winter, and a feast and celebration were held. Campbell was in charge of the post for the winter, aided by at least four clerks, and hoped to better trade by bringing peace between the Crow and Snake Indians. He was anxious to leave the "unsettled life" of the mountain trade as soon as possible and was determined to have a profitable winter season.[26]

Wyeth and Milton Sublette were received hospitably by William at the mouth of the Yellowstone the previous August and passed at least one sociable evening together. Wyeth decided to go downstream as soon as possible and traded his bullboats to McKenzie at nearby Fort Union for a twenty-foot sailing canoe. Milton, however, was suffering from a foot injury and remained with William to accompany him aboard the keelboat to St. Louis. They had some business to transact, including a few items for the Rocky Mountain Fur Company, but the statement frequently given credence that William persuaded his brother not to "encourage any interloper [Wyeth] in the [fur] trade, but to continue to buy his [William's] goods," may be inaccurate. It seems that Milton's agreement with Wyeth was made partially with the understanding that Sublette and Campbell might in the future have a difficult time taking supply trains to the mountains if they intended to concentrate upon trade on the Upper Missouri. Aboard the keelboat, William may have convinced his brother that such was not the actual situation. Despite their differences at times, he and Milton were devoted to each other, and there on

[25] Annie H. Abel (ed.), *Chardon's Journal at Fort Clark, 1834–1839*, 359, 364.

[26] Letter of September 12, 1833, Private Campbell MSS; Settlement of Accounts between W. L. Sublette and the Rocky Mountain Fur Company, September 9, 1833, Sublette MSS.

the keelboat returning to St. Louis, each ill, they may have resolved many misunderstandings.[27]

While on his return trip to St. Louis, Sublette also had the opportunity to investigate conditions in the new fur posts, of which there were at least thirteen, begun under his jurisdiction during the summer. Located in strategic spots along the river, wherever the tribes gathered to trade, most posts showed promise. On September 25, at the Mandan Villages, he stopped to see John Dougherty, his agent, and was "wind bound" there at least three days. Despite his continued poor health, the stopover enabled him to examine closely Dougherty's operations. The Indians in the area were at peace, trade in buffalo robes was brisk, and Dougherty was anxious to complete construction of the post before spring. Sublette agreed with him and sent a messenger back to Fort William to ask Campbell to send down by bullboat or canoe some much-needed supplies. If Dougherty could have them before winter, his trade would be more profitable, and he would have more robes to forward to St. Louis the following spring. Two other Sublette and Campbell agents along the river did not equal Sublette's expectations, and he sought to replace them immediately. His men had to be on their toes, since McKenzie was determined to retain the trade of the region for the American Fur Company and had recently visited the tribes in that country.[28]

Late in October or at least by November 2, Sublette reached Fort Leavenworth, where he mentioned McKenzie's Upper Missouri distillery. The authorities at the post had heard the same tale from Wyeth a few weeks earlier and were not surprised. Sublette remained at Leavenworth only a short while and on November 5 passed Independence on his way home. Each spring and autumn Independence was "exceedingly bustling" with Santa Fé–bound wagons—wagons that parked in the dusty streets about the town square and carted supplies along the rough road leading

[27] American Fur Company Ledger V, 1831–36, pp. 150–55, AFC MSS; Settlement of Accounts between W. L. Sublette and the Rocky Mountain Fur Company, September 9, 1833, Sublette MSS.

[28] W. L. Sublette to Robert Campbell, September 25, 1833, Campbell MSS (Semsrott); Letter of September 12, 1833, Private Campbell MSS.

from Independence to the river. John W. Agnew, the American Fur Company outfitter in town, was almost a neighbor to some of Sublette's business friends on the square.[29]

He stopped in Lexington to see the Aull brothers and gave them orders for pork and salt to be shipped upriver the following spring and arranged with Mr. Meek of the Steam Mill Company to add fifty barrels of flour to the shipment. At Arrow Rock, Jefferson City, and St. Charles he sold small numbers of buffalo robes, possibly also some beaver, and was home by mid-November. The brief stops he made on his return trip—important since they enabled him to extend his outstate business contacts—delayed him long enough to miss Ashley in St. Louis. Ashley did, however, leave a message telling him that beaver was bringing a good price and that if he did not see fit to sell his fur in St. Louis, he should ship it East, where Ashley could find a ready market. Sublette approved of the suggestion and prepared most of his fur for shipment to Ashley and Tracy. Local St. Louis merchants bought small amounts of skins and castors, but he believed the Eastern Seaboard would be the better market Ashley predicted. He was willing to chance selling buffalo robes in St. Louis, although beaver was another more valuable question.[30]

In the meantime he resided at his farm and saw to it that Milton rested there under the care of Dr. Bernard Farrar, physician to William Clark and to many old, prominent St. Louis families. Between November 22 and December 6, Dr. Farrar made daily visits to the farm to care for Milton's foot; the medical bill for his services was probably paid by William. Friends dropped by from time to time to see both Sublettes. Dr. Benjamin Harrison and Black Harris came in from the mountains, carrying letters from Fitzpatrick to Sublette and Ashley. Fitzpatrick told of his

[29] Henry L. Ellsworth to E. Herring, November 8, 1833, Indians Envelope, MSS, MoSHi; Aull Brothers Letter Book III, February 21, 1833–December 19, 1835, p. 106, MSS, Commercial Bank of Lexington, Missouri.

[30] Account of Sublette and Campbell with J. & R. Aull, November, 1833, Aull Brothers Letter Book III, pp. 105–107, MSS; Cash Receipts of W. L. Sublette's Yellowstone Outfit, 1833–34; W. H. Ashley to W. L. Sublette, November 8, 1833; W. L. Sublette in Account with W. H. Ashley, 1833–34, Sublette MSS.

loss to the Crow Indians and asked Sublette to make certain Wyeth met his obligations for 1834. Fitzpatrick was "uneasy" about the entire western situation and his mistrust of the American Fur Company was growing daily.[31]

Sublette intended to leave St. Louis in time to be in Philadelphia by New Year's Day, 1834. He met his lawyer, Henry S. Geyer, several times in November and December to talk over legal affairs, but those affairs did not delay his departure. Nonetheless, he was three weeks late reaching Philadelphia. Inclement weather, impassable stage routes, or his brother's sickness all might have played their part in disrupting his schedule, but it is more likely that he waited in St. Louis to receive every possible last-minute particle of news drifting down by express from the Upper Missouri and the mountains. Exactly how much news he received from Campbell is difficult to determine, but the situation on the Upper Missouri was unpredictable.

Campbell encountered many difficulties in that winter's trade. McKenzie said that at first, in December, the Assiniboins rushed to Fort William to trade, but that Campbell's offerings were a disappointment. He thought also that Campbell was short of horses and was buying up any he could lay his hands on, stolen or not. In fact, McKenzie expected Campbell to be in the red by spring and wrote him off as "not . . . very detrimental to our interests." Despite the report that Campbell had sent parties to the Crows as well as to Fort Jackson, farther up the Missouri, McKenzie relied upon his agents to counteract successfully any such moves. His only real worry was that Campbell had a large liquor supply on hand and would use it to the best advantage.[32]

William Laidlaw, American Fur Company factor at Fort Pierre, generally agreed with McKenzie's view. He maintained that the Indians treated Sublette and Campbell's agents badly and that the agents traded very few robes despite their willingness to give higher prices. Although he was convinced that Sub-

[31] Farrar and Walker Day Book, 1832–36, entries of November 22–December 6, 1833, MSS, MoSHi; Thomas Fitzpatrick to W. L. Sublette, November 13, 1833, Sublette MSS.
[32] Abel (ed.), *op. cit.*, 359–60, 365–68, 371.

lette and Campbell could not profit from the river trade and re-garded their employees as "the refuse of our people that we would not take upon any account," he feared, as did McKenzie, the power of alcohol and suggested that the opposition's mountain trade might be enough to sustain their river-trade losses. Inter-estingly enough, by mid-winter Campbell was short of the very liquor the American Fur people so feared in his possession.[33]

Campbell kept up a strong winter competition and planned in the spring, when navigation was open, to go down-river to his other posts and agencies. It was clear to McKenzie, Laidlaw, and their associates that the only way to win was to undersell or over-trade their competition. The company men knew that the part-ners had Ashley's support, as well as other eastern business back-ing, and that they might continue to wage a bitter battle for some time.[34] Astor had greater financial resources, but was it worth while to risk them if it were not absolutely necessary?

[33] William Laidlaw to Collin Campbell, October 30, December 8, 1833; to P. Papin, December 28, 1833; to P. Chouteau, January 10, 1834; to James Kipp, February 24, 1834, U. M. O. Letter Book B, 1832–35, P. Chouteau MSS.

[34] W. L. Sublette to Robert Campbell, September 25, 1833, Campbell MSS (Semsrott); Robert Campbell to James Bridger, February 28, 1834, Sublette MSS.

The "Partition of Poland"

JOHN JACOB ASTOR was seventy in July, 1833, and he doubted that the American fur trade would have many more productive years. The quarter-century New York charter under which his western enterprise had been organized was due to expire, reorganization would be necessary, and he wanted to dissociate himself from his company before the fur market collapsed. Ill health and the death of his wife further encouraged him to take such a step—a step he finally agreed to in June, 1834, when he sold his western and northern fur departments respectively to Pratte, Chouteau and Company and to Ramsay Crooks "and associates."

The year 1834 was an important one to the American Fur Company, since it marked also, on or about the first of February, the completion of a far-reaching agreement with Sublette and Campbell. In New York City, early that year, Sublette met representatives of the American Fur Company in several closed-door sessions. A document was drawn up in which he agreed, for Campbell and himself, to give up their trade and posts on the Upper Missouri, in exchange for which the American Fur Company agreed "to retire from the mountain trade" for one year.[1]

[1] Letter of February 14, 1834, Private Campbell MSS; J. C. Cabanne to L. Fontenelle, April 9, 1834, Drips Papers, 1832–60, MSS, MoSHi.

Hugh Campbell remarked, "The article itself looks much like a treaty of peace betwixt sovereign potentates—perhaps . . . a little resembling the partition of Poland."[2] The American Fur people had "paid well for a cessation of hostility" in the West; had given Sublette and Campbell, Fitzpatrick, Bridger, and the other Mountain Men at least a temporary free hand south of the Upper Missouri.

Sublette's accomplishment was startling. But what had made it possible? Certainly Astor's plans to retire and the reorganization of his company contributed; yet other factors probably were of greater importance. In 1833–34, the company was in "bad political odor" with the federal government over the Indian liquor laws. Also, and more important than that, was the fact that Sublette and Campbell through their operations convinced the company that they could secure unlimited credit to purchase new equipment and thereby indefinitely continue their open competition. The American Fur Company men in St. Louis were frightened by the prospect and supported the "partition." McKenzie was disgusted by the turn of events, but in this instance his voice did not prevail against the St. Louis members and the New York City home office. With a little prodding and a few well-placed suggestions, Sublette won his point.

The possibility suggests itself that Sublette and Campbell had planned such a coup since the spring of 1833, and that their Upper Missouri operations were a blind to cover their grand strategy. During the autumn of 1833, Campbell proposed to McKenzie a very similar agreement. Nevertheless, after two meetings they had ceased negotiations, since McKenzie maintained his point of view: rather than buy out competition, he would "work them out by extra industry & assiduity." Thus, Sublette and Campbell must have reached an agreement on strategy before Sublette left Fort William for St. Louis, and the strategy seems to have been that they would both, each in his own area, work for an agreement with the Astor men, cover up their own difficulties, and strike fear into the heart of the American Fur Com-

[2] Letter of February 14, 1834, Private Campbell MSS.

pany. To say, however, that Sublette and Campbell's entire Upper Missouri project was directed to that end from early 1833 would be an exaggeration. They had invested too much to risk in such an uncertain diplomatic move; their over-all plans suggested permanency. It seems, rather, that they took advantage of a situation that they themselves had created both by accident and by intelligent deliberation.[3]

Other business, as well as the great agreement, had taken Sublette to the East. He planned to oversee the sale of his beaver, he had business decisions to reach with Ashley and Hugh Campbell, he had to arrange for supplies to be sent west in 1834, and he had to keep an eye on Wyeth and brother Milton. He knew that the Rocky Mountain Fur Company was in critical condition, especially after he received Fitzpatrick's dismal report, and much would depend upon his ability to get enough supplies to the Mountain Men at the year's rendezvous. As a result, by January 22, William and Milton were in Philadelphia, where they spent a day with Hugh Campbell and then proceeded to New York City for a week's negotiations with the American Fur interests. In all probability, Milton, as a representative of the Rocky Mountain Fur Company, sat in on some of those monumental conferences.[4]

After the New York City negotiations, Sublette returned to Philadelphia to spend two weeks with the Hugh Campbell family. Hugh was very attached to him for his kindness, good judgment, honor, and constant friendship—qualities not recognized by his enemies. Wyeth, who had returned to Boston to outfit his 1834 supply expedition to the mountains, held not nearly such a high opinion of Sublette. Openly their relations were cordial, yet careful and filled with skepticism. Wyeth had left a colony of men on the Columbia River, and it was his intention to rejoin them after the coming rendezvous. A group of Boston business associates put up the necessary capital for the formation of the Colum-

[3] Abel (ed.), *op. cit.*, 355, 359, 363–64.
[4] Letter of February 14, 1834, Private Campbell MSS; Thomas Fitzpatrick to W. H. Ashley, November 13, 1833, Sublette MSS.

bia River Fishing and Trading Company under his direction. Milton, after the New York City conferences between his brother and the Astor interests, joined Wyeth in Boston to supervise, as he had been advised, preparations for the expedition. Wyeth hoped that William might consent to a joint expedition to the mountains that year, but did not reach Philadelphia in time to discuss the plan. Milton was in Philadelphia on February 14, two days before William left for home, but said little or nothing about Wyeth's proposal.[5]

Sublette, when his accounts were settled or arranged temporarily with Ashley and Tracy and his goods forwarded to St. Louis, left Philadelphia. As soon as he reached home, he set to work feverishly to organize his supply train of approximately twenty men, which he intended to lead personally to the annual rendezvous on Hams Fork of the Green. Milton, who had agreed previously to go west with Wyeth, now agreed as a brotherly gesture to travel up the Missouri on an American Fur Company boat to take Campbell the news and papers relating to the "partition." Since Sublette and Campbell had relinquished their river interests, Sublette would not send supplies upriver to Campbell, but would, instead, concentrate efforts upon trade in the mountain country.[6]

Wyeth tended to underestimate the critical condition of the Rocky Mountain Fur Company. Sublette, on the other hand, was convinced that his friends were on the brink of dissolution and that "the arrangement [which they had made] with Captn. Wyeth [was] likely to operate against the goodness of the debt due [Sublette and Campbell] by the company."[7] Sublette had just divided the western country with the monopolistic American Fur Company. Was he to lose his share to the dwarf Wyeth organization? He knew that neither Fitzpatrick nor his brother Mil-

[5] John McLoughlin to John McLeod, March 1, 1833, McLeod MSS; Tucker and Williams to Wyeth, December 22, 1832, MS, Oregon Historical Society, Portland.

[6] Letters of February 14, April 5, 1834, Private Campbell MSS; Jackson and Sublette to Frederick A. Tracy and Company, 1833–34, Sublette MSS.

[7] Letter of April 5, 1834, Private Campbell MSS.

ton was pleased with the Wyeth contract. If Wyeth should arrive first at the Green, Sublette and Campbell's future interests would be in jeopardy. The solution was simple: Sublette had to beat him there; show him up as second-rate. The contention that he bribed Fitzpatrick to turn down Wyeth's goods at the rendezvous reflects the true character of neither Fitzpatrick nor Sublette.

The quarrel with Wyeth also involved Sublette's self-respect, since Wyeth was an easterner first helped into the western country by the very man he now challenged. Westerners had regional pride even then and as in later years "viewed a business transaction of intersectional or international application as being to no small extent a competitive trial of intellect."[8] As far as Sublette was concerned, Wyeth was not his business equal, not really strong enough to maintain his position in the West, not experienced enough— and he proved to be right. The West set its own requirements, and Wyeth would have to meet them. He was oversensitive and thought in terms of a western trading empire to stretch from the Columbia Valley to Santa Fé, and that, to Sublette, would and must never do.

St. Louis, in the spring of 1834, wore an obvious garland of prosperity. Dozens of steamboats were tied at the levee, loading and unloading foodstuffs and bar lead; Indians, boatmen, and traders wandered the streets; settlers passed through the land office; and suppliers outfitted their western parties. To some visitors the town was not to be distinguished from any eastern city: they noticed the well-kept gardens and the well-dressed better citizens. But other travelers looked beyond the glitter and noise to mention that only a few of the streets were paved, while other thoroughfares were "extremely dirty," and that it was not unusual to see the remains of dead animals in the gutters. Rather than the gardens, they saw homes surrounded by pools of muddy rain water in which city waifs floated toy boats.

By early April the season's westward movement was under way in earnest. Two or three parties outfitted for Santa Fé, a company of dragoons readied itself for reconnaissance duty, and

[8] Philip Ashton Rollins, *The Cowboy*, 88.

a trapping party prepared to meet Bonneville in the West. Wyeth and his men passed through the city on their way to Independence, "contending" with the other expeditions "for precedence in starting." Also, there were some other noteworthy individuals in town, most of them adjuncts to the expeditions. Revs. Jason and Daniel Lee were bound for Oregon and were going west in Wyeth's company, as were Thomas Nuttall, a Massachusetts botanist, and John K. Townsend, a Philadelphia ornithologist.[9]

Since both Sublette and Campbell were opposed to anything which might attract undue attention to themselves or to the fur country, when Sublette led his party west from St. Louis in late April, his departure went largely unheralded in the general confusion. He passed through Lexington on the thirtieth of the month, by the first week in May entered Indian country, and traveled as quickly as possible northwest along the Kaw, Blue, and Platte rivers. Near Grand Island his men hunted buffalo, and he taught his raw recruits how to take "tongue, bosses, and hump ribs." They were impressed with his leadership, since a few days before he led them safely through a menacing Pawnee war party and frequently astonished them with his accurate, almost uncanny, vision while on the march. They spent the night of May 29 encamped a short distance below Scott's Bluff, braced against a violent, howling wind. Luckily for their timetable, the inclement weather soon was over, and they could push up the North Platte —game abundant along the way—to the mouth of Laramie Fork.[10]

Sublette planned to build a fur post on the Laramie—a post, or rather the primary link in a new chain of posts, that he hoped would give Campbell and himself control of much of the central mountain trade. He may have planned to meet Campbell there on the Laramie. If he did, he was disappointed, since Milton Sublette, whom he depended upon to carry the news of the "partition" upriver to Campbell, instead had stuck to his plans to travel west with Wyeth. He had gone only as far as the Little Ver-

[9] Letter of April 5, 1834, Private Campbell MSS.

[10] Letter of May 14, 1834, Private Campbell MSS; "Anderson's Narrative of a Ride to the Rocky Mountains in 1834" (ed. by Albert J. Partoll), *Frontier and Midland*, Vol. XIX (1938), 54–55.

million, however, when his recurrent leg ailment forced him to return to St. Louis, and Campbell did not receive official news of the "partition" until later.[11]

At the Laramie, Sublette, on June 1, immediately "laid the foundation log of a fort" and christened it "Fort William" in honor, it seems, of himself and two other Williams in his command: William Marshall Anderson, chronicler of the expedition, and William Patton, who was left with fourteen men to plant corn and build the fort. Buffalo were abundant all year near Laramie Fork, and the site was ideal for trading purposes. Sublette took the remainder of the party across the Wyoming Black Hills to the rendezvous, over a region of wild sage, scattered scrubby pines, grizzly bears, and petrified logs. They passed an occasional Indian camp, and near the Red Buttes girded themselves for possible danger, since the countryside was hostile. He advised his men to "keep wide awake"—Anderson added "watch and pray"— but the only alarm of an attack, and it was a hoax, was sounded at sunrise on June 11, when they were bedded down just west of South Pass.

From South Pass, Sublette led his party to the Green River Valley and encamped near the rendezvous site on Hams Fork. Six trappers rode in from Fontenelle and Drip's camp, and Sublette's scouts reported increasing numbers of men in the vicinity and plentiful wild game. Early on the fourteenth of June, Louis Vasquez, Fitzpatrick, and several companions dashed shouting into camp, dismounted, and burst into Sublette's tent for a boisterous reunion. For the next two days the men from the camps exchanged visits, after which both Sublette and Fitzpatrick moved their followers upstream to the general rendezvous site. It is extremely difficult to locate the exact meeting place in 1834, as well as in many other years, since, in order not to exhaust food and fuel supplies, rendezvous sites would move as meetings progressed.

The rendezvous, composed of "Whites, French, Yankees, Nez Percés, Flatheads, and Snakes, or Shoshones," formally

[11] "Diary of Rev. Jason Lee–Part I," *Quarterly of the Oregon Historical Society*, Vol. XVII (June, 1916), 120.

opened on June 17–18 and was a rousing success. Diluted alcohol sold, as the best liquor available, at three dollars a pint, and the Indian chief Bull's Head opened festivities when, suddenly, he drove a buffalo bull through the main camp for the entertainment of Sublette's party. Edmund Christy came to the meeting with a large number of Indians, who filled the atmosphere day and night with their yelling, singing, and cursing. Another chief present was Ara-pooish of the Crows, who had been wounded with Sublette at Pierre's Hole. As Anderson commented: "The scene [of the chief's meeting with Sublette] was uproarious, shouting, laughing, slapping and joking each other, then winding up by cursing the Blackfeet with a hearty and vicious eloquence."[12]

Wyeth was the serious problem at the rendezvous. Fitzpatrick, upon Sublette's arrival, repudiated his supply contract with Wyeth and arranged to take his goods from his old friend. Wyeth's caravan had left western Missouri nearly ten days in advance of Sublette's. It was June 18 or 20, however, before it reached the rendezvous. Wyeth and his men claimed that Sublette had deliberately raced them to the rendezvous—ungentlemanly conduct, but they were right—in order to beat them out of their contract with the Rocky Mountain Fur Company. It is doubtful, however, that Sublette had taken any secret route to the West; rather, he knew the trail and made better progress. Wyeth had not encountered any unusual difficulties on the way and had made good time, but Rev. Jason Lee noted that Sublette always seemed to be one or two days ahead.[13]

At least as far as Mr. Lee was concerned, the Sublette-Wyeth quarrel was of little significance. At the rendezvous the minister

[12] "Anderson's Narrative of a Ride to the Rocky Mountains in 1834," *loc. cit.*, 55–62. The Huntington Library, San Marino, California, owns the original unpublished diary of William Marshall Anderson. The author was not granted permission to see the original or to examine the Sublette accounts appended to that document.

[13] *Niles' Weekly Register* (Baltimore), October 11, 1834; Archer B. and Dorothy P. Hulbert (eds.), *The Oregon Crusade*, 130–31; Charles Henry Carey, "The Mission Record Book of the Methodist Episcopal Church, Willamette Station, Oregon Territory, North America, Commenced 1834," *Quarterly of the Oregon Historical Society*, Vol. XXIII (September, 1922), 233.

was received by Sublette "with all the gentlemanly politeness which had always characterized his conduct towards me."[14] The two supped together or "took tea" as another companion noted, after which Sublette introduced his men.[15] The following day, or the day after, Mr. Lee again visited Sublette's camp to purchase a mule, remained for the evening to witness an Indian dance festival, and decided to stay overnight in Sublette's tent. The clergyman's contention that some of the Mountain Men were opposed to his missionary plans for Oregon clearly did not include Sublette, since he mentioned "of his own accord" that Fort William on the Laramie might be an excellent missionary site and also gave Mr. Lee an article on the Western Colonization Society. When Mr. Lee departed for the Columbia on July 1, he entrusted Sublette with several letters to be carried to St. Louis.

Sublette had won his point: Wyeth was beaten and knew it. The remaining important business to be negotiated at the rendezvous concerned the Rocky Mountain Fur Company. On June 20, Sublette witnessed its dissolution and the formation in its place of a new business compact among Fitzpatrick, Bridger, and Milton Sublette. Gervais and Fraeb settled most of their accounts with William, since they were leaving the company, and the new partners asked Fontenelle to supply their goods for the coming year. Sublette, now that the debt owed him by the Rocky Mountain Fur Company was nearly eradicated, was willing to relinquish the next year's supply duties to another group. He saw Wyeth and his men leave for the Snake River, where they intended to construct a trading post near the junction with the Portneuf. Fort Hall, the result of their labor, later was sold to the Hudson's Bay Company when Wyeth dissolved his enterprise.[16]

Sublette, probably on July 9, left the rendezvous with sixty to seventy packs of beaver. At Fort William he could see that construction of a "square . . . of pickets, 18 feet high, with little

14 "Diary of . . . Lee . . . ," *loc. cit.,* 139.
15 Cyrus Shepard Journal, 1834, p. 100, MS, Coe Collection, Yale University Library, New Haven.
16 Rocky Mountain Fur Company Dissolution of Partnership, June 20, 1834; Thomas Fitzpatrick's Notice of Dissolution, June 20, 1834, Sublette MSS.

bastions at two diagonal corners and a number of small houses inside" proceeded rapidly. His men stationed there learned the hard way that the agricultural possibilities of the countryside were quite limited and that crops demanded irrigation. Strong prevailing winds, especially during the dry summer, were scarcely conducive to anything but short prairie grass, dwarf cacti, and cottonwood trees along the watercourses. After a quick survey, Sublette continued down the Platte and Blue rivers, and by August 23 probably reached the settlements in western Missouri. He was definitely in Lexington two days later, since he saw the Aull brothers on the twenty-fifth and sent his fur ahead in two wagons. The wagoners were to return to Lexington with merchandise from St. Louis.[17]

He was home before the end of the month, and Campbell was there waiting for him. News of the "partition" reached the Upper Missouri late in the spring, and Campbell had hastily relinquished his holdings to McKenzie. By late June he had completed his business at Fort William on the Missouri and with his personal belongings and several companions set out for St. Louis. He passed Fort Clark on the eleventh of July, Council Bluffs on the twenty-seventh, and by August 7 was home in St. Louis. No doubt he was overjoyed to return to the civilization he so dearly loved, although he was prepared to spend four years in the mountains if need be, and certainly had many things to discuss with Sublette. The Ashleys were then at Columbia and expected to be in St. Louis before long. All signs pointed to a happy reunion.[18]

The only dark cloud on the horizon was Milton's health. He had returned to the Sublette farm after his unsuccessful attempt to ascend the Missouri and had passed the summer there under the constant care of Dr. Farrar. Milton's condition was serious: osteomyelitis seems to have developed and, although he was given the best care the age would permit, Dr. Farrar had no choice but to

17 *Missouri Republican* (St. Louis), August 26, 1834; Louis Vasquez to B. Vasquez, July 9, 1834, Vasquez Papers, 1797–1860, MSS, MoSHi; H. S. Schell, Memoranda Forts Laramie and Kearny, 1870, MS, Bancroft Library.

18 W. H. Ashley to W. L. Sublette, September 5, 1834, Sublette MSS; Letter of February 10, 1835, Private Campbell MSS; Note of Joshua Pilcher to P. Chouteau, Jr., July 27, 1834, Chouteau-Maffitt MSS.

amputate his left leg. The operation was not performed until February 4, 1835, and consequently William was under considerable anxiety throughout the winter for his brother's health. Moreover, Uncle Solomon Whitley died in St. Charles in the autumn, and his loss was deeply felt.[19]

Both Sublette and Campbell were eager to settle down into a more normal pattern of life and to arrange their affairs so that they "could entirely withdraw from the Indian country." Some of the Mountain Men, however, expected them to continue in the trade for a while and possibly even to take an expedition west in the autumn of the coming year. They retained some mules and horses, but at least for the present did not intend to plunge back into the wilderness. Clearly, they were a bit uncertain what they wanted to do. Astor had retired, an act of Congress had just reorganized the field service of the Office of Indian Affairs, and they had to consider many peripheral facts before they acted.[20]

When not looking after Milton, William devoted his time to his farm. On November 29, he removed a quitclaim William Russell held to his land and in December negotiated three building contracts. In the first one, dated the thirteenth, he contracted for four log cabins, each fourteen by sixteen feet, to be built two-together in the usual style of double slave cabins, at a cost of four hundred dollars. Sublette agreed to furnish the plank for floors and shingles for the roof; the builder Lindsay Lewis was to complete the job by May, 1835. In the second contract, of December 23, John Lewis, possibly Lindsay's brother, promised to build two additional cabins, each twenty-four by sixteen feet, at the same cost and by the same date. The most important contract, however, also drawn up on the twenty-third with Lindsay and Samuel Lewis, involved fourteen hundred dollars in payment for a stone and lime house, fifty-five by forty-five feet. The house

[19] Bill of Dr. Farrar to Milton Sublette, February 24, 1836 [?], Chouteau-Papin MSS; Farrar and Walker Day Book, 1832–36, Entries of May–September, 1834, January, 1835, MS, MoSHi.

[20] Letters of October 28, 1834, February 10, 1835, Private Campbell MSS; Louis Vasquez to B. Vasquez, July 9, 1834, Vasquez Papers, 1797–1860, MSS, MoSHi.

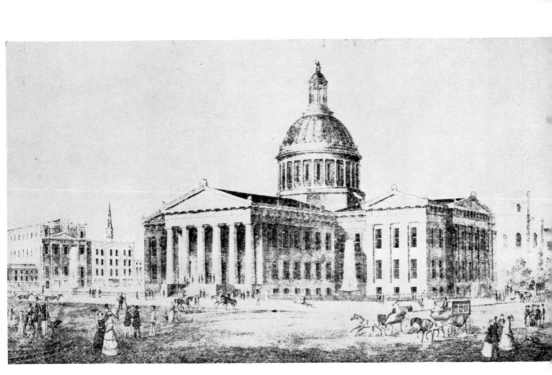

St. Louis courthouse

Boatmen's National Bank of St. Louis

"Verdict of the People," from a painting by
George Caleb Bingham

was to contain a basement and two upper stories and was to be completed within six months. The entire structure was to be architecturally attractive and substantial. Its two-foot-thick outer walls enclosed three rooms on the basement level. There were to be six fireplaces on the first floor, stone caps over each door and window, and an arch over the main entrance. This would be Sublette's new home at Sulphur Springs, to replace his temporary quarters there, and would be a worthwhile addition to the countryside.[21]

The New Year, 1835, opened prosperous and promising, and the partners decided it would be best, after all, to continue in the fur trade a bit longer. They had an inescapable obligation to send supplies to Fort William on the Laramie and might as well prepare to make the best of the season. Before the end of January, Campbell was in Philadelphia, where he visited his family and purchased a few supplies. His brother Hugh advised him not to return to the mountains under any circumstances, but to give up the fur trade for some small village business. Robert rejected Hugh's suggestion and traveled to New York City to make further arrangements. He had agreed to return to St. Louis in time to take the spring supply train to Fort William. Sublette suggested that later in the summer he might take an even larger party to the rendezvous.[22]

By April 1, Campbell was in St. Louis, but did not take a substantial party to the West. Instead of perhaps twenty-five or thirty men, only two accompanied him when he left for Fort William on the ninth. New arrangements had been made whereby William Sublette and Campbell were to sell the post to Fitzpatrick, Bridger, and Milton Sublette. When Campbell reached the fort in May, final arrangements were concluded for the transfer.[23] By that time the Oglala Sioux had moved in numbers to the

21 Original (Deed Record) U, p. 140, MSS, St. Louis CRDO; L. Lewis Contract with W. L. Sublette, December 13, 1834; John Lewis Contract with W. L. Sublette, December 23, 1834; Lindsay and Samuel Lewis Contract with W. L. Sublette, December 23, 1834, Sublette MSS.

22 Letters of May 7, 1834, February 10, 1835, Private Campbell MSS.

23 Letter of April 6, 1835, Private Campbell MSS; Missouri Intelligencer and Boon's Lick Advertiser (Columbia), July 25, 1835.

145

Laramie plain, supposedly as a result of an invitation issued to them the previous year by Sublette and Campbell. According to the rumors afoot in the mountain country, Campbell sent men to visit the Sioux and Cheyennes in order to bring about such a move. The Sioux chief Bull Bear led many of his lodges from the Black Hills in response, but it would be difficult to prove that Sublette and Campbell actually encouraged the migration.

The operation of Fort William also posed a threat to the new mountain firm of Bent, St. Vrain and Company. Operating on the upper Arkansas, they would have to compete with whatever group controlled Fort William. Bent and his associates planned to spread their activities into Wyoming, but now their road was blocked at least temporarily. Once the transfer of Fort William was completed, however, the Indian migration and the plans of Bent and St. Vrain were no longer problems of much consequence to Sublette and Campbell. Those problems were a legacy to Fitzpatrick and his associates.

Campbell spent fifteen days on the Laramie and then with Andrew Sublette, twelve other companions, and several packs of buffalo robes, descended the Platte and Missouri one thousand water-miles to St. Louis. The navigation of the river was dangerous in certain areas, but they constructed a "batteaux" and with the aid of smaller craft floated down-river in safety. They met an American Fur Company party including Oregon-bound missionaries Dr. Marcus Whitman and Rev. Samuel Parker on June 27, and less than three weeks later were again in St. Louis. Campbell completed the round trip in a little over three months—something of a record for the journey. For the first time buffalo robes sold better than beaver on the St. Louis market, and local merchants willingly took his entire stock.[24]

Sublette spent most of the spring and early summer at home nursing Milton through successive operations and watching the business scene. He managed to secure for Campbell and himself a share in the Fontenelle-Drips expedition of that year, saw Ira

[24] Diary (author unknown) of May 14 to July 13, 1835, entry of June 27, 1835, MS, Oregon Historical Society, Portland.

G. Smith about some details of Jedediah Smith's estate, was again in touch with Jackson, and carried along the day by day affairs of his partnership. Business in St. Louis continued to flourish, and a building boom was under way. The local press recorded the daily arrival of boatloads of immigrants, homes and business locations were scarce, craftsmen were in general demand, and in the confusion the more "nefarious" members of society found easy "pickins" amongst the frontier populace. A traveling clergyman who passed through the city in April compared it favorably with Albany and stressed the increasing influence of shrewd eastern businessmen. He took a dim view of the older Creole culture evident in the city, but praised the fur and lead trade.[25]

Sublette and Campbell paid close attention to the local and national economic situation and carefully considered their partnership's future. No decision was reached immediately, however, since Campbell had returned from the West with an intermittent fever said to be the result of overexertion and exposure to the severe natural elements of prairies and mountains. He moved to Sulphur Springs to be under Sublette's care and gradually recovered enough to travel to Philadelphia, where he hoped to sell the residue of the year's fur catch. Hugh Campbell expected both Robert and William to spend the winter in the East, but Campbell made the journey alone. Upon his arrival in Philadelphia and despite the attention of friends whom he met along the way, he suffered a relapse and was placed under a physician's care in Hugh's home.[26]

Someone had to remain in St. Louis to evaluate the changing aspects of western trade, and since Campbell had gone east and was ill, Sublette had little choice but to uphold the partnership.

[25] L. Fontenelle to C. Cabanne, October 21, 1835, Chouteau-Papin MSS; Jackson-Sublette and Smith-Sublette Temporary Settlements of April 25, 1835, Sublette MSS; Letter of April 6, 1835, Private Campbell MSS; Samuel Parker, *Journal of an Exploring Tour Beyond the Rocky Mountains . . . in the Years 1835, '36, and '37,* 23–24; *Daily Evening Herald and Commercial Advertiser* (St. Louis), June 5, 9, 1835.

[26] Letters of July 27, September 27, 1835, Private Campbell MSS; W. L. Sublette to Robert Campbell, February 9, 1836, Campbell MSS; Robert Campbell's Will of July 27, 1835, Sublette MSS.

Even though Hugh Campbell regarded fur traders and merchants as a "wire-working set of fellows," he supplied Sublette regular information, nonetheless, on the eastern fur market. The beaver market was dull as a result of the new fad for silk hats—"all the go" of the day—and buffalo robes remained in high demand.[27]

In the autumn Sublette took a short trip west to Independence and stopped on the way at Columbia and Lexington. He visited the Ashleys, his cousin William Burch, the Cooks in Callaway County, and other scattered friends up and down the lower Missouri Valley. In Independence he transacted business, swapped a few horses, and then returned to Lexington to visit friends and negotiate a land purchase. He again saw the Cooks, passed through Columbia, and by November 6 was on his way home. His river tour enabled him to see how the state had grown. Boonville had added several brick structures in recent years; New Franklin was springing up across the river; Liberty had a number of "decent dwelling houses" and a few busy stores, in addition to a flourishing horse market; and Jefferson City, though still struggling to be born, boasted a new statehouse the size of a small academy and a governor's mansion even smaller.[28]

In central and western Missouri he met trading companies newly arrived from the West and gleaned from them firsthand information on the fur and stock trade. Santa Fé traders at Independence related news of the Southwest, and at Columbia he met two old friends, Fraeb and Gervais, who had just returned from the mountains. They told him of the year's fur take, but could not answer his questions about Booneville. He did learn, and this was of more importance to him since he had a financial interest in their success, that Louis Vasquez and brother Andrew Sublette were seen last on the South Fork of the Platte. On July 29, they had renewed their trading license and were out to prove that a small partnership still could be successful in the trading region.[29]

[27] Letter of August 2, 1835, Private Campbell MSS.
[28] W. L. Sublette to Robert Campbell, November 2, 1835, Campbell MSS; Charles A. Murray, *Travels in North America During the Years 1834, 1835, & 1836,* I, 245, 247.

Sublette probably reached St. Louis during the second week in November and seems, even then, to have reconsidered going east; yet his St. Louis obligations simply were too great to warrant the trip. He had a case pending in the Missouri Supreme Court, which he lost on reversal, and Milton was involved in another in the St. Louis Circuit Court. William was summoned twice as a witness and, simultaneously, served as an administrator of a friend's estate. Also, Stewart was in town from the West, and we may presume had a spirited reunion with Sublette. At times travelers found St. Louis "extremely dull," lacking in both gaiety and hospitality, but Stewart wrote ahead to tell Sublette of his return, and William probably planned something to enliven his visit.[30]

During the autumn of 1835, Milton was up and around, aided by a cork left leg a Philadelphia craftsman had made for him under order from Hugh Campbell. Milton was determined not to be a cripple forever confined to wheeled transportation and did not intend to spend his days in seclusion. In fact, he believed himself fit enough, by the following spring of 1836, to re-enter the fur trade. He would not be deterred by anyone, went west, lost contact with William, and succumbed, on April 5, 1837, to his illness. Placed in a grave not far from Fort William on the Laramie, he became the second of the five Sublette brothers to die in the mountain trade.[31]

Brother Solomon Sublette, in contrast, was in much better health and by 1836, anticipating his twenty-first birthday, turned to William for advice and assistance. Solomon wanted a business of his own—he seemed not to realize his lack of business sense—and knew his older brother would help. William was willing to try,

---

[29] W. L. Sublette to Robert Campbell, November 2, 1835, Campbell MSS; File of B. L. E. Bonneville, Capt. U. S. A., 1831–35, Records of the Adjutant General's Office United States Army, Record Group No. 94, MSS, N. A.; William Clark to Elbert Herring, August 3, 1835, Letters Received, 1824–41, Records of the Office of Indian Affairs, Record Group No. 75, MSS, N. A.

[30] File of *John R. White* v. *Milton Sublette*, File 75, MS, St. Louis CCC; William Drummond Stewart to W. L. Sublette, October 16, 1835, Sublette MSS.

[31] Letters of April 6, September 27, 1835, Private Campbell MSS; *Daily Picayune* (New Orleans), December 15, 1843; *Daily Missouri Republican* (St. Louis), June 16, 1837.

and suggested he open a clothing and shoe store in Independence
—a suggestion Solomon liked. While he waited for William to
order for him shoes, boots, headgear, and Indian goods valued at
fifteen hundred to three thousand dollars, he took a temporary
position as clerk in St. Louis. But, as might be expected, he
was unable to succeed in Independence, and by late spring, 1838,
was looking for more adventurous pastimes. A friend encouraged
him to forego a shopkeeper's life; to "throw away" his goods and
rejoin his old pals in a whirl of parties, mint juleps, card games,
and women. Solomon gave in, had his whirl, left William with
his unsettled financial obligations, and was off to Arkansas to
engage in the mule trade.[32]

[32] W. L. Sublette to Robert Campbell, January 4, 12, 1836, Campbell MSS;
I. T. Peck to Solomon Sublette, June 28, 1836, Sublette MSS.

Sublette and Campbell

T HE CHRISTMAS SEASON, 1835, was a quiet but busy one at Sulphur Springs. Solomon was home with William, Milton divided his time between St. Louis and his outstate business commitments, Andrew was in the West, and Campbell remained in Philadelphia. Robert was still in poor health, and it would be March before he recovered sufficiently from his "ague & fever" to return to Missouri. In his absence Sublette drew up a new partnership agreement—the old three-year agreement was to expire January 1, 1836—which Campbell approved in absentia. By the new contract, also of three years, the two agreed to become bona fide merchants. Each was to contribute slightly over $9,700, to share equally all gains and losses, and to have the right to dissolve the partnership at any time by mutual consent. For the present, until Campbell's return, Sublette concentrated upon two subjects: he tried to settle certain outstanding debts due the partnership, and he searched for a favorable downtown business site. If they were to do a profitable spring business, they had to have a conveniently located establishment. A simple warehouse or storeroom would no longer suffice.[1]

[1] W. L. Sublette to Robert Campbell, January 4, 12, 1836, Campbell MSS; Sublette-Campbell Agreement of January 1, 1836, Sublette MSS.

Throughout the winter Sublette watched the fluctuations of the mountain trade and pressured the successors of the American Fur Company to pay the debts they owed his partnership. On January 12, he visited Chouteau and hinted that if the debts were not paid, it might be necessary for him to prepare another western expedition which would go to the rendezvous of 1836 and secure beaver in payment. The threat caused Chouteau to pay some outstanding notes, but Fontenelle had not as yet reached St. Louis, and Chouteau was unwilling to settle the remainder until they could confer. Sublette grew more and more anxious, since he had to know one way or another what was to be done before finally committing himself to an expedition. Fortunately for him, Chouteau paid another note on February 26, leaving only Fontenelle's notes outstanding to Sublette and Campbell. But Fontenelle, who was by then in St. Louis, seemed unable to "leave off Frolicking fer two days to arainge them"; both Sublette and Chouteau were disgusted.[2]

On the twenty-seventh, Fitzpatrick reached St. Louis, bringing news of Vasquez and Andrew Sublette. Fitzpatrick and Fontenelle then were business associates, as a result of a rather recent amalgamation of Fitzpatrick, Bridger, and Milton Sublette with Fontenelle and Drips. Sublette warned his old friend Fitzpatrick that if Fontenelle's debts were not paid, "I will then make arrangements for the mountains." Fitzpatrick's answer was to dissolve his agreement with Fontenelle, but the debt remained to plague Sublette.[3]

Once again the spring brought St. Louis numerous westward-bound travelers. A new missionary group, composed of Dr. Whitman, Rev. Henry H. Spalding, and—surprise of surprises—their wives, reached St. Louis on March 30 and left again the following day aboard the steamboat "Chariton" for Liberty and Independence, where they hoped to join a fur caravan to Green River. In St. Louis they asked advice of several Mountain Men,

[2] W. L. Sublette to Robert Campbell, January 12, February 9, 27–29, 1836, Campbell MSS.
[3] *Missouri Republican* (St. Louis), May 14, 1836.

including, it seems, Sublette, and were told to "turn back," since no caravan was regarded as strong enough to protect the missionaries' wives from the Indians. Sublette feared that the women had little if any chance of surviving the arduous journey, but in that instance he was wrong—they made it to Oregon.[4]

Stewart wrote during the winter that he planned to return to the mountains in the entourage of some former American Fur Company men. Would Sublette provide him "Indian trinkeets," horses, and mules? The request was not difficult to fill, since the equipment he desired was readily available and Sublette esteemed Stewart's friendship. William brought him two fast horses, possibly some mules as well, and when Stewart, later in the season, went west with two light wagons, he and an elusive German companion were well outfitted.

Sublette's problem of finding an acceptable business location was not solved as easily as he expected. He had thought about possible sites for many months and the previous June of 1835 had attempted to buy a storehouse recently vacated by the St. Louis firm of Kyle and Edgar. At that time he was unsuccessful, and it was not until January, 1836, that he had a second opportunity, this time to buy, along with a certain Captain Holt, a twenty-thousand-dollar downtown mercantile house. On second thought, however, Sublette believed the price to be too high and refused the offer. He and Campbell had known for many months just what they wanted: a wholesale establishment with a large Indian goods department. Since he had not been successful in finding such a place, he now decided not to act until Campbell was well enough to assist him. Also it might be best, he thought, to sample the prospects for the year's fur trade before plunging into a business dependent upon fur returns.[5]

Campbell, contrary to his usual preference, had returned to

---

[4] H. H. Spaulding, "Narrative of an Overland Journey to Fort Vancouver and Lapwai in 1836, Together with an Account of the Beginning of the American Protestant Missions Beyond the Rockies," MS, Oregon Historical Society, Portland.

[5] W. L. Sublette to Robert Campbell, January 12, February 27–29, 1836, Campbell MSS; Letters of June 19, July 4, 1835, Private Campbell MSS.

St. Louis willing to take a party west if necessary to guarantee payment of debts due Sublette and himself. He also, especially for his partner's sake, thought he might learn something of Vasquez and Andrew Sublette and their future plans. While William remained at home, Campbell could see what the fur hunt of 1835–36 had produced and, incidentally, might turn a small profit by taking a caravan to the rendezvous. The caravan would be small and no great loss to them if the fur catch were diminutive. Despite Campbell's willingness to go, the most reliable information available suggests that he did not carry out his plan. He was still in St. Louis on May 13, much too late to have started for the mountains.[6] The few furs and robes he and Sublette received that year were conveyed down-river to them rather late in the season. Hugh Campbell kept them informed on the eastern fur markets—he still was a bit baffled by the "secrecy" of their business operations—and presumably they sold their part of the year's catch at a fair profit.[7]

Reports from the West were promising enough to encourage them to take their long-delayed step: early in September they opened a store at No. 7 Main (First) Street, opposite what had been the St. Louis branch of the United States Bank. They advertised "an entire new stock of goods consisting of domestic and foreign dry goods, shoes, hats, &c., which they [would] sell on accomodating [sic] terms, by wholesale or retail." The building, a brick one, had been operated as a business house by N. B. Atwood, its previous occupant, and was situated on a lot 38 by 160 feet. The building and lot were purchased by Sublette and Campbell for $12,833.[8]

[6] References in the St. Louis courthouse records place Campbell in St. Louis as late as May 13. Alter, *op. cit.*, 157–58, places Sublette at the rendezvous, but William remained in St. Louis during the spring and summer. The Sublette papers and the St. Louis courthouse records prove that point. Alter possibly mistook William for Andrew Sublette.

[7] Ramsay Crooks to Pratte, Chouteau & Co., August 24, 1836, American Fur Company Letter Book V, MSS; Unknown Person to Ramsay Crooks, August 31, 1836, American Fur Company Letter Book III, MSS, New York Historical Society; Letter of July 19, November 3, 1836, Private Campbell MSS.

[8] *Missouri Argus* (St. Louis), September 16, 1836; *Missouri Republican*

The time was auspicious for a business-opening, since the general spirit of progress and prosperity, common for so many years, continued and grew. Up and down the Ohio and Mississippi valleys, "pretty" little towns expanded in their provincial pride, and the larger cities profited from crowded—at times over-crowded—steamboat landings. Although their business sections might be plain in design, no one could mistake the buzz of activity. Louisville boasted an elaborate lock system on the Ohio River and New Orleans a handsome business exchange building and many fine, open-fronted stores, but only St. Louis was located advantageously enough to tap the first flow of trade from the Upper Missouri. According to the *Arkansas Gazette*, St. Louis seemed "to be enthusiastic in everything." Its enterprising citizens watched affairs in Texas and were pleased to hear that a daily stage line had been ordered to begin service to Louisville. That September St. Louis was thronged with strangers—their sensitivities were bothered by swarms of early autumn mosquitoes, but their spirits remained high.[9]

In general, business conditions in St. Louis were prosperous from 1836 to 1840, and the "kaleidoscopic years" to 1837 carried with them enough momentum to continue western prosperity until 1840–41, at a somewhat diminished pace. From 1837 on, however, there was a major national economic crisis. At first it confined itself to the East and South: at least until 1842–43 its full force was unrealized in the West. One westerner wrote to a friend a year after the depression began and mentioned the vast amount of building in progress in St. Louis, the shortage of residential space, the speculation in all fields, and the general prosperity. The difficult times inevitably would be felt in the West, although for St. Louis the year 1839 began "pregnant with prosperity," and the worst was yet to come.[10]

(St. Louis), September 6, 1836; Original (Deed Record) X, pp. 80, 301, MS; General Record (Deed Record) K–2, p. 348, MS, St. Louis CRDO.

9 *Arkansas Gazette* (Little Rock), October 25, 1836.

10 Letter of Frederick Graff to Charles Graff, June 29, 1838, St. Louis Miscellaneous Envelope, MSS, MoSHi; Dorothy B. Dorsey, "The Panic and Depression of 1837–43 in Missouri," *Missouri Historical Review*, Vol. XXX (January, 1936), 133, 137.

Sublette and Campbell, under license from the county court, continued to operate their business at No. 7 Main Street throughout the entire period. Their ideal position in the very heart of the commercial district was heightened by their excellent reputations—reputations respected by competitors both in St. Louis and in nearby rural areas. A few blocks from their store were expensive ladies' shops on Market Street, stocked with an abundance of "rich . . . and fine fancy wares," and closer to their business house were a bookseller and stationer, a dry goods company, and a prosperous grocery. The partners stocked a wider and wider variety of goods, including everything from Indian looking glasses and palm leaf hats to heavier dry goods and luxury items. In June, 1840, they received a small shipment of new, "superior" blankets from Boston and put them on display as proof of their fine taste. That portion of their goods sold and shipped from St. Louis was sent by water along the Missouri, Mississippi, Illinois, and Ohio rivers but was only a small part of the thirty millions in trade goods carried in the year 1841 alone by the hundreds of steamers operating from the city. At times, however, they lost goods sent by river transportation. In 1840, part of a cargo of dry goods they shipped up the Ohio settled on the river bottom when the steamer "Miami" struck a snag.[11]

Hugh Campbell thought both his brother Robert and Sublette were novices in the mercantile line and freely advised them how best to operate their business. In most instances his suggestions were sound. He told them to beware of the second year's trade, especially in the spring of 1838; to sell only for cash "or acceptances which can be converted into money"; and to collect promptly all debts due them "without regard to circumstances." Their credit was good, and he wished to keep it so, but, unfortunately, although they did take his advice, they did not use it as completely as they should and soon suffered the consequences in a number of suits for debt.[12]

[11] *Daily Evening Gazette* (St. Louis), July 13, 1838, December 20, 1839, August 19, 1840; *St. Louis New Era*, June 11, 22, 1840; *Daily Missouri Republican* (St. Louis), January 7, 1839; Record of St. Louis County Court No. 2, 1836–41, pp. 123, 208, 244, MS, Register's Office, City Hall, St. Louis.

In the late autumn of 1838, Sublette made one of the first of many short trips he would be forced to take up the Missouri River to Independence. By stage and steamboat he managed to visit most of the principal river towns, saw some old friends, and enjoyed the welcome change from everyday business routine. His expense account totaled nearly three hundred dollars, but in return he collected debts of better than nine hundred, and brought back, late in November, a slave girl purchased, in all probability, near Independence.

The partners not only carried on their wholesale-retail business in St. Louis, but also continued, at least until 1840, to invest in the fur trade. In mid-June of 1839, the local press noted that a boat employed by them had just "arrived from the Platte . . . ladened with furs and robes" and that another, which may have been theirs, was due shortly. They remained in intimate contact with Andrew Sublette and Vasquez, paid bills for them to firms in St. Louis and at Independence, and stood their power of attorney. It was common knowledge that William and Andrew had worked together for years and that Sublette and Campbell still gained something from the fur trade. The last sale of furs directly attributed to them was transacted in August, 1840, when two lots of deer and raccoon skins, possibly taken in barter from local residents, were sold in St. Louis.[13]

The partnership had legal difficulties almost from the very beginning, although the amount of trouble was intensified by the darkening economic picture. They were forced, by 1842, to bring suits for debt in at least four Illinois and eleven Missouri counties. Five cases in Illinois were heard in Adams, Macon, Jefferson, and McLean counties, and three of the five cases were decided in favor of Sublette and Campbell. They had to take lands in each instance in payment, and the lands usually were difficult to resell. In Missouri at least thirty-two cases were considered, scattered amongst the following counties: Chariton, Cole, Gasconade, Jack-

12 Hugh Campbell to W. L. Sublette, February 24, 1838, Sublette MSS.
13 *Daily Missouri Republican* (St. Louis), June 19, 1839; *Arkansas Gazette* (Little Rock), September 11, 1839; License of Vasquez and Sublette, July 15, 1837; License of Vasquez and Sublette, June 30, 1838, DMDI, MSS, MoSHi.

son, Lafayette, Marion, Ray, St. Charles, St. Louis, Ste Genevieve, and Saline. All of the counties contained important river trading communities, some of whose merchants had given promissory notes to Sublette and Campbell and had defaulted in payment. Only one case was tried in each of five of those counties, but thirteen cases, of which three were significant, appeared in St. Louis County. Excluding the three significant cases, of the remaining twenty-nine the partnership won twenty. Seven were dismissed and two were lost on technical grounds on appeal to the Missouri Supreme Court. In one-fifth of the cases won, landed property was taken: in one case the property of a stage line was attached and in many of the others personal property from buckets to horses.[14] As the traveling partner in his business, Sublette was called upon to appear before various county courts from time to time. Most of the debts involved were under eight hundred dollars, and at least one case, tried in St. Louis, directly involved a woman, Hannah Fletcher, who defaulted on a purchase of "carpet . . . and . . . Green Baize [woolen fabric]."[15]

Of the three important St. Louis County suits, the earliest, dated 1839, was an action brought by Sublette and Campbell against a debt owed them by their old mountain friends Henry Fraeb and Edmund Christy. Fraeb consistently refused to appear in court, and when a judgment against him finally was given, "no good chattels land or tenements" of his in the county could be located.[16] A second case in the same court also involved the fur trade. In 1842, the partners brought suit against Vasquez and Andrew Sublette for goods sold them, but they had dissolved their agreement the year before, having been hard hit by the depression and the general decline in the trade, and could not pay in cash the $2,751.77 in debts plus costs granted by the court. Eventually, in 1845, seventy-seven and one-half acres of land

[14] See extensive citations of all cases and county courthouse records listed in the bibliography.
[15] File of *Sublette and Campbell* v. *Hannah Fletcher*, File 236, MS, St. Louis CCC.
[16] Executions, 1837–42, No. 72; File of *Sublette and Campbell* v. *Henry Fraeb*, File 43, MSS, St. Louis CCC.

in St. Louis County was taken from them in payment and transferred to Sublette and Campbell.[17]

The third St. Louis County case involved the Bank of Mineral Point, Wisconsin. One of the first in its region, it was chartered in 1836 with a capital of two hundred thousand dollars and was located in a small red-brick building on High Street in Mineral Point, a booming lead-mining center of southwestern Wisconsin. Since 1839, the bank had issued notes. Although an investigation in 1840 "had shown it to be sound," it collapsed the following year when its cashier and teller suddenly absconded. The vaults were found empty, and close examination revealed large drafts on the banks of several other cities. Sublette and Campbell held fifteen small notes against the bank, for which they requested payment in 1842, but the bank was then in process of dissolution and could make no immediate restitution. Although the court decided in favor of Sublette and Campbell, the bank in 1845 requested a new trial. The Missouri Supreme Court upheld the lower court's decision, but it is questionable whether the notes were ever paid.[18]

One large debt, over thirty-five hundred dollars, was settled out of court. James and Elizabeth Hibbard granted Sublette and Campbell a mortgage to five town lots in Fenton, Missouri, on one part of which was located a steam sawmill, and a deed to a nearby small farm. Most of the property was disposed of by Campbell after Sublette's death. In the instance of the Hibbard property it seems that the partners personally directed negotiations, but, because their legal difficulties were so numerous and scattered, at other times they found it necessary to employ trusted agents. One such agent was J. P. Helfenstein, their devoted chief clerk and bookkeeper, who collected debts, witnessed deeds, and

[17] File of *Sublette and Campbell* v. *Louis Vasquez and Andrew W. Sublette*, File 288, MS, St. Louis CCC; General Record (Deed Record), P-4, p. 41, and T-3, p. 55, MSS, St. Louis CRDO.

[18] Files of *Sublette and Campbell* v. *Perpetual Insurance Company*, File 372, v. *The Mineral Point Bank*, File 192, MSS, St. Louis CCC; David D. Van Tassel, "A Study of the Influence of the Frontier on a Wisconsin Mining Town" (M. A. thesis, University of Wisconsin, 1951), 52–53.

stood security before the courts. The St. Louis legal firm of Bowlin and Hudson was retained in certain suits, since James B. Bowlin of the firm was Sublette's close friend and a well-known Democratic leader. William M. Campbell served as their attorney in St. Charles; Thomas Burch, a relative of Sublette's, aided in Ray County; C. R. Morehead, another close friend, and Micijah Tarver, a dearly beloved intimate of the Sublette family, gave their assistance as called upon; and last but not least Abiel Leonard, eminent lawyer and citizen of the Boon's Lick country, was ready to advise and serve.[19]

As a speculative venture the partners invested surplus business capital in other lands. In 1838, they purchased a town lot in the new settlement of Columbus, Illinois, and the same year bought a city lot in Christy's addition to St. Louis, "fronting 26 feet on Franklin Avenue." Sublette originally had purchased the Franklin Avenue lot in 1836, holding it in trust for the partnership. At other times they speculated in lands for Stewart: 156.50 acres in December, 1836. This tract was held in his trust until August, 1839, when it was resold at cost.[20]

It was evident to Sublette and Campbell, by early 1841, that general economic conditions in St. Louis were more difficult and that their cash receipts would continue to dwindle as long as the heavy hand of depression weighed upon western business. Notwithstanding their close connection with local and state government and their right to "sell drafts" on various banks such as the Farmers and Mechanics in Philadelphia, for which they were sole western agents, their credit balance continued to fall. Sublette undertook at least five debt-collecting trips to central and western Missouri between 1839 and 1842—one five months in duration— and Campbell gave whatever assistance he could, but he had more immediate family obligations. He was not as well known in far western Missouri as Sublette: "one of the chivalrous sons of the

[19] Adams to Abiel Leonard, September 21, 1844; Robert Campbell to Abiel Leonard, November 9, 1844, Leonard Collection, 1769–1928, MSS, UMWMC.

[20] William Drummond Stewart to W. L. Sublette, April 14, 1839, Sublette MSS; Record of Sales U. S. Land Vol. 5, 1836–39, p. 8, MSS, Office of the Secretary of State, Jefferson City, Missouri.

West and . . . the hero of Washington Irving's Rocky Mountain sketches." It was the policy of the partners, or rather of the partner remaining in St. Louis, not to make any important business decision if the other were absent.[21]

Sublette and Campbell extended their partnership by mutual agreement in 1839, but their most difficult years were ahead of them, and rather than risk greater losses in 1842, they agreed to dissolve their long, close association. They hoped that after collecting their assets they could balance their late losses, perhaps exceed them, and realize some profit. On January 15, 1842, they drew up a written dissolution whereby Campbell, for $6,656.82, payable in three notes, purchased the goods and furnishings of the partnership. He was empowered also to keep the books of the old agreement until they were closed, and the store on Main Street was divided into two units for the use of each respectively for two years or until a further decision could be reached.[22]

Much of the success of the dissolution depended upon business in the spring of 1842, and to bolster their prospects, Campbell went east to exchange a small quantity of gold, to purchase some essential items, and to see his relatives. Sublette remained in St. Louis and attempted, with Helfenstein's aid, to collect debts. He had little or no success. Business conditions grew more stringent, and the store was closed temporarily until Campbell could return and open his half. Mrs. Campbell said that "[She] went down [the] street and . . . wouldn't even look at the store it looked so gloomy." Campbell found it impossible to borrow in the East: "never" had he "felt so much anxiety about money," and hoped against hope that Sublette, who by May was in western Missouri, would collect enough on debts to close the books and cover the spring's expenses. A few individuals stopped at the store to see Campbell after he returned and paid their debts, although most simply pleaded inability to meet their obligations, and all spoke of the hard times. Writing to Sublette on June 4, Campbell men-

[21] Letters of October 19, 1839, June 17, 1840, January 25, 1841, Private Campbell MSS; W. Gilpin to H. D. Gilpin, December 1, 1841, Sublette MSS.
[22] Sublette-Campbell Dissolution of Partnership, January 15, 1842, Sublette MSS.

tioned that he had not collected a dollar in over a week and said that on the previous evening a mob had gathered in the city with the intention of attacking local brokers.[23]

Sublette had more success than he had anticipated: large debts were hard to collect, but he had received payment of some small ones. At the same time he considered the current prospects of the mountain trade and was told by his old friend Bridger, just in from Green River, that the trade was still profitable and could be very lucrative to an experienced, ambitious mountaineer. Sublette realized the possibilities "on the head waters of the Platte" and seriously considered taking a supply train west in the autumn —so seriously that he secured forty-two head of horses and mules. Yet, "for want of money and Business not wound up," he was forced to return home in early September.

Both partners lent money to the business from their private accounts, their fortunes dwindled, and they did not wish to borrow in St. Louis. They decided to apply to Stewart for a four-thousand-dollar loan, to be guaranteed by real estate mortgages, and Stewart immediately complied through a bank in New York. Philadelphia, and as the gloomy year 1842 closed, they made Hugh Campbell provided them other sums and drafts through forceful attempts to balance their books. On December 1, their ledger revealed many outstanding, uncollected accounts, despite all their exertions, and a final settlement was not reached until eight years later.[24]

For a half-dozen years since 1842, Sublette and Campbell were allied closely to the new Bank of the State of Missouri. Certainly the alliance increased their community standing and helped their business prospects, but it also involved them in the heated controversies over the bank and the money question. For many years, because its first state bank had failed in 1821, the state of Missouri had consistently refused to recharter another. Hard coin

[23] Letters of January 18, 26, 1842, Private Campbell MSS; "Correspondence of Robert Campbell, 1834–1895," *loc. cit.*, 27–31, 33, 34.

[24] Balance Sheet from Sublette and Campbell Ledger, December 1, 1842; Balances and Statements from Sublette and Campbell's Books, February 1849, and April 1850, Sublette MSS.

flowing in from Santa Fé encouraged the anti-paper-money factions, and the state maintained itself on much of a hard-money psychology. A branch of the second United States Bank opened in St. Louis in 1829—Ashley was a director—but it was not until 1832, when Jackson vetoed an attempt to recharter the second bank, that Governor Miller recommended the establishment of a new state bank as a substitute for the "oppressive" national institution. A legislative committee reported in favor of his suggestion, although public opinion in the state was split into no bank, national bank, and two active state-bank factions.[25]

In the state election of 1836, the bank was a principal issue, and the Democratic candidate for governor won on a pro-state bank platform over Whig opposition and the disapproval of many Democrats. Representative James B. Bowlin, Sublette's friend from St. Louis, the following year pushed the bill through the legislature and into law. It was justified as a means to aid agricultural prosperity and was approved by Senator Benton, who had just led the attack in Washington to kill the second national bank. He viewed the new state bank as an instrument of the many, not of the few; as a bank that would have public interests in mind. The new state bank, set up at a time when so many others were failing throughout the nation, was capitalized at five million dollars and was to have a twelve-man board of directors, plus the president. He and seven others were to be chosen biennially by the legislature.

Following the approval of the act on February 2, 1837, the legislature immediately selected its quota of directors in the "parent bank" of St. Louis and the branch at Fayette. Edward Walsh was elected a director on the first ballot. On the second, cast on Thursday the second, Edward Dobyns, Lewellen Brown, and Sublette were nominated, but Dobyns won with sixty-two votes to Brown's nine and Sublette's three. Nonetheless, on the third ballot Sublette was chosen by eighty-one votes, and the board of

25 F. F. Stephens, "Banking and Finance in Missouri in the Thirties," *Proceedings of the Mississippi Valley Historical Association*, Vol. X (1918–21), 122–27; James Neal Primm, *Economic Policy in the Development of a Western State: Missouri 1820–1860*, 19.

the St. Louis branch, as finally constituted, included Walsh, Dobyns, Sublette, Samuel S. Rayburn, John O'Fallon, and Hugh
O'Neil. Both leading pro- and anti-bank newspapers in St. Louis
admitted that the choice of directors and president—John Brady
Smith, a native Kentuckian and a "man of stern integrity, serious, dignified and sturdy"—was thoughtful and intelligent. Stock
subscriptions were opened in St. Louis at the Chouteau House
on Main Street near Vine and in ten other Missouri communities, but sales were slower than expected. Many St. Louis businessmen preferred a national bank; others no paper-money bank
at all. Finally, on March 15, it was announced that books would
remain open indefinitely and as a result the necessary amount
was subscribed by late spring, and the Governor of Missouri
promptly subscribed the state's share.[26]

Late in February the directors held their first meeting and
initiated a program for the operation of the bank. Tellers, book-
keepers, and other employees were hired, and the bank slowly
expanded its circulation throughout the spring. The state appointed its four directors, the stockholders appointed their two,
but as might be expected in such an institution buffeted by diverse
political winds and personalities, there was immediate suspicion
that this or that board member was involved in *sub rosa* stock
transactions.[27] At an October 23 meeting two members requested
information on O'Neil's stock dealings and, according to the *Missouri Argus*, "a pause followed and Mr. O'Neil was seen to whis-
per to Sublette who sat beside him," after which William objected to the proposed examination. A vote was taken and Sublette was sustained, but the implication was clear.[28]

Sublette attended only half of all board meetings, which was
average attendance, yet his financial interest in the bank grew.
As of October, 1840, he had drawn $2,074 in notes on the bank

---

[26] *Missouri Republican* (St. Louis), February 8, 20, 1837; *Missouri Argus*
(St. Louis), February 10, 1837; John Ray Cable, *The Bank of the State of Mis-
souri (Columbia University Studies in History, Economics, and Public Law,
Vol. CII, No. 2)*, 161–63.

[27] *Daily Missouri Republican* (St. Louis), July 1, 1837.

[28] *Missouri Argus* (St. Louis), November 1, 1837.

in his own name and another $7,128 in the name of his partnership. In the years 1841–42, Sublette and Campbell owed the bank more than any other Missouri firm of which bank directors were members. Their liabilities to the bank reached a peak of $11,181 in January, 1841, and then fell gradually, whereas their deposits with the bank were never much above $1,500. The figures are not too complete, but they reveal the ups and downs of the partnership as it attempted to meet bank failures and note fluctuations. Although directors of the bank were at times allowed to overdraw, "No loans were ever made to any officer or director whose account was overdrawn; and no officer or director . . . had ever let his paper go to protest. The directors were . . . accustomed to borrow quite heavily from the bank."[29]

As the panic grew in the East, specie became scarce; boatmen refused to handle freight if paid in western bank notes; and the Bank of Missouri, to save itself, restricted loans to meet decreased deposits. The directors withdrew all possible funds from other banks, converted their notes into specie, and managed to survive the panic "without serious injury." A committee of three examined the bank and reported that it was as sound as could be expected. Their entrenched belief in hard money—a belief Sublette as a director, re-elected to the board in December, 1838, accepted—prevailed over the times. Risks were not to be taken, and when, in the autumn of 1839, the bank refused to receive anything but its own notes and specie or notes of specie paying banks, there was a loud cry from Missouri merchants who had invested heavily in other notes. The order was successful, but in the next directors' election of December, 1840, Sublette was not chosen. For one reason, he had been active in the presidential election. Van Buren, his choice, had lost to the Whig, William Henry Harrison. Also, Sublette may have asked to be relieved in order to devote more time to his business and his farm, but, as seems more likely, he was chastised by the legislature, in response

[29] *Journal of the House of Representatives of the State of Missouri . . . One Thousand Eight Hundred and Forty*, Appendix G; *Journal of the House of Representatives of the State of Missouri . . . One Thousand Eight Hundred and Forty-Two*, Appendices B, C, F.

to St. Louis public opinion, for his determined hard-money views. He was dropped from the board temporarily, but Campbell was sent to the bank in his place.[30]

In spite of the "great juggling in the money affairs" of St. Louis during 1841–42, the bank continued to pay specie on its notes. It was the outstanding example of western state bank stability and much in contrast to certain neighboring institutions. The Bank of Shawneetown, Illinois, was an example of an unreliable one upon which Sublette and Campbell held several notes —notes soon of little value. Campbell wrote frequent letters to Sublette, whenever William was in western Missouri, warned him of fluctuating bank-note values, and advised him to get rid of unstable notes. Such fears and uncertainties were common to the business community at that time. Were Kentucky notes superior to Indiana's or vice versa? What was to be done in such a paper storm?

When the legislature met in December, 1842, to choose a new board of bank directors, there was considerable political bickering: charges and counter-charges fell thick and fast. Campbell was "indifferent about . . . re-election as director," but stressed the selection of hard-money men and asked Sublette to use his influence in that way. But Sublette used more than his influence on others and by the end of the balloting had been returned to the board by a vote of 127 to 1. Campbell also was re-elected—the bank incorporation act of 1837 prohibited two men in a trading partnership from serving on the board at the same time, but their partnership had been dissolved—and four years later would become president of the board. Both Sublette and Campbell opposed F. M. Kennett, who was selected president in 1842, since they regarded him as a soft-money man. Nonetheless, the Bank of Missouri had stood its period of trials and emerged a sound "Gibraltar of the West," following a steady but extremely cautious policy that they had helped establish.[31]

[30] *Journal of the Senate of the State of Missouri . . . One Thousand Eight Hundred and Forty-Two,* Appendix A; *Journal of the House* (1840), Appendix G.

Between 1837 and 1840, they took a leading part in the organization and establishment of three other institutions: the Marine Insurance Company, the St. Louis Insurance Company, and the St. Louis Hotel Company. All three were chartered by the state legislature in 1837, and once again Representative Bowlin was responsible for introducing the proposals as necessary to the "state's expanded economic program." Sublette and Campbell were included on the original list of over one hundred stockholders in the St. Louis Hotel enterprise, and Sublette was one of the eleven commissioners appointed to open books for capital stock subscriptions in the St. Louis Insurance Company. When the third institution, the Marine Insurance Company, opened at No. 62 North Ninth Street, he was on its thirteen-man board of directors.[32]

As businessmen, bank directors, and corporation investors, it was almost inevitable that they should enter local politics. Of the two, Sublette was by far the more avid politician. He had political ambitions, some political experience, and could point to a father and a grandfather who had served in political capacities. Through Ashley he met established leaders and budding politicians and, having retired from the mountain trade, was willing to devote part of his time, energy, and money to the cause of the Democratic party. In 1833 he had written Campbell to "d——d the Yanke's as will as the Nullifiers," and was regarded as a Jackson man, a Benton man, and a hard-money Missouri-Kentucky Democrat.[33]

Prior to 1837, he took little part in politics. True, he attended

[31] Letter of T. H. Benton to Governor Reynolds, November 10, 1842, Benton Family Papers, MSS, MoSHi; *Daily Missouri Republican* (St. Louis), December 9, 1842; Robert Campbell to W. L. Sublette, December 11, 1842, Sublette MSS.

[32] *Journal of the House of Representatives of the State of Missouri . . . One Thousand Eight Hundred and Thirty-Six,* 156, 250, 265, 269, 316, 324, 362, 391; *Journal of the Senate of the State of Missouri . . . One Thousand Eight Hundred and Thirty-Six,* 197, 199, 210, 223, 226, 229, 236, 239; *Laws of the State of Missouri . . . One Thousand Eight Hundred and Thirty-Six,* 180–81, 213–14, 221; *Missouri Republican* (St. Louis), February 13, 20, March 21, 1837, May 5, November 12, 1838.

[33] W. L. Sublette to Robert Campbell, January 11, 1833, Campbell MSS.

the January 8, 1835, ball and supper in St. Louis to commemorate Jackson's victory at New Orleans a score of years before, but otherwise seldom participated. Ashley ran for governor the following year against L. W. Boggs, but was beaten, and Sublette seems not to have participated in that contest. Although Ashley was his dear friend, he was considered to be a new Whig, certainly not a Jackson Democrat, and for that reason Sublette might have refrained from active campaigning.[34] Some of his politically minded friends, however, in May of that year sent his name to the Secretary of War, recommending him as a prominent, able westerner who deserved an officer's appointment in the dragoons. The President had been authorized by Congress to raise an additional regiment of dragoons, or mounted riflemen, to maintain order on Missouri's northern border. The incident behind the Congressional action—the so-called Heatherly War—was chargeable to five white outlaws who had filled the Missouri frontier with thoughts of an Indian war. Sublette did not receive the appointment and may not have been too eager to participate in such a border incident.[35]

His first real political interest centered in the state and Congressional campaigns of 1838. A meeting held at the courthouse in December, 1837, was the opening gun in the state campaign—a meeting Sublette attended. William Millburn, a Benton partisan, presided, and Sublette served on a temporary twenty-man resolutions committee that reported planks in opposition to a national bank, for a general national bankruptcy law, and of course in favor of the re-election of Senator Benton. Shortly after the December meeting, he worked with a number of other men to prepare the annual eighth of January dinner at the National Hotel. Over two hundred loyal Democrats turned out for the gala occasion, dined and spoke, and proposed endless toasts. Sublette

[34] *Arkansas Gazette* (Little Rock), September 15, 1835, September 6, 1836; *Missouri Republican* (St. Louis), January 16, 1835.

[35] The letters to the Secretary of War were sent by George W. Jones (May 28), L. F. Linn (May 24), W. H. Ashley and A. G. Harrison (May 24), and A. H. Secier (May 27), Letters Received; the Secretary of War to A. G. Harrison and W. H. Ashley, May 25, 1836, Letters Sent, Secretary of War, 1836, Records of the Office of the Secretary of War, Record Group No. 107, MSS, N. A.

raised his glass to "The American Eagle: May She never lose a feather whilst protecting what Washington guaranteed American [Liberty]. May she raise up chicks of Democracy, and feed them on the flesh of Tories."[36]

At a courthouse meeting earlier in the evening before the dinner, his political star was lighted. As a member of the thirty-man resolutions committee, he helped form an address to the people and reported on candidates for the state general assembly. Van Buren and Benton were lauded, the idea of a national bank was attacked again, and shortly after the meeting and dinner he was selected to run for the Missouri Senate to fill a vacancy created by the resignation of Senator Eliott Lee of St. Louis County. The opposition "Whig Reform and Internal Improvement Ticket" nominated John F. Darby, an able St. Louis lawyer and politician. Darby, a native of North Carolina, had settled in Missouri in 1818, studied law, and met "rapid . . . success" as a legal mind. Three-times mayor of St. Louis, he had more legal and political experience than Sublette.[37]

Another important figure on the political scene was Ashley—candidate for re-election to Congress. He died unexpectedly, however, on March 26, at his home near Boonville. His shocked friends in St. Louis met at the courthouse on the fifth of April to express "deep grief" and to offer their sympathy to the Ashley family. Sublette, with five others, was chosen to confer with the Ashley family and to plan a funeral sermon. Deeply grieved, he did what he could. Campbell assisted with Ashley's estate, Sublette stood partial security for Campbell's bond, and the partnership, as soon as possible, settled its accounts with the Ashley heirs. Another candidate was nominated in Ashley's place, and the campaign of 1838 continued at a quickened pace.[38]

Although Sublette fought a hard, determined campaign, his energy was wasted: the year was unpropitious for his political

36 *Missouri Argus* (St. Louis), December 23, 1837, January 6, 1838; *Southern Advocate* (Jackson, Missouri), January 27, 1838.

37 *Missouri Republican* (St. Louis), February 10, 28, 1838; *Missouri Argus* (St. Louis) January 13, 1838; *John Fletcher Darby of Missouri*, 334–37.

38 *Missouri Republican* (St. Louis), February 10, 1838; *Missouri Saturday News* (St. Louis), April 7, 1838.

career. He paid to have election tickets printed in German to appeal to that growing segment of the Missouri electorate and attended several mass meetings: one was held on July 31 to voice approval of Benton, and another on August 4 to stimulate voters' enthusiasm. At the second meeting, held in the Old Market Square, the Whigs turned out to interrupt deliberations, and the result was tumultuous. The following Monday, August 6, the Democracy was called to the polls "to do its duty" on the first day of the three-day election, and what an election it was! The polls, situated in the brick courthouse between Fourth and Fifth streets, were flooded with voters who overflowed the front portico, pushing and shoving in the intense August heat. Voting was viva voce in that sharply contested election, and both parties resorted "to all the plans in their power both Fair & Foul." So many voters were turned away by the crowd, that both parties hired carriages to take their supporters to other polling places outside the city. Steamboats were requisitioned to carry others downstream to the polls at Carondelet, where there was quite a political "battle" on the second day of the contest.[39]

The first returns appeared on August 7, and by the ninth it was clear that the Whig ticket, despite "the office holders and the managers of the Bank in the field against [them]," had won the day. Darby's lead over Sublette, substantial from the beginning, mounted each day, and in the official count, published August 13, he had 1,895 to Sublette's 1,177 votes. William carried only one of the five townships in the senatorial district. He lost Carondelet, where there were so many voting irregularities, by a large margin, but not enough to have cost him the contest. Clearly, he had lost in a state campaign which saw a general Democratic victory except in the more populous urban trade centers. Six months before the election, Hugh Campbell had written Sublette that he hoped he would be defeated "by such a decided majority that [he would] hereafter decline such honors." Hugh considered

[39] *Missouri Argus* (St. Louis), July 31, August 2, 6, 1838; "The Journal of Henry B. Miller" (ed. by Thomas M. Marshall), *Missouri Historical Society Collections*, Vol. VI (June, 1931), 255, 261-62.

politics a "farce"; that a businessman "should have nothing to do with the legislation of the country." His wish for Sublette came true: Darby won.[40]

Sublette felt the loss more than he admitted and decided not to run for office in any future campaigns, but to remain politically active without serving. During the autumn he participated in two committees: one gave a dinner on October 9 at the City Hotel for Governor-elect Boggs; the other invited Benton to a public dinner, but the Senator, usually unwilling to attend such time-consuming events, sent his thanks and apologies which the committee discussed and accepted. At the Boggs dinner Sublette toasted "The Dry Land Pirates and Squatters of the Platte: May Henry Clay know their worth through the ballot box of Missouri." After that public wish and the Benton exchange, he spent a politically inactive winter at the farm.[41]

For William the really important political work of 1839 centered in his support of the nominees and platform approved by the Democratic state convention, which met at Jefferson City in the early autumn. Earlier, in the summer, he had served on another committee—a committee of fifty to congratulate Benton on his political work and to invite him once again to a testimonial dinner. Benton declined, busy as he was with a political turn around the Missouri county circle. After the state convention, the St. Louis Democrats met at the courthouse on October 24, voted to accept the convention's work, and appointed vigilance committees to oversee the coming elections. Sublette was chosen a member of the twenty man Ward 2 committee, and in such capacity attended at least one ward meeting held the following spring at Mr. Brown's schoolhouse. At the first meeting on March 12, the names of the ward's nominees for city office were read and accepted. At the second meeting on April 10, he was one of ten selected to take part in a county meeting at Manchester.[42]

40 Hugh Campbell to W. L. Sublette, February 24, 1838, Sublette MSS; *Missouri Republican* (St. Louis), August 7, 8, 9, 13, 1838.

41 *Missouri Argus* (St. Louis), October 11, 31, November 1, 1838.

42 *Missouri Argus* (St. Louis), July 31, November 1, 1839, January 22, March 13, April 14, 1840.

The Manchester meeting of May 1, 1840, was held in an onrushing political storm. Although the hard-money faction was in control of the gathering and proposed nominees to the Missouri House and Senate favorable to it, the soft-money faction of the Democratic party was by then in opposition both to Benton and to the state bank's specie circular. The currency question seemed to be all important, and dissatisfied Democrats held meetings of their own. Not only that, but a group of Whigs appeared at Manchester and were permitted to present their candidates to the crowd.[43]

On the national level the major parties had chosen their presidential candidates, and the hard-money men were pleased with the Democratic choice. Van Buren had been renominated, and to celebrate the event, a meeting was held on August 7, at the courthouse where Sublette and his friends, with "repeated cheers" and "great applause," resolved in favor of Van Buren, Benton, and an independent treasury act. A committee of ten—Sublette was a member—was formed to collect funds to print Benton's letters on the treasury bill. Late in September the committee met and by the end of the year had a pamphlet of Benton letters available for distribution.[44]

Sublette was sent as a delegate of Ward 2 to the Democratic state convention, which met on October 8 at Jefferson City. At least one unknown spokesman for the frontier democracy of western Missouri recommended him to the convention "as amongst the fittest of the prominent men of our state to be placed on the general ticket for congress." But William would not accept. In November, although Thomas Reynolds, Democratic nominee for governor, won and Van Buren carried the state, the Whigs took the presidency. Temporarily at least, by applied political action, slogans, and "ballyhoo," they had stolen the Democratic mantle as spokesmen for the common people.[45]

[43] *Daily Commercial Bulletin* (St. Louis), May 4, 1840.

[44] *Missouri Argus* (St. Louis), August 10, September 26, 1840; *Missourian* (St. Louis), March 7, 1844.

[45] *Missouri Argus* (St. Louis), October 1, 1840; letter entitled "Give the Pioneer a Voice," 1840, Sublette MSS.

As a token of his thanks, newly elected Governor Reynolds appointed Sublette honorary aide-de-camp for the second division of the state militia. This "commission" of April 1, 1841, carried with it the title of "Colonel"—a title which stuck to Sublette's name. Otherwise his political life that year was uneventful. He attended the regular eighth of January meeting at the courthouse, where a resolution was adopted commending him—also Dobyns and O'Neil—for their hard-money tactics in the bank. O'Neil died the following June, and his friends met twice at the court-house to honor his services.[46]

Throughout the remainder of 1841 and all of 1842, Sublette was too busy with his partnership and his farm to devote much time to politics. Even though former President Van Buren was in St. Louis in June, 1842, and Sublette was appointed to his reception committee, William was too occupied with duties in western Missouri to wait upon Van Buren and had to receive accounts of the visit from Campbell. Nor did he participate in the Democratic state convention that year—a good sign of his preoccupation with other matters.[47]

[46] Sublette's Aide-de-Camp Commission, 1841, Sublette MSS.

[47] *Jefferson Inquirer* (Jefferson City), June 9, 1842; *Western Atlas and Evening Gazette* (St. Louis), June 15, 1842; *Daily Evening Gazette* (St. Louis), June 10, 1842.

A Progressive Gentleman-Farmer

THROUGHOUT the spring and summer of 1835, carpenters worked steadily to finish Sublette's new home at Sulphur Springs. "A flight of stairs four feet wide running from the Basement floor to the Garrett" was constructed, shutters were hung, door and window frames were raised, and venetian blinds were installed. Two master carpenters, Thomas Herd and Jacob Sash, used as their building guide the plan followed in "Col Johnsons" popular "Brick House . . . on Fifth Street." They had to hurry, however, since Sublette expected them to be finished by October 1, at the latest.[1]

One of his friends remarked that he was not only a "chivalrous" son "of the West," but a "*rich* acquaintance" as well: an accurate term considering the home he planned and his estimated yearly income, at that time, of approximately twenty thousand dollars. He intended to live fashionably, yet conservatively, and divided his time, as best he could, between his store on Main Street and his farm beyond the city limits. Although in the eighteen thirties and early forties male attire was rather effeminate, he dressed much as he lived—conservatively—and when weather permitted, donned his best clothes and commuted to town, leav-

[1] Herd-Sash-Sublette Agreement, April 10, 1835, Sublette MSS.

174

ing his horse with downtown St. Louis liverymen. In inclement weather he used a vehicle. His sleigh, gliding swiftly across the snow, provided a smooth winter ride, but without snow the roads were extremely bumpy, and his barouche had to keep to the limited thoroughfare, where the safety of all passengers depended upon the driver's competence and the misty glow of "brass mounted coach lamps." At times, owing to the demand of business, social obligations, or ill-health, he remained in the city, roomed at an inn or hotel, and dined at his favorite restaurants.[2]

Sulphur Springs was his dream of Arcadia—a dream common in his day—an old dream of a golden agricultural age. Over the years he transformed his acreage from a semiwilderness into a prosperous farm and watering place. In his old age he hoped to reside there permanently, surrounded by well-tilled fields and superior livestock. His accumulated fortune, income from his partnership, and whatever he might derive from operating part of his farm as a watering place would be more than enough, he thought, to provide for his every comfort. From year to year the amount of land he held in St. Louis County varied according to purchase and sale, but Sulphur Springs proper, all 779 acres, was seldom touched. In fact, in July, 1836, he bought 273 acres of the remaining Gratiot lands adjoining his farm. He resold seventy of them immediately for a substantial profit, but the next year, added a little over eight acres, also originally Gratiot land, in the nearby Barrier Des Noyes tract.[3]

Between 1835 and 1842, he sold or leased tracts to John Forstaken, George K. Nye, Thomas Asby, Dr. John Tagart, Owen Williams, and Daniel Thomas. Forstaken purchased 20 acres in 1839, but the following year defaulted on his notes and lost the land to Sublette. William then resold the land to Nye, and this time the sale was valid. Asby leased a small tract in 1840, with the understanding he would cultivate 10 acres and build a log cabin and stable upon the remainder. Dr. Tagart bought

2 W. Gilpin to H. D. Gilpin, December 1, 1841, Sublette MSS.

3 Original (Deed Record) X, pp. 276, 298, and Z, p. 176, MSS, St. Louis CRDO.

139.20 acres in 1837 and met his notes on time, while Williams and Thomas held 15 acres for only two years.

Within St. Louis, Sublette held a few scattered lots in addition to the Main Street lot owned jointly with Campbell. The lots, held in speculation, at times brought him fair profit. One, located on the square south of the courthouse, he purchased in 1835 and resold three years later for nearly double the price. Two others, lots fourteen and fifteen in Christy's Addition, he resold: one to his partnership, as mentioned, and the other to Thomas Fitzpatrick. In 1843 he purchased two others, twenty-nine and thirty, in Randolph's Addition to the city. Fortunately for him, during his lifetime his city properties were never subject to any extensive legal difficulties, as were so many of the tracts jointly held with Campbell.[4] Certainly he was party to some minor cases in the St. Louis Circuit Court—cases not involving Campbell—but they were largely over promissory notes.[5] Outside of St. Louis County he was party to two suits for debt—Campbell was not involved—in Adams County, Illinois, and Ralls County, Missouri. He won both cases, but neither was large.[6]

His greatest speculative land ventures were undertaken in central and western Missouri, with the aid of John M. Robinson, a surveyor, and Daniel Dunklin, public land surveyor for Missouri and Illinois. In 1834–35, William inspected 200 acres of public land held by the United States Land Office at Lexington and on October 26–27 of the second year purchased the tract for $1.25 an acre. Evidently he was satisfied, since three years later he appeared again at the same land office and purchased 120 additional acres at the same price. Leaving Lexington, he traveled to Fayette, bought another 40 acres, and the next year, 1839, took up two additional tracts, each of 40 acres, from Thomas

---

[4] Original (Deed Record) Z, p. 177, F–2, p. 195, I–2, pp. 264–65, S–2, p. 378, E–3, p. 401, MSS; Deed Record V, pp. 185–86, MSS, St. Louis CRDO.

[5] File of *St. Louis Gas Light Co.* v. *Wm. L. Sublette*, File 222, MS; File of *Wm. L. Sublette for John F. Darby* v. *Hiram Darby*, File 529(2), MS, St. Louis CCC.

[6] Common Law Chancery & Peo. Record, 1837–39, p. 305, MS, Adams CCC; Circuit Court Record B, pp. 8–9, MS; File of *Wm. L. Sublette* v. *T. S. Barkley and H. A. Barkley*, Case No. 1036, MS, Ralls CCC.

Andrew W. Sublette in his Mexican War uniform

Sir William Drummond Stewart, from the portrait by
Henry Inman, 1844, in Perthshire

and Rebecca Goode of Cole County.[7] His deepest plunge into speculation was in company with thirteen others. Together they formed a land company to secure a sizable area near Westport Landing. He had become well acquainted with the area while in the fur trade and believed that a new town could be located there, in spite of the opposition of Independence and Westport. The original owner of the tract had died in 1838, and upon the settlement of his estate Sublette and his friends gave $4,220 for the land. They "laid it off into a town and named it Kansas, but owing to disagreement among themselves, nothing was done until 1846." In the meantime the region grew in population and importance: land values mounted, and Sublette secured another niche in history as one of the original developers of Kansas City.[8]

By the summer of 1835, his home and slave cabins were nearly completed, and he moved into his new residence. It was situated a few hundred feet from the tiny River des Peres and was surrounded by rich valley lands and gentle, sloping hills. A beautiful stand of good native timber covered much of the farm, and beneath the soil was a commercially marketable horizontal vein of coal two to five feet thick. A large, sparkling mineral spring was located nearby "in the bed of [the River des Peres] opposite to a high bank." The potentialities of Sulphur Springs were evident: his "manor house" stood in the midst of a gentleman-farmer's domain.[9]

His cultivated fields, largely lying along the course of the river, were never farmed extensively during his lifetime, yet some of them were worked each year. Corn was planted in the "bottom field" and oats, timothy, potatoes, and cabbage in others. Drought,

[7] Lexington Cash Entries Nos. 5571, 5573, September 7, 1838, and 16564, 16580, May 1, 1843, Cash Entries for the Lexington Land Office; Fayette Cash Entry No. 19935, November 10, 1841, Cash Entries for the Fayette Land Office, Records of the General Land Office, Record Group No. 49, MSS, N. A.; Missouri Contracts, 1815–43, p. 328, MS, Office of the Secretary of State, Jefferson City, Missouri.

[8] Record I, p. 158, MS, Jackson CRDO; Dean E. Wood, *The Old Santa Fé Trail from the Missouri River*, 48–49; Alexander McCoy, *Pioneering on the Plains* (pages not numbered).

[9] Alphonso Wetmore, *Gazetteer of the State of Missouri*, 256.

excessive water, and insect pests such as the army worm, which "was perhaps the most dreaded," caused periodic troubles, but he took measures against them and carefully supervised his slaves and hired agricultural workers. Several of the laborers resided at the farm as permanent gardeners or lived in the neighborhood. Other artisans and craftsmen, some of whom temporarily lived at the farm, were employed to keep the buildings in repair. Stonework, plastering, minor carpentering jobs, and repairs were always necessary, and in 1837 they built a new double log cabin and possibly also a small mill.[10]

He began to plant fruit trees as early as 1835 and to use better varieties of seed. Although many of the trees did not grow well immediately, he constantly experimented with the best available strains and within a few years produced an attractive orchard. He was careful to buy his seeds from the most reliable dealers, usually from D. and C. Landreth and Company of 85 Chestnut and Federal in Philadelphia, "general dealers in Seeds," who advertised in the *Cultivator*, a well-known progressive farming periodical of the time, one Sublette read. With Hugh Campbell's assistance he placed seasonal orders with them for fruit trees, grains, flowers, berry bushes, and a wide variety of kitchen-garden seeds. By selectivity he became one of the most progressive farmers in the county.[11]

Farming methods were crude, but he followed what up-to-date information was available in the *Cultivator* and developed a superior farm. Extensive cultivation was retarded, however, since he lacked improved farm machinery other than the usual hand tools. Harrows were primitive, reapers nearly unknown, and his workmen could cradle grain at a rate not much above two acres per day per man. In 1842, only five years after John Deere created an improved steel plow, Sublette paid to have two of his

[10] A. W. Sublette to W. L. Sublette, April 11, June 5, July 1, 1842, Sublette MSS; "Correspondence of Robert Campbell, 1834-1845," *loc. cit.,* 31-32.

[11] W. L. Sublette to Robert Campbell, January 30, 1836, Campbell MSS; A. W. Sublette to W. L. Sublette, June 5, 1842, Sublette MSS; Letter of April 7, 1836, Private Campbell MSS.

"laid with steel." The earlier wooden and cast iron types were cumbersome, tending to stick and drag in heavy soil.[12]

To his experimentation with seeds and tools he added a third project: stock raising and breeding on a rather extensive scale. There were usually five to eight horses at Sulphur Springs—necessary for transportation and farm work—and also a small herd of pigs, no doubt of the common, "ungainly type, with long legs and snout, sharp back, of a roaming disposition, slow and expensive to fatten." Also there seems to have been a small herd of sheep at the farm, but his significant stock was a herd of improved, imported Shorthorns. By 1842, he owned twenty-five of them, and the same year received two silver cups for the best cattle exhibited at the St. Louis County Agricultural Fair.[13]

"The leadership in the improvement of cattle . . . came from a few wealthy men who made a hobby of progressive farming. Their attention was directed to the importation of representatives of English stock or common animals by selective breeding": a true statement as far as Sublette's cattle were concerned. The first "approved pedigreed Shorthorns" were brought from Ohio to Missouri in 1839, by Nathaniel Leonard of Cooper County.[14] Sublette corresponded with Leonard and served as an intermediary in the shipment. A few months later William imported the first pedigreed Shorthorns to reach Missouri directly from England. They were the basis of his award-winning herd.

Stewart, in Scotland in December, 1839, shipped Sublette the first of his new herd: "a very fine Spring bull and a Heifer," Fieryman and Malibran. They were loaded aboard the ship "Hen-

---

[12] A. W. Sublette to W. L. Sublette, July 10, 1842, Sublette MSS; File of Estate of William L. Sublette, File 2052, MS, St. Louis PC.

[13] Certificate of Merit from the St. Louis County Agricultural Fair to W. L. Sublette, October 18, 1842, Sublette MSS.

[14] B. O. Cowan and W. L. Nelson, *Shorthorn Cattle in Missouri* (*Monthly Bulletin*, Missouri State Board of Agriculture, Vol. XII), 6–7; John Ashton, *History of Shorthorns in Missouri Prior to the Civil War* (*Monthly Bulletin,* Missouri State Board of Agriculture," Vol. XXI), 14, 20, 26, 29; B. G. Leonard to N. Leonard, May 20, 1839[?], Abiel Leonard Collection, 1786–1933, MSS, State Historical Society of Missouri, Columbia.

rietta," out of Liverpool, comfortably stabled, provided plenty of feed, and entrusted to the care of an old farmer. At New Orleans, Loyal Case and Company, received them, transferred them to the steamboat "Alton," and forwarded them to St. Louis, where a liveryman stabled them until Sublette could take them to Sulphur Springs. In all probability Stewart sent them as a token of his esteem, since it was common for him to exchange gifts with Sublette. When first he returned to Scotland in 1839, he seems to have taken with him several presents from Sublette: tame deer, a large turtle, caged redbirds, and a quantity of seeds. Two years later they exchanged farm products. Sublette sent him a seed shipment, and in return he tried to buy William "a horse of the draught breed." A little later in the year Stewart wanted to buy his friend "a cart stallion," and in the spring of 1842 Sublette sent him four deer and some buffalo. As a reciprocal token in their international exchange program, Stewart promised him that he would look around for a good breed of pig and that, perhaps, the two of them might "get up some farming speculation together."[15]

Generally speaking, however, Sublette was more interested in agricultural security than in agricultural speculation. From time to time, he marketed a little livestock or food, but was not a regular dealer in either one. Visitors noted a number of "exotic" animals at Sulphur Springs—animals he ordered brought in from the mountains for the entertainment of his friends and family, but animals that were not for sale. His menagerie included buffalo, deer, cranes, wild and domesticated geese, and even swans. At least one visitor was surprised by a tame, young female antelope which frolicked freely about the house to the delight of the host and his guests. Others referred to bears staked out on chains—an interesting attraction—and all were pleased with Sublette's living memories of the mountain trade.

Since his circle of friends was a wide one composed of old mountain companions, business associates, politicians, bankers,

15 William Drummond Stewart to W. L. Sublette, February 13, 1839, August 23, November 3, 1841, April 3, 1842; W. L. Sublette to William Drummond Stewart, April 15, 1842, Sublette MSS; *Missouri Argus* (St. Louis), March 7, 1840.

and farmer-neighbors, there were frequently guests in his large stone house. Hugh Campbell was there; Joseph Williams, just in from Oregon in 1842, visited at the farm; and so did the western artist Alfred Jacob Miller. Stewart, before his return to Scotland in 1839, frequented the farm and, in fact, seemed to consider it his second home. His hours with Sublette were enjoyable, care-free ones. As Stewart said: "I think I never was better off than with the bottle of claret & the joint for dinner & the hundred eggs for breakfast when we lived together." Although he was not to see Sublette again until 1843, he not only sent him gifts but on one occasion sent two German immigrants, possibly Rev. Bishop Stephan and Dr. Marburg from New Orleans, with a letter of introduction and a plea for Sublette's help.[16]

Campbell was frequently at the farm, but after February 25, 1841, had a wife and additional family obligations. Both Sublette and Hugh Campbell opposed the marriage, since they believed she was too young and too "fond of admiration." Yet, Robert persisted in his courtship, the young lady's mother reluctantly consented, and all parties concerned accepted Virginia Jane Kyle of Philadelphia as the new Mrs. Campbell. She proved to be an excellent wife and a capable, though young, mother. James Alexander, her first child, was born May 14, 1842.[17]

At times relatives stopped at the farm, although most of William's contacts with them were limited to letters. On his frequent travels in rural Missouri, he visited the McKinneys in Callaway County, dropped in to see cousin William S. Burch and family of Columbia and Jefferson City, and on special occasions saw the family of Littleberry Sublette in Clay County. Otherwise he saw only brother Andrew, who for a time helped him operate the farm, and sister Sophronia, who made her home with him after 1840. Andrew, after leaving the fur trade in 1841, settled

16 Joseph Williams, *Narrative of a Tour from the State of Indiana to the Oregon Territory in the Years 1841-2*, 92; *The West of Alfred Jacob Miller* (ed. by Marvin C. Ross), 129; Elijah White to J. C. Spencer, May 11, July 2, 1842, Letters Received, 1824–41, Records of the Office of Indian Affairs, Record Group No. 75, MSS, N. A.
17 Campbell Family Bible, Private Campbell MSS.

down for a time to a farmer's life at Sulphur Springs, but he was still young, ambitious, and determined to re-enter the Far West. Andrew liked to tipple and was more willing to sign a pledge to live a farmer's quiet life than he was to sign another pledge in June, 1842, when he attended a "big temperance meeting . . . up the Country."[18]

Sister Sophronia had had marital difficulties and had taken shelter in Sublette's home. Theresa, her only child, was with her and had attended school in St. Louis, probably since early 1837, and Uncle William footed the bill for her tuition. At the same time he supported two young boys in another St. Louis boarding school, possibly as a gesture to financially embarrassed friends. Sophronia repaid her brother, in part, by supervising his household. There was always an abundance of food and drink on hand, easily replenished from fields, orchards, and streams, and with the aid of household slaves she directed her brother's kitchen. Sublette installed in her domain a large, modern cookstove, purchased in Pittsburgh, and supplied her with tableware, silverware, glassware, and whatever she needed for proper housekeeping.

Although divorce was then much more serious and less frequent than now—even condemned in some communities—Sublette supported Sophronia when, on March 29, 1841, she brought such a suit in the St. Louis Court of Chancery. She complained that Grove Cook, her husband, had "been guilty of gross and wanton ill treatment towards [her] . . . and [had] offered such indignities to said complainant, as to render her condition intolerable." She contended further "that said Grove [had] for more than two years past been guilty of and addicted to habitual drunkenness: That he [had] abandoned [her] . . . and refused to support her."[19]

When Grove failed to appear at the July term of the court, the presiding judge decreed that he should appear in the next term or else the divorce would be granted without consent. By that time, however, Grove was well on his way to California as a last-minute member of the Bartleson-Bidwell expedition then traveling

[18] A. W. Sublette to W. L. Sublette, June 19, 1842, Sublette MSS.
[19] Chancery Record No. 2, 1838–45, p. 97, MS, St. Louis CCC.

west from Missouri. According to one member of the party, Cook had "begged to be allowed to pay his way by driving [a] wagon," and was accepted on that basis. He abandoned his family, but in California he rebuilt his life. He settled near Santa Cruz, where he bought a distillery, amassed a large fortune in land, participated in the revolution against Mexico, and engaged in quicksilver mining, especially after 1848, at his Rancho de los Capitancillos. On December 28, 1845, he was married to Rebecca Kelsey in a ceremony at Sutter's Fort; and when he died, seven years later at Santa Cruz, it was as an honored citizen who had outlived his wayward youth.[20]

Meanwhile, on October 4, 1841, the St. Louis Court of Chancery granted Sophronia a divorce, "absolutely . . . from the bonds of matrimony." Sublette offered her the permanent security of his home, which she accepted willingly and expressed her gratitude by saying that her brother was "the only person I have to Thanke for the menney comforts I enjoy." She returned to Sulphur Springs to take up her duty as housekeeper, which was not a light task because the interior of Sublette's home was furnished elaborately as the time required. He spared no effort to display samples and souvenirs of western life, including three pairs of elk horns, several skins, and Indian oddities. The rooms were filled with large pieces of cherry furniture, the windows were heavily draped and curtained, and the floors were covered with carpeting and matting. "Oil lamps with cotton wicks" and tallow and wax candles lighted the rooms and halls, and in the flickering glow his Indian trophies cast their spell.[21]

Slaves performed farm and household tasks and were well cared for by their master. Sublette's parents and grandparents had been slaveholders, and he did not question slavery as an institution. Although he owned only a few, "principally young," even

20 *Missouri Argus* (St. Louis), March 3, 1841; *Alta California* (San Francisco), February 21, 1852; *Narrative of Nicholas Cheyenne Dawson* (ed. by Charles L. Camp), 9–10, 43; *New Helvetia Diary of Events from 1845–48*, 26.

21 Chancery Record No. 2, 1838–45, p. 113, MS, St. Louis CCC; Sophronia Cook to W. L. Sublette, November, 1842, Sublette MSS; File of Estate of William L. Sublette, File 2052, MS, St. Louis PC.

the ownership of a handful was in Missouri, where large holdings were rare, a mark of class. He at no time actively participated in the slave market, since most of his were acquired through natural increase. In other instances he hired slaves, usually by the year, to perform additional tasks, but he provided all of them soundly constructed cabins, good medical care, and, at death, burial near the main house. As with so many other slaveholders of his day, he had to strike a tenuous balance between property and humanity. He was realistic enough to know that slaves were valuable property to be protected, yet, at the same time, human beings to be respected.

Although there were some household industries at Sulphur Springs in which the slaves were useful, most utensils were not made at the farm but were purchased from St. Louis merchants or were ordered from the East. By 1840 the value of household industries in St. Louis County had fallen to thirty-eight cents per capita—a sure sign of decline—but certain commodities, soap in particular, must have been produced at the farm. Much of the slaves' clothing also must have been made at the farm from the large amounts of cloth on hand or from the carded wool available. Those slaves not employed in the house, barns, or fields assisted the white hired hands to produce ice, lumber, and coal.

Sublette's coal mining industry was by far the most important of the three and was very profitable. As early as 1819–20, coal was mined in numerous St. Louis County localities. In December, 1835, at the time his buildings were under construction, William began to develop his coal—also fire clay?—deposits. The initial cost of sinking a shallow pit and supporting and equipping it, was nearly five hundred dollars. At first he planned to utilize a horse-drawn coal wagon to carry the coal to market, but switched to oxen when he discovered they were more adept.

In the summer of 1836, owing to the press of business in town, he entered into a two-year partnership agreement with John Gant and William Stoney to mine and sell coal from the deposit recently opened on his farm. Within five months Gant gave up the partnership, and Sublette drew up a new eighteen months' contract with Stoney—share and share alike. Under this contract the mine was operated successfully and profitably. During the months of September through February, four wagons—the remainder of the year, two wagons—regularly carried coal to market in St. Louis. The loads were weighed at official city scales, and each wagon driver received in return a weight certificate which he was to transfer to the purchaser. The cost of weighing and certifying was twenty-five cents a load, but well worth it since coal prices were good.[22]

Upon conclusion of the agreement with Stoney, Sublette made a new one early in the autumn of 1838 whereby the mine, plus a new one recently opened at the farm, was leased to Abraham Stephens. Stephens was to mine the coal; Sublette was to purchase it from him at the mine. By this agreement coal marketing was vested solely in William's hands, but the risk was slight because coal sales continued to flourish. Late in 1839 or early in 1840, Sublette opened a third mine "between the two old mines" and permitted Stephens to work it for two years, not under lease but under a partnership similar to the earlier one with Stoney. Profits were to be divided equally, Stephens was allowed to live rent free in one of the cabins at the farm, and in return he promised to keep two coal wagons in operation. By early 1842, however, the depression was in full force and Stephens was unable to meet his part of the contract. After some negotiation, Sublette turned over all three mines to Elias Stitts and G. W. Shepherd, who agreed to work them three years and to pay him one-fourth of a cent for every bushel mined.[23]

Sulphur Springs also boasted more than enough timber to provide fuel, fencing, and building material for the farm—in fact, so much timber that it could be marketed in St. Louis. Cordwood was cut, loaded on coal wagons or in separate vehicles, and carried into the city. In volume, however, its sale and distribution was

[22] Sublette-Gant-Stoney Agreement, August 15, 1836; Sublette-Stoney Agreement, January 1, 1837, Sublette MSS; St. Louis, *City Ordinance 348*, August 19, 1837.
[23] Sublette-Stephens Agreement, March 1, 1840; Sublette-Stitts-Shepherd Agreement, March 1, 1842, Sublette MSS.

much less than that of Sulphur Springs coal and was handled directly by Sublette or brother Andrew. Wood sold at $4.00 a cord in 1839, but, like every other commodity, was hit by the depression and by December, 1842, was reduced to a "dull" $2.25 a cord. At that time Sublette had "one team halling coal" and another wood and corn. In that way he hoped to increase his falling income, although the most profitable years had passed.[24]

In the winter a third commodity, ice, was gathered at the farm and stored for the summer months, when it was used by the family or sold to neighbors. John York, Sublette's gardener, and William R. Benson, one of the coal haulers, both helped with ice production. A heavy midwinter freeze brought family and workmen alike to the river to gather as much as possible and store it, packed in straw, in underground sheds.

The volume of Sublette's trade to St. Louis depended upon the condition of the Old Manchester Road, alternately muddy or dusty, leading into town. Horses and mules were not strong enough to pull loaded wagons through the deep, sticky mud, but he learned that oxen were, if the wagons were in good repair. On return trips from the city, his wagons carried loads of fodder to supplement what was available at the farm, some staple household items, and farm equipment. He realized that better roads were a key to the success of his farm and so exerted every effort for road improvement. In August, 1836, the county court appointed him to contract for a stone bridge to be built "over the Camp Spring branch, one mile from St. Louis" on the Old Manchester Road. Within less than a year he reported the bridge completed for less than the estimate, and the court, very well satisfied, in the spring of 1838 appointed him, with two others, "to view a proposed alteration" in another road. They recommended that no alteration be made, lest it greatly inconvenience the public, and their suggestion was accepted.[25]

There was, however, another reason why Sublette favored

[24] A. W. Sublette to W. L. Sublette, December 2, 9, 1842, Sublette MSS; *Daily Evening Gazette* (St. Louis), January 29, 1839.

[25] Record of St. Louis County Court No. 2, 1836–41, pp. 42, 86, 178, 198, MS, Register's Office, City Hall, St. Louis.

county road improvements. Sulphur Springs, as previously noted, was not only his home and farm but was, as well, especially between 1838 and 1842, a leading St. Louis resort and watering place. Good roads meant good business. He always recognized the resort possibilities of his farm and could remember from boyhood days the valuable assets of the springs at Crab Orchard. Before elaborately developing his springs, he sought competent analysis of its waters. He sent two samples to Hugh Campbell, who had them analyzed and returned a favorable report: the water was said to resemble that of White Sulphur Springs, Virginia, or as stated in the *Gazetteer of the State of Missouri:* it "has the taste and smell of sulphurated hydrogen . . . To certain [aged persons] it may be serviceable, particularly those effected with complaints of the liver." Samples were sent into St. Louis for public examination, and within a short time the springs were patronized for their curative powers.[26]

Following the water analysis, during the summer of 1835, Sublette, assisted by a crew of workmen under E. Town, started to erect "large and commodious" guest buildings near the springs and within close walking distance of his nearly completed home. The St. Louis Grays, a volunteer militia organization, held its summer encampment there in July, and the word spread that the springs were worth a visit. Sublette hoped to lease the grounds and buildings of the springs proper to some enterprising manager. Many of the hotels in St. Louis were said to be "filthy" and "disagreeable," but Sulphur Springs was to be an exception. Thomas W. Thompson, a well-known hotel manager, took over operation of Sublette's new resort from E. Town; furnished it on Sublette's surety; and on July 20, 1837, announced that he was prepared to receive visitors, about sixty of whom he could accommodate as boarders.[27]

For those local citizens anxious to escape the whirl of city life the springs offered a variety of quieter entertainment, but

[26] Wetmore, *op. cit.*, 256; Letters of July 4, 25, 1835, Private Campbell MSS; *St. Louis Commercial Bulletin & Missouri Literary Register*, July 10, 1835.
[27] *Missouri Republican* (St. Louis), July 20, 1837; Thompson-Sublette Agreement, May 18, 1837, Sublette MSS.

for the more spirited was provided a ninepins alley and a race track, both illegal within St. Louis. In September, 1838, Sublette and several friends organized the St. Louis Jockey Club and the following month commenced races at the springs. A large purse was put up, plus other "novel" attractions, and the crowds flocked to the event. Six months later a spring meet was held, lasting several days, for both full-gaited and trotting stock. Sublette, as had his grandfather Whitley many years before at Sportsman's Hill, watched some of the country's best horseflesh race over his track.[28]

His principal difficulty was to keep a good manager at the resort. Thompson lasted only a short time, and his successor, Edmund Leonard, was heavily in debt and not very dependable. In March, 1838, William leased the springs for five years to Owen W. Grimes, who promised to keep the springs clean, to build a porch on the rear of Sublette's house, and to pay two hundred dollars the first year and one thousand dollars each year thereafter in rent. In addition, Grimes was permitted to graze his stock on the pasture, to use some of the timber, and to farm a few of the fields.[29]

Almost immediately Grimes began to default on his promises, or so Sublette said, and had to be taken to court. The case finally was dropped, but he still owed Sublette a little over one thousand dollars. Everything regarding the lease seemed to go from bad to worse early in 1842: Grimes failed to meet his note payments, and on March 1 the lease was dissolved by mutual consent. He remained at the springs until mid-April in order to whitewash and paint the buildings for a new lessee John C. Branner, who had taken the resort for three years under conditions similar to those in the Grimes lease. Branner, Sublette discovered, was without ready money or credit and spent most of his time in St. Louis "about the groceries trying to get some one to join him to open" the resort. Since the money market was tight and the lease strict,

[28] *Missouri Saturday News* (St. Louis), September 29, 1838; *Daily Evening Gazette* (St. Louis), May 3, 1839; *Daily Missouri Republican* (St. Louis), June 24, 1839.
[29] Sublette-Grimes Agreement, March 17, 1838, Sublette MSS.

few were disposed to help him. Andrew, in William's absence on a business trip, tried to dissolve the lease, but the "trifling old curse [Branner]," as he said, refused to submit. Andrew ordered him out of the resort and "threatened to club him," but the old man remained in one of the cabins and refused to leave until paid for some repairs he had made. After considerable bickering, the lease was broken, and in July Branner moved.[30]

Andrew proposed that William permit him to open the tavern in the hotel, but William, recognizing his brother's propensity for hard liquor, refused. By that time Grimes was back in town, trying to take benefit of the bankruptcy law, after having returned empty handed from a borrowing trip to Kentucky, and was talking wildly about taking up a new lease to the springs. Dr. Thomas Hereford, a respectable Alabama physician, was also in town, and he was anxious to negotiate for the springs. Andrew believed he was just the man for the lease: he had "money and negroes" and "those who knew him spoke well of him." William agreed with Andrew when he met Dr. Hereford, and on September 13, 1842, leased him ninety acres, including the resort buildings and springs, for five years. The doctor was given timber rights, rights to the coal beds, and consent to improve the buildings; in return Sublette was to receive rent payable in nine installments.[31]

Dr. Hereford brought a large family with him when he opened the resort at the springs—a family Sublette was happy to welcome, since his life was in some ways rather lonely. Certainly there were guests at the hotel when the springs were open, but business was erratic for years. True enough, he had visitors to enliven his days, and Andrew and Sophronia were at the farm; yet he had passed forty and missed a wife and family. For a while he was concerned with brother Solomon, who was back in St. Louis after four years of roving the West. In 1839, Solomon was in Arkansas, then the "*Ultima Thule* of southern agricultural

---

30 File of *Wm. L. Sublette* v. *Owen W. Grimes*, File 35, MS, St. Louis CCC.
31 Sublette-Hereford Agreement, September 13, 1842; A. W. Sublette to W. L. Sublette, June 15, 24, July 10, 1842, Sublette MSS.

expansion in the United States," where he speculated in horses and mules and, as usual, failed. From there his gypsy-like nature carried him to Independence, then to Santa Fé, partially financed by William, and back again to Independence by October, 1842. William accused him of "negligence or selfishness" in failing to write; Solomon claimed he had written and accused Andrew and Sophronia of negligence on their part. He was home again, however—he had turned down the offer of a job in Texas—and the family quarrel was healed quickly.[32]

Solomon's return did not alter William's loneliness. He had admitted in a letter to Campbell, in 1837, that he "was never seriously in love in [his] life nor would [he] permit [himself] to be so for [he] never was in a situation to get married as that which [he] could wish." For a long while he was preoccupied with business and western trade, but in 1840 he was in a "situation" to take a wife. If we discard the supposition that he had one or more Indian wives and children by them, a supposition common to the Mountain Men and, admittedly, many times exact, the fact remains that he had few serious romantic interests. Both Hugh and Robert Campbell encouraged him to marry some "western belle," although he appeared to be more interested in some of the eligible eastern women he had met in Philadelphia. He enjoyed their merry, carefree company, and at least on one occasion had toyed with the prospect of marriage to a certain bank-stock heiress. But the eligible ladies quickly married more persistent suitors, to his "dispair," and so the years had passed.[33]

St. Louis social life placed him in contact with the city's leading families—an enviable position for a promising bachelor. During the winter season there were always "divrs & Sundry Balls & parties" which he could and did attend.[34] He subscribed to a series of "Select Cotillion Parties" given in 1837–38, and financed

[32] S. P. Sublette to W. L. Sublette, May 1, 1839, October 31, November 28, 1842, Sublette MSS.

[33] "Correspondence of Robert Campbell 1834–1845," *loc. cit.*, 19; Hugh Campbell to W. L. Sublette, February 24, 1838; W. L. Sublette to Robert Campbell, November 2, 1835, January 12, 30, February 3, 1836, Sublette MSS.

[34] W. L. Sublette to Robert Campbell, January 30, 1836, Campbell MSS.

part of Governor Bogg's Christmas ball in 1838. Such elegant gatherings permitted young belles wide choice of companions—companions who might later escort them to the St. Louis Theatre, one of the "best-looking" in the country, or, perhaps, take them to a summer picnic such as the one Sublette attended on the Fourth of July, 1842, at Kemper College.

He improved his community standing through jury service and service in the Central Fire Company, after 1837, where he might be seen at drills dressed in a "fire hat white coat or round about." Volunteer fire companies were important social institutions in that age of poorly organized municipal services. Moreover, nonpartisan civic functions at times also required his attention. He was one of seven marshals appointed to oversee the laying of the new courthouse cornerstone in 1839, and two years later served on a committee which called a public testimonial meeting for Circuit Judge L. E. Lawless, who was about to retire from the bench.[35]

Had Sublette been rebuked in love? Not entirely, since one young lady sought to be his wife. She wrote, early in 1837, "When you ride out to the Sulphur Spring think of the walks we have had around the spring and then it will bring some fond recollections of your country Mary . . . *Remember Me.*" His "country Mary," who penned those words, was Mary A. Town daughter of resort-builder E. Town. When the elder Town gave up his position at the springs, probably as the result of the death of his wife, Mary was forced to leave St. Louis for a home with relatives in Kentucky and Ohio. From there she wrote Sublette tender words of love, imploring him to write her or join her: ". . . You are well aware of the love and esteem I have for you, there is know [sic] other person has a place in this heart . . . how many tears it made me shed that you would not confide in me so much as to let me have the [?] scrap of paper from your hand. . . . I hope it will not be many more days and nights before we shall see each

35 *Missouri Argus* (St. Louis), February 12, 15, 1841; *Daily Evening Gazette* (St. Louis), October 6, 21, 1839; Central Fire Company to W. L. Sublette, December 4, 1837, August 29, 1838, Sublette MSS.

other again." And, some months later: ". . . my heart . . . could not be moved nor won by any other, neither shall it ever be whether you alter your mind or not, mine shall remain constant as a *dove* to the last. . . . Days of absence sad and dreary clothed in sorrow's dark array Days of absence I am weary when thou art far away." She wrote no more after 1837, but drifted out of his life, leaving him a ring, a memory, and a packet of letters he was requested to burn.[36]

Sublette may have refused to marry the young lady because she was of more common stock—not a woman of position and prestige—or because illness interfered. In the autumn of 1836, he placed himself under the care of Dr. William Beaumont, the eminent physician. Dr. Beaumont confined Sublette to a rocking chair while he performed a series of operations upon him for "Fistula in Anno," and Sublette was probably still confined to a chair "with a writing desk attacht thereto" when Mary Town began her correspondence. He was "much pleased" with Dr. Beaumont as a "sergent [surgeon]" and was up and around again by late spring. On other occasions, Dr. Beaumont was called in to prescribe, especially in 1841 and 1842, since Sublette's health grew worse each year, partially as a result of his dangerous western exploits.[37]

His diet did not contribute to better health. Although he was not usually a heavy or immoderate drinker, he had acquired a taste for certain delicacies uncommon in civilized areas. He commissioned his friends coming from the West and his employees to bring in packages of buffalo meat prepared according to the Indian method in thin slices and dried on a framework over an open fire. There was a supply of pemmican in his larder which he served along with the buffalo meat at home and in his office to old mountain friends. As it was, most of the food Americans ate at that time was "badly cooked," lacking in imagination, and oftentimes swimming in grease. They ate in a hurry and, if they

[36] Mary A. Town to W. L. Sublette, October 31, 1836, March 14, 1837, Sublette MSS.

[37] "Correspondence of Robert Campbell, 1834–1845," *loc. cit.*, 12–13, 18.

192

"A Beaver Hut," a drawing by Charles Bodmer

Solomon, Frances, and Fannie Sublette about 1856

could afford it, waded through every edible item the neighborhood could provide. Everything considered, he would have been fortunate if he escaped dietary troubles.

Sulphur Springs, however, was a pleasant place to convalesce after his recurrent illnesses. There was a piano in the parlor, where guests could gather to sing contemporary melodies from "Social Song Books"; there were maps in the study and a small library, quite possibly including works of Irving, Cooper, and Scott; there were cards; and, for ready reference, the latest issues of the *Missouri Argus*. In such comfortable surroundings he passed many an hour and day.

When in better health, and the weather permitting, he may have attended Sunday services at one of the Presbyterian churches scattered about the county or in St. Louis. His "candid belief," as he once wrote, was that "all things are for the best as God made us for his purpose and knows best how to dispose of us if it should be for the benefit of others, as I am smartly inclined to believe in fore-ordination." There is no accurate proof of his membership in any particular religious congregation, but circumstantial proof, based upon his Kentucky religious background, upon the fact that he married later in a Presbyterian service, and that a niece was baptized in the same faith, all strongly suggest his Calvinism. But whatever his denomination, he was tolerant of others—a tolerance built upon years of close association with men of many beliefs. He had won the respect of Rev. Jason Lee, many of his fur-trade companions were Roman Catholics, his dear friend Campbell was a Presbyterian, and his other dear friend Stewart was baptized a Roman Catholic in 1837 at the Old St. Louis Cathedral. Kemper College, a Protestant Episcopal institution, stood near Sulphur Springs, and Sublette was the respected friend and neighbor of its teachers and students. Hugh Campbell's remark that he "seemed equally successful in acquiring the good will of ladies and gentlemen the learned & unlearned" was a most accurate estimate in religion as well.[38]

[38] Entry of November 20, 1837, Baptisms, 1835–44, MSS, Old (Roman Catholic) Cathedral, St. Louis; Letter of May 7, 1834, Private Campbell MSS.

Back to the Green

SPRING, 1843—the Millerites believed the end of the world was at hand and bought muslin for ascension robes. Most Americans ignored Millerist predictions and preferred to think about more earthly things. The depression was nearly over, and national economic equilibrium was in sight. Sublette's midwinter business trip to western Missouri had not been too productive, since many firms and individuals had refused to pay their long-standing debts; still, he had had some success and, more important, had been fortunate enough to lease Sulphur Springs the previous autumn. During the first week in January he and Dr. Hereford agreed to slightly different, but still very reasonable, terms in light of existing conditions. Meanwhile, the Doctor moved into a house near the resort. Mrs. Hereford and most of the Hereford children remained in Tuscumbia, Alabama, patiently waiting for regular spring traffic to open on the Mississippi so they could move to St. Louis.[1]

"Frank," Frances S. Hereford, however, was with her father, and she, the eldest daughter of the new proprietor of the springs,

[1] Bettie Carter to F. S. Hereford, February 19, 1843; A. L. Christian to F. S. Hereford, March 3, 1843, Sublette MSS; Certified Statement of Thomas A. Hereford, June 6, 1846, in File of Estate of William L. Sublette, File 2052, MS, St. Louis PC.

194

was an attractive, dark-haired southern beauty with a graceful figure and an eye for an advantageous marriage. She met Sublette either in the summer of 1842 or after he returned from his business trip. Although she had a beau at home, she realized that the lord of Sulphur Springs would make an excellent husband. She listened carefully to some of her Alabama friends, who advised her to "catch some good amiable and rich man . . . as a full purse is very useful." The Herefords were said to have tempers "equal to brimstone," but she seems to have hidden that characteristic behind her large, sad eyes. Certainly, they said, she would make some lucky man "a most accomplished wife."[2]

Late in May the Herefords reopened the springs as a watering place. The water was reanalyzed, the favorable results were published in the St. Louis press, and guests were invited to visit and stay for a rest. But they had to bring references; Dr. Hereford did not want the undesirable at his resort. Medicinal waters from the springs, now said to resemble most those of certain English wells, were available to all who could afford them. Sublette, his mind for once free of worries about the resort, spent his time with Frances and thought about a long vacation.[3]

He and Stewart had planned a western trip since 1840, but each year family or financial troubles upset their intentions. At first Stewart considered returning to the United States in the autumn of 1840 to take an expedition to the mountain rendezvous of 1841 and asked Sublette to buy him "strong mules" and carts. His plan failed to materialize, and he immediately made another: he would be in St. Louis by late spring, 1842, and hoped Sublette would have men and equipment ready—at least "six good horses, mules & carts." Once again he had to change his plans, to his great disgust, but wrote William to keep what equipment he could and to dispose of the remainder. Sublette's answer was that "all was ready for the Prairies"; that he would continue to wait until Stewart was there. Meanwhile, he arranged to winter

<hr />

[2] Thomas Hereford to Solomon P. Sublette, September 18, 1854; A. L. Christian to F. S. Hereford, March 3, 1843, Sublette MSS.

[3] *Daily Missouri Republican* (St. Louis), May 19, June 21, 1843.

the horses and mules in western Missouri. Fortunately, Stewart concluded his time-consuming duties in Scotland and by the fall of 1842 reached the United States. He stopped first at Baltimore and Cincinnati to recruit "for the mountains," then moved to New Orleans to await an ice-free channel on the Mississippi.[4]

In Havana and New Orleans Stewart added more men to his company of "companionable adventurers" and, granted favorable weather, planned to be in St. Louis by March. He forwarded an India-rubber boat, ideal for crossing western rivers, but, unfortunately, most of his supplies were lost when the steamboat "J. M. White," upon which he was traveling upriver, sank while en route to St. Louis. Nevertheless, he survived and in St. Louis took quarters in "a large bed room" at the Planters House, saw Sublette, and happily set to work to replenish the lost supplies. The city was alive with activity, since a large emigrant party of perhaps one thousand people was scheduled to leave for the West within a few weeks. The "Oregon fever" raged in many parts of the nation, and companies formed in Missouri, Illinois, Ohio, Iowa, and the East.[5]

Not only were hundreds of emigrants bound for Oregon, but John James Audubon, the famed naturalist, was on his way West, and John Charles Frémont was said to be assembling a new western expedition. When Audubon arrived in St. Louis, he stayed at the Glasgow House, but avoided most social functions. At noon, April 25, he started up the Missouri aboard the "Omega" with a large band of trappers bound for Indian country. He may have seen Sublette and Stewart in St. Louis, yet did not join their party. The "Omega" reached Independence on May 2;

---

[4] *Ibid.*, June 6, 1839; William Drummond Stewart to W. L. Sublette, November 26, 1839, August 23, November 3, 1841, February 20, April 3, 1842; W. L. Sublette to William Drummond Stewart, April 15, 1842; Robert Campbell to W. L. Sublette, December 11, 1842, Sublette MSS.

[5] Letter of February 26, 1843, Private Campbell MSS; William Drummond Stewart to W. L. Sublette, February 13, 1843, Sublette MSS; *Niles' National Register* (Baltimore), April 1, May 6, 1843; *Wabash Express* (Terre Haute), March 29, 1843; *The Radical* (Bowling Green, Missouri), April 15, 1843; *American & Commercial Daily Advertiser* (Baltimore), April 17, 1843; *Daily Evening Gazette* (St. Louis), April 20, 1843.

slightly west of there, at Chouteau's Plantation, deposited some freight for the Stewart-Sublette expedition; and then continued upriver to Fort Union.[6]

The Stewart-Sublette expedition was publicized widely as a well-supplied, tastefully arranged summer's "excursion," not much of a profit-making venture. Sublette, as mentioned, having wintered a herd of horses and mules in western Missouri, now sent brother Solomon to Arrow Rock and points west to purchase more animals. William had on hand "rigging" for several carts and draught animals, but not enough, and entirely lacked many other supplies. In three days, April 27–29, he bought nearly six hundred dollars' worth of goods from St. Louis trading houses, especially from Campbell, who had by then reopened his half of the old store. Stewart's purchases were equally large, if not larger, and many of the items paid for were surplus luxury goods not usually carried in quantity on a western expedition: cigars, playing cards, quills, paper, and ink. One item high on the list was liquor—good liquor—of all types. They purchased a keg of sloe gin, two of cognac, one of rum, a barrel of alcohol, one dozen bottles of champagne, and two of port wine. Stewart reminded Sublette not to forget whiskey, since "we are a thirsty party," and suggested that he take it into Indian country under his permit which allowed him to carry "with him as much spiritous liquors as he may deem necessary for the use of himself and Party." If they could prevent it, no one would starve or go thirsty in the mountains; theirs would be a well-fed, well-drunk party.[7]

By late April most preparations were made, including Sublette's last-minute business arrangements. He co-ordinated his old account with Hugh Campbell into one lump sum, payable in installments; Vasquez and Andrew Sublette finally gave him a promissory note for their outstanding debt; and Campbell agreed to go up the Mississippi during the summer to see some "hard

<hr />

[6] *The Radical* (Bowling Green), April 15, 1843; *Audubon and His Journals* (ed. by Maria R. Audubon and Elliott Coues), I, 454–55, 468.

[7] "Correspondence of Robert Campbell, 1834–1845," *loc. cit.*, 44, 50; William Drummond Stewart to W. L. Sublette, May 1, 1843; D. D. Mitchell to his agents, April 28, 1843, Sublette MSS.

customers" who still owed debts to the old partnership. Robert, however, did not look forward to much success on that trip.[8]

Navigation was open, prairie grass was abundant, and the time had come to leave for the Green. Suddenly, tragedy struck —an unexpected death in Sublette's immediate family. Sister Sophronia had been ill the previous autumn of 1842, but had recovered under the care of Dr. Beaumont. She was careful not to expose herself to "the cold as it brings on the ague," yet her precautions were insufficient. In the spring her health grew worse, and Dr. Hereford was called in for consultation, followed by Drs. Prout and Coalter of St. Louis. Dr. Hereford made daily calls after April 11, but Sophronia died on the twentieth of causes unknown, possibly of pneumonia, tuberculosis, or some malignant fever. She was interred with simple services at the farm late in the afternoon the following day. Her daughter Theresa remained in St. Louis until early May, when she left with her uncle John Cook to take up residence with relatives. The "painful and mournful" shock of Sophronia's passing further delayed Sublette's departure, and he left under a cloud of sorrow.[9]

By May 1, most of the men who intended to accompany the expedition had gathered in St. Louis. Many were new to the West, others old, but all were willing to take their chances. Some of them were young St. Louisans: notably Clark (William Clark) Kennerly, Jefferson Clark, William C. Kennett, and John Radford. Brother Andrew Sublette was not going, although William had been granted permission by the Superintendent of Indian Affairs at St. Louis to take trading goods with him and possibly could have used Andrew's experience with the Indians. Andrew was to remain at Sulphur Springs to look after the family interests and to operate the grocery and "dram shop," under belated permission from William.[10]

[8] Letter of January 31, 1843, Private Campbell MSS.

[9] Sophronia Cook to W. L. Sublette, November, 1842; A. W. Sublette to W. L. Sublette, December 2, 1842, Sublette MSS.; *Daily Missouri Republican* (St. Louis), April 21, 1843.

[10] Record of St. Louis County Court No. 3, 1841–44, pp. 424–25, MS, Register's Office, City Hall, St. Louis; Trading License of W. L. Sublette, May 1, 1843, Sublette MSS.

Matthew (Matt) C. Field, "Phazma" of the *New Orleans Picayune*, was journalist of the expedition, so designated by Stewart, who equipped him for the mountains. Field's health was poor; he was underweight and wanted to give up both tobacco and liquor and thought the trip would be ideal for his general constitution. He reached St. Louis on April 25, five days from New Orleans aboard the steamer "Missouri," and settled at the Planters House amidst a "raging excitement" of spring business. A friend, George W. Christy of New Orleans, "a graduate of Harvard University, and a gentleman of great taste in Natural History," arrived with him or shortly thereafter.[11]

Others flocked to St. Louis from the East. Dr. Charles Mersch, Dr. Stedman Tilghman, who kept a sketchbook of the party, and the brothers Adolphus and Theodore (Dale) Heermann all came from Baltimore. John Hill, "a gentleman from Washington City ... of a highly respectable family ... wealthy," was there. Another very important member was Charles A. Geyer, an European botanist, who intended to travel with the expedition to the "Upper Colorado," where he would leave the party to go to the Hudson's Bay Company posts on the lower Columbia. Geyer was accompanied by another botanist Friedrich Luders.[12]

Two military observers, Lieutenants Richard Hill Graham

[11] The narrative of the expedition of 1843, from St. Louis to the rendezvous and back to St. Louis is drawn principally from the following sources: Sublette Account Book and Diary, 1843, Sublette MSS; *Weekly Picayune* (New Orleans), May 8–November 20, 1843; *Daily Picayune* (New Orleans), April 1, 1843–March 14, 1844; *Daily Missouri Republican* (St. Louis), May–November, 1843; *Niles' National Register* (Baltimore), May–November, 1843; George Engelmann Letter Book G, 1843, MSS, Missouri Botanical Library, St. Louis; Letters of Matthew and Cornelia Field (Harvard Microfilm Collection), 1843, MSS, MoSHi; Ludlow-Field Collection, 1842–44, MSS, MoSHi; Field Diary, MSS; Report of Graham and Smith, November 12, 1843, Letters Received, Adjutant General's Office, 1843, Records of the Adjutant General's Office, Record Group No. 94, MSS, N. A.; Diary of W. Clark Kennerly, August 17–October 13, 1843, MS, MoSHi; Bessie K. Russell, "My Hunting Trip to the Rockies in 1843," *Colorado Magazine*, Vol. XXII (January, 1945), 23–38; "Correspondence of Robert Campbell, 1834–1845," *loc. cit.*, 3–65.

[12] J. V. Hamilton to A. Drips, September 17, 1843, Drips Papers, 1832–60, MSS, MoSHi; Charles A. Geyer, "Notes on the Vegetation and General Character of the Missouri and Oregon Territories ... During the Years 1843 and 1844," *London Journal of Botany*, Vol. IV (1845), 482, 659.

and Sidney Smith, both of the Fourth Infantry stationed at Jefferson Barracks, wanted to go with the expedition. They applied for leave "until the end of September or middle of October" and were granted the request extending until October 15. The army's point of view was that it was "desirable . . . [to] get as much information as possible of the country." Tension grew over the Oregon question, and the two lieutenants would be in excellent position to return with a detailed report—a report subsequently produced.[13]

The expedition was to leave St. Louis in two parts: one under Stewart's command and the other under Sublette's leadership. The first group, called Stewart's "private expedition," was to travel by steamboat to Independence, encamp, and await Sublette's smaller party, traveling overland along the river's south bank. Stewart hoped that a few days in camp near Independence would acclimate his men to outdoor life. Meanwhile, the prairie grass would grow and the prospects of forage for their stock would improve.[14]

A "fortnight late," Stewart's party left St. Louis aboard the steamer "Weston" and six days later reached Madame Chouteau's Landing below Westport. Nearly everyone in the party was happy, carefree, and filled with enthusiasm, although heavily laden with equipment and trading goods. The St. Louis *Missouri Republican* wished that "their most sanguine hopes of enjoyment be realized," and Edmund Chouteau, at the Landing, gave them game for dinner and "initiated some of the new ones into the mysteries of a merry hunters breakfast." Christy and George E. Hepburn, of New Orleans, were "tasteful musicians" and provided entertainment. One of the doctors in the company brought along a "fracture machine" and other necessary instruments in

[13] First Lieutenant R. H. Graham to Brig. Gen. R. James, April 8, 1843, Letters Received, Adjutant General's Office, 1843; Special Orders No. 29, April 19, 1843, Special Orders, 1840–51, Records of the Adjutant General's Office, Record Group No. 94, MSS, N. A.

[14] "Correspondence of the Reverend Ezra Fisher" (ed. by Sarah F. Henderson and Nellie E. and Kenneth S. Latourette), *Quarterly of the Oregon Historical Society*, Vol. XVI (September, 1915), 93; *Savannah Daily Republican*, May 27, 1843.

anticipation of falls, cuts, and bruises, since the caravan might frolic into trouble rather easily. The only immediate discordant note concerned a mysterious Mr. Matthew, who caused considerable animosity on the steamboat and continued to do so in camp. Geyer disliked him, and Stewart's servant fought him on two occasions. Sir William finally decided to force him out of the expedition, but found that he had decamped of his own accord.

Father Pierre Jean De Smet and two Jesuit companions, Fathers Peter De Vos and Adrian Hoecken, outfitted and bound for mountain missionary work, stopped to dine with Stewart on May 10, and the following day Sublette's party arrived "with about 50 mules and drove them towards the camp." He had left St. Louis on the first, passed through Jefferson City to gather mules his friends had purchased—prices were quite high—and then had stopped at Boonville, Arrow Rock, Marshall, and Lexington before reaching Independence. He was accompanied by three Mountain Men and two slave boys, aged eleven and fourteen, and, except for his stock transactions and river crossings, had finished an uneventful trip. He brought a choice pony for Geyer, but the botanist intended to hike to Oregon and refused the mount, and Sublette resold it for forty dollars.[15]

There was no clear consensus about how long they planned to remain in the mountains. Geyer was "uncertain," and Field wrote home that he might go on to Fort Vancouver and added that Stewart might winter in the mountains. Some of the men, however, intended to return home in the autumn, and Sublette planned to be with that group. There might be important business at Sulphur Springs, and he had a growing romantic interest in Frances Hereford. He knew that he had "made a good impression" on her and that if he asked her to marry him, she would accept. Andrew also was interested in Frances and wrote on May 6 that he might consider asking for her hand. Before William left, a friend wrote him suggesting that he relinquish his outfit to brother Solomon, who was in his company, and return post-

[15] *Life, Letters, and Travels of Father Pierre-Jean De Smet, S. J.* (ed. by H. M. Chittenden and A. T. Richardson), I, 44.

haste to St. Louis. As he said to William, "You never will be happy until you are married . . . you never will do better, if you would hunt the wide world over—She is most amiable in deed."

Sublette, however, decided to complete the expedition before proposing marriage to Frances. Temporarily, while Stewart and most of the men moved to "Camp William," located near the Methodist (Shawnee) Mission on the prairie beyond Westport and about one mile from the state line, Sublette remained at Westport and Independence, negotiating for last-minute supplies. The party under Stewart made its final preparations at Camp William. Stewart was "in fine health and spirits," and, except for two incidents, the camp was peaceful. One young man dislocated his shoulder trying to mount a mule, and another fellow was thrown in jail. He had embezzled forty thousand dollars in treasury notes in New Orleans and was on his way west to escape the law. The men in camp visited the Shawnees, entertained themselves by "cottillions, reels and waltzes" to tunes sung and played by their comrades around the campfire, or repaired gear and bargained with visiting tradesmen. Rains accompanied by high winds which shook their tents like water-soaked wash did not dampen their spirits.[16]

Frémont and his party reached Kaw Landing on May 18, encamped, and by the twenty-first had met with Stewart and Sublette. It was understood that either Frémont's party, guided by Fitzpatrick and "Kit" Carson, would precede Stewart's to the West or, as Campbell believed—he had furnished groceries and dry goods to Frémont in St. Louis—the two expeditions would leave together. One member of Stewart's party remarked that "we are to travel part of the way in company with a corps of the United States soldiers, under Captain Frémont"; and Field wrote his wife on May 12, "We only await to be joined by young Frémont." Certainly there seems to have been a travel agreement between the parties. It is also certain, however, that Frémont left Kaw Landing on May 29, bound for St. Vrain's Fort on the south

[16] *The Journals of Theodore Talbot, 1843 and 1849–52* (ed. by Charles H. Carey), 5.

fork of the Platte, and left unaccompanied by the Stewart-Sublette party. He moved to the West in a hurry on the advice in his wife's letter, in order not to lose command of his small, highly mobile unit. Stewart and Sublette had delayed their departure waiting for him; now they had to make up for lost time.[17]

As soon as Stewart and Sublette knew they were to proceed without Frémont's expedition, Stewart broke camp, packed his tents, including his own "very elegant" one, and directed his men northwest across the prairies. He wished to avoid the hundreds of emigrants bound for Oregon. The settlers streamed along the trail, used the grass for their stock, and, as far as the Mountain Men were concerned, generally got in the way of other expeditions. Sublette remained at Westport until the twenty-seventh, two days before Frémont's hasty exodus, and then traveled to Round Grove, where he picked up Stewart's five-day-old trail.[18]

Solomon was with William, as were a half-dozen other men, at least two of whom drove carts loaded with food, ammunition, and personal belongings. Just beyond Round Grove they left the main Santa Fé road to take the wagon-rutted trail Sublette had used so many times to the mountains. At first they traveled with six wagons bound for Oregon and California and on the evening of the twenty-ninth reached Papin's Ferry on the Kansas River, where they found forty wagons in transit across the rain-swollen stream. After a short delay, Sublette crossed on the ferry and led his party another three miles to camp on the Soldier River near the blazing fires of a large Oregon party. In the morning he sent his wagons ahead under Solomon's care, while he dropped down the Soldier to meet Stewart's party, which had ascended the Kansas by a muddy road.

On the banks of the Soldier, Sublette took control of the entire party, including a score of carts and several two-horse, or two-mule, wagons and led them across the stream. Stewart's cara-

[17] Charles W. Upham, *Life, Explorations, and Public Services of John Charles Frémont*, 107–108; Allan Nevins, *Frémont, the West's Great Adventurer*, I, 142, 147.
[18] *St. Louis New Era*, May 30, 1843; Peter H. Burnett, *Recollections and Opinions of an Old Pioneer*, 102.

van had reached the Kansas on May 27, some sixty to seventy miles above its mouth, and there, with considerable difficulty, crossed the river. Once reassembled on the opposite bank, they encamped near the ruins of an old Indian agency, then turned west at fifteen to twenty-five miles a day to reach the Soldier, where Sublette met them. Slightly more than half of the entire party was composed of gentlemen travelers, and the most accurate estimate of total strength, excluding Stewart, the two Sublettes, the missionaries and their associates, and the trappers who later joined the expedition in the mountains, would probably be sixty to sixty-two.[19]

After crossing the Soldier, and eight miles to the west, they met Solomon Sublette and his carts, accompanied by the two Jesuits, De Vos and Hoecken, and their companions, who had said farewell to Father De Smet and were now on their way west. Stewart and Sublette were willing to have them join their party and increase their strength. There on the banks of a small stream they spent the night of May 29, in advance of the main Oregon party—a position they were to retain all the way to the mountains.

At sunup they broke camp and crossed the stream by fashioning logs into baggage rafts. The wagons crossed body deep in water, and everyone had a wet time, but it was only the beginning. All the streams in the area bulged at the banks and had to be bridged, forded, or floated. Despite the high creeks, they covered nearly twenty-five miles on the last day of May and bedded down on a tributary of the Blue. The two following days were quiet ones on the trail. Then, on June 3, while crossing the Big Vermillion, a cart bogged down. It was repaired, but they made camp in the rain—a "hard days march" with a wet ending. However, their troubles with carts were far from over, since the Jesuits' wagons and carts frequently stalled in the muddy stream banks and had to be pushed and pulled by hand.

Geyer and Alexander Gordon, another botanist in the party, enjoyed themselves completely, at times miles from the main

[19] Richard Rowland to his Sister, January 9, 1844, MSS, Oregon Historical Society, Portland.

party in search of plants. The region was well timbered, and grape vines grew in profusion along the watercourses, amidst linden, sycamore, box elder, ash, and walnut trees. On the ridges were clumps of dwarf chestnut, oak, and blackjack, its shiny leaves glistening in the sun; and in fertile spots were cultivated gardens belonging to half bloods and French traders. Most of the other men were as pleased as the two botanists with life along the trail. They tried to overlook the wet spring weather, mules and horses which ran off and had to be pursued and recaptured, and even "an imperfect guide" who once led some of the party in the wrong direction. They found that nature provided a varied diet, even though the buffalo "lords of the prairie" were "yet far in advance," and Field admitted that he and his companions were "well and growing fat."

At night the wagons were placed in a circle, and the men simply spread their blankets under the vehicles and used their saddles as pillows. Stewart usually pitched his tent, but the others took to theirs only in inclement weather. Guards alternated on night duty, although the party was too large to fear any serious Indian troubles. They did have a minor Indian "scrape" on the afternoon of June 5, an hour beyond nooning, at a timbered spring near the Vermillion. A war party of seventy Osages and Otoes, in pursuit of a horse-stealing Pawnee band, rode up and pounced upon three Pawnees who had been riding in the rear of the caravan. The Jesuits interceded, secured the release of the three unfortunates, and gave them shelter. Again the expedition proceeded, but the Osages followed and made several attempts to take the Pawnees before they gave up the chase at sundown. The following morning another band of Osages met a hunting party from the expedition, but the Indians were friendly and their leader, at least, spoke English.

While encamped on the Big Blue at Rocky Creek on the evening of June 6, they were pleasantly surprised by a visitor from the upper Platte. John Rishan, an employee of Sibille and Adams, came in leading a caravan of five or six wagons loaded with buffalo robes. He was on his way to market at St. Louis and brought news from the mountains. When he broke camp, two of Sublette's men went with him out of disgust for the "pleasure tour" they had found to be too uncomfortable. Stewart and Sublette let them go and continued west across the Little and Big Sandys of the Blue—difficult and wet crossings—and by June 10 were two hundred miles west of Independence.

Forty miles up the Blue they struck directly north-northwest twenty miles towards the valley of the Platte. Their route took them across vast, rolling prairies devoid of timber. Driftwood and dry buffalo chips provided their only fuel, and during their first night on the Platte, June 14, rain fell in torrents and many in the party spent unpleasant hours standing ankle-deep in water. The fires had gone out, they munched on crackers washed down with whiskey, and tempers grew short. There was one nearly violent quarrel, and the men standing watch did so more out of respect for their leaders than from a sense of duty. Thirteen of Stewart's men promptly headed for home—enough was enough.

In the morning the expedition moved upstream towards the forks of the Platte. Their road "lay over almost one unbroken flat, the soil being sandy and occasionally somewhat marshy, the average width of the Valley about seven miles. There was no timber on the Platte, not a tree to be seen on its banks." On the eighteenth as they "leisurely" rode along, advance scouts sighted a herd of buffalo, and the expedition held its first hunt. Part of the herd rushed by the wagons and startled two mules to flight. Both were located in the morning, but neither was retaken.

Clark Kennerly, one of the favorite young men, almost lost his life in an accident the night after the buffalo hunt. While un-saddling his pony, he caught his foot in the saddle rope; the pony bolted, dashed through the camp dragging the young man with him, and at last he was cornered in the horse corral. Sublette and the others, fearing the worst, ran up and untangled Kennerly, but found he was not seriously injured. Later in the evening, when the last of the horses entered the camp laden with buffalo meat, one horse objected to its pungent load, and all stampeded. Everyone ducked for cover, some fearing it was an Indian attack, but no one was trampled.

In accordance with their plan to follow the Oregon Trail and Frémont's route of 1842 as closely as possible, they forded the South Fork of the Platte at a point about forty miles upstream. Since the river was high with melted snow and rainwater, they decided to use Stewart's two India-rubber boats and to swim the stock across. The operation took two days, but was successful, and on the evening of June 25, they encamped on the north bank in an enormous field of wild flowers.

At dawn they broke camp and headed cross-country to the south bank of the Platte's North Fork. Their first day's march took them through a hot, waterless tract, and late in the afternoon when they reached a "wild romantic gorge" leading away three miles to the river, some fifteen or eighteen of the men followed the gorge to Ash Hollow. They relaxed at the Hollow until sunset and then set out for the main camp on the trail. Cyprien (Louis Cyprien) Menard, a lone horseman from the main party, mistook them for Indians, hid himself until they passed, and while hiding, lost his horse. Left alone in a most dangerous situation, he shouldered his saddle and started up the Platte, intending to rejoin the expedition somewhere along the way.

Sublette and his companions had no choice other than to move forward along the river. Parties were sent to search for Menard and returned with his horse and coat, but by the morning of the twenty-eighth they feared he was lost permanently. They had entered dangerous Sioux country and dared not delay their advance. Then Sublette, who rode in the lead, suddenly stumbled upon a whitened buffalo skull upon which Menard had written a message with a charred stick. Ten men, including Father Hoecken, who bundled food into his clothing, dashed forward up the valley and five or six miles farther sighted a second skull and message. Near there they found Menard, physically exhausted but in "good spirit," on the river bank huddled over a small fire, cooking four turtles. The main party joined the searchers at Menard's fire, and all bedded down for the evening near the Prairie Church, a geological formation ten miles east of Chimney Rock. A thunderstorm struck at sundown, followed by a rainbow and a "beautiful sunset": an appropriate ending to a most trying day.

The morning was "bitter cold" for the first of July, but they ignored the weather and, with Menard in a wagon, slowly moved towards Scott's Bluff. They nooned by the river, shot a few buffalo, and then sent a party ahead to locate a short, safe way through the hills surrounding the bluff. Due to the topography of the region, expeditions were forced to leave the river to pass through the "Valley of Jehosophat" behind the highlands. They made the valley passage the following day—Sunday—but Sunday was no day of rest on the Platte.

Sunday evening they encamped at Horse Creek and nooned on Monday, the third, near the Platte in an inviting spot where there was sufficient wood, "bubbling spring" water, and plenty of forage. Although they were within fifteen or twenty miles of Laramie Fork, they decided to remain where they were and to celebrate the Fourth of July on the Platte. Preparations for the important day were started immediately. Two enormous plum puddings were mixed, the larder was opened in all its profusion, and liquor was brought out as the hour approached when the nearby hills would resound with their merriment.

At sunrise they hoisted an improvised flag in the center of the camp, fired a twenty-six-gun salute, and welcomed into the Far West the sixty-seventh anniversary of independence. The men were dressed in their best, but as the day passed, the finest clothing was rumpled and torn. Some went swimming; others took to wild foot and horse races. To accommodate everyone at dinner, an oilcloth was spread on the grass in two connected tents, and the men sat Indian-fashion on the ground. Others dined in four separate tents, and then all joined together for toasts. Stewart and Sublette proposed the Union; Christy delivered an appropriate address, followed by an original ode, other "sentiments and songs'" and in Stewart's honor they sang "God Save the Queen," with new words unlikely to ruffle the tender feelings of anyone present. They had started the day with "Libations at Sublette's" and continued it with libations in many places. It was "a great day for the prairies"; even the teetotalers got "glorious."

Bright and early, after a much-needed night's rest, they were off to the Laramie, where they encamped near Fort Platte, about one mile below Fort Laramie. While some in the party visited a nearby Sioux camp or swam in the river, Sublette and Stewart purchased fresh horses and supplies from the post. They remained in camp on the Laramie until late in the afternoon of July 8, enjoying fresh meat, butter, and milk, although prices were high in anticipation of a heavy Oregon emigration. There also, close to the fort, William and Solomon found the grave of Milton Sublette, its cross "prostrate and broken." Solomon, who was to remain at the post while William continued to the mountains, erected a more "christian" monument over his brother's last resting place.[20]

When the party finally broke camp on the eighth, they proceeded into the Wyoming Black Hills, but traveled only a dozen miles the first day. They halted in an ideal camping spot "on a green hillock in a wide dry sandy valley, between high, wild-looking rocky hills, half bare, and half covered with short black pine shrubbery." Lively echoes thundered down from the hills across the dark pines and cedars and the scattered clumps of ash and cottonwood. The next day's travel took them thirty miles over scattered hills towards the upper reaches of the North Fork of the Platte; and the following day another twenty miles carried them past one of the sources of the river—a spring whose waters poured "from between tremendous rocks, out upon a shelving lawn of green." A Cheyenne war party was in the neighborhood and "stricter care" had to be taken; but no attack materialized, and they spent the night, after finishing a supper of buffalo ribs, in a riverside hollow.

At dawn they could see extended upon the horizon snow-

20 "Journal of Pierson Barton Reading" (ed. by Philip B. Bekeart), *Quarterly of the Society of California Pioneers*, Vol. VII (September, 1930), 165; Joseph Bissonett to Sibille and Adams, July 25, September 13, 1843, David Adams Family Papers, 1809–69, MSS, MoSHi.

capped peaks—their destination to the west. Camp broke in early morning and the day's travel was more difficult than usual, across rugged countryside under a blazing sun. That night they encamped near a lake by the side of a deep gorge bearing russet-colored water, and most of the party gathered in a little natural arbor to drink milk punch, harmonize, and drift to sleep on buffalo robes. Weather was very favorable for travel the next day, but the country was filled with cacti and sage, "the latter giving forth a strong, sickening odor." They spent the night beneath enclosing hills, enjoying the moonlight. Travel the following day was uneventful, and the encampment on Deer Creek differed little from the previous night's.

By July 15, they reached a crossing-place on the North Fork. Before swimming the stream, however, they spent better than a day in camp in order to dry a supply of fresh buffalo meat. Some men hunted; others splashed about in the river, ignoring the myriads of mosquitoes and ground toads; and one band of horsemen rode to a distant snow field in the hills and returned with large snowballs wrapped in bundles, which the sun-drenched men in camp turned into "fixins" for a round of mint juleps. At daybreak on the seventeenth, Sublette ordered them to prepare to cross the river: not a difficult crossing and one that they completed, with aid of the rubber boats, by late afternoon. That night they settled down on the north bank near a grove of "gigantic pines" bordered by piles of boulders. All in all, as Field remarked, it was "a great day on the fork."

The eighteenth was an eventful Tuesday. An overturned "mess cart" delayed them in the morning, and scarcely a quarter of an hour later they noticed a mounted party approaching. The strangers proved not to be Indians, as they feared, but a fur caravan on its way to Fort Laramie. They nooned together near the Red Buttes in "high spirits," but later in the afternoon a heavy gloom fell over the entire camp. François Clement, a fifteen-year-old protégé of Stewart's, accidentally shot himself in the chest. He lingered on through the afternoon, resting in the arms of Stewart and Dr. Tilghman, and died in the evening. The following morning he was buried in an unmarked grave.

The region beyond the buttes was desolate. Two carts upset, and the drinking water the party found after digging for it was mineral infested. Their first camp beyond Clement's burial spot was made in "great depression . . . on account of yesterday's melancholy accident." The following day's route wound over ridges of fossiliferous rocks, through woodless, waterless country in which the very soil itself was covered with a fine, white mineral powder. Sage choked the trail and cacti dotted the landscape. There were "many sandy and swampy ravines" to cross, and in between a strong, dust-laden wind swirled about them. Fresh game was scarce, and hunting parties failed to return with much more than a few grouse.

At Independence Rock, Field witnessed a "rowdy spree" between several members of the party—a sure sign that tempers were short. Discipline was hard to maintain in such a heterogeneous party, and it was inevitable that in such a diverse group some would grumble, swear, and quarrel. There is no reason to suspect that either Sublette or Stewart was unnecessarily tyrannical or demanding. If anything, the opposite was true, yet back home the newspapers by mid-July carried stories of trouble in the expedition. How the stories started is not clear, but it seems that the few men who left the party on the Platte must have carried exaggerated tales to the St. Louis press. Stewart was described as "overbearing" in his command, and it was said that some "of his company threatened to shoot him if he persisted in his tyrannical course."[21]

The men encamped at Independence Rock would not learn of the stories until they returned to St. Louis. As it was, some were "dispirited" with the long trip, and nearly all had resolved by then to return east in the autumn. Fortunately, the country beyond Independence Rock improved, and so did their morale.

21 *Daily Evening Gazette* (St. Louis), July 13, 1843; *Old School Democrat and St. Louis Herald,* August 17, 1843; *Savannah Daily Republican,* August 19, 1843.

They moved west along the grassy banks of the Sweetwater, constantly surrounded by high mountain peaks, and realized they were within ten days of their destination. On July 26, they sent a three-man express to Fort Bridger to invite Miles Goodyear and other trappers in the area to gather together their Indian friends for a rendezvous on the Green. Twenty-three miles to the west of the place from which they had dispatched the express, Stewart and Sublette made camp on the Sweetwater and remained there until noon of the twenty-ninth, drying buffalo meat, reading, and playing cards. One man accidentally shot off his finger, but otherwise everything was quiet.

They moved ahead again on the twenty-ninth. Suddenly, two horsemen rode up with news that the Snake Indians would be at the rendezvous. That evening camp was placed on a "rich neck of land formed in a bend of the Sweetwater, encircled by willows, and overtopped by mountains all around." It was a beautiful yet dangerous location, since hostile Indians were said to be in the area.

Rain, hail, and snow, with intermittent thunderstorms, battered them for days. During those hours of inclement weather, they traveled at least thirty miles and on the evening of August 1 spent a cold night south of Frémont's Peak. They had crossed South Pass almost "without knowing it." By noon of the second they were on the Big Sandy, camped there, and the following morning the priests left them and started west. Sublette and Stewart directed their party up the valley of the Green to a campsite on the New Fork, where there were antelope and "plenty of wild geese to be had for the catching." The following day they moved fifteen miles north across several streams to the middle reaches of Piny Fork and early on the fifth encamped near a fire-blackened pine grove.

They had little to do but await the arrival of the raw material of every rendezvous: hunters and Indians. One uninvited, marauding Indian band appeared and lurked near the camp until persuaded to leave, but nothing else happened. Stewart and Sublette realized that their men would soon tire of waiting and so moved camp up Piny Fork to the shores of Frémont Lake, where they could rest, explore, and fish. The carts were sent over the hills, while some of the men followed the banks of the fork to where it issued from the lake in roaring, bubbling cascades. Many of them immediately went fishing and angled for large lake trout they could see swimming in the crystalline water. Later in the afternoon an express arrived to announce that a group from Bridger's Fort would soon be there, and two days later a band of thirty, under Goodyear and Chief Cut-Nose, rode in screaming and shouting.

Stewart, Field, Christy, and several others explored the edges of the lake during the second week in August, and by the ninth or tenth the rendezvous was under way formally. Most of the initial trading with the Snakes was completed by the fourteenth, after which the camp moved from the lake across Piny Fork to a new site on an island where there was room for greater festivity. Indian women, children, and dogs roamed the nearby meadows and enjoyed the contests of skill between their warriors and the white visitors. Many of the men hunted; others held foot races, played ball, smoked and drank—sometimes to excess—or took skins to Jack Robertson's Indian wife, who was the most skilled seamstress in the camp. Gradually, however, grass and wood grew scarce, the nights grew colder, and the rendezvous ended.

Before disbanding, however, they held three days of horse racing over a rough, ill-defined course full of badger holes. An Indian lodge was placed at one end of the track to serve as a judges' stand, and all comers were welcome. Betting was heavy in peltries and trading goods, and, late in the afternoon of the fourteenth, at the rap of a tin pan the first horses were off. On the following day Sublette entered his horse "Tom," but Tom ran last in a field of five led by a young Indian brave, wearing only a red handkerchief, who rode bareback on Robertson's horse "Siskeedee." The main attraction of the third day was a mile race for the nine poorest horses in camp—a wild, hilarious event—followed by a match race between James Ogle's "Harlequin" and Dr. Tilghman's "Scatter Dust."

On the eighteenth of August, Stewart and Sublette started on their return trip to St. Louis. Game was plentiful, and the mosquitoes less bothersome since the days were cooler. On the banks of the Big Sandy an Indian band attempted to drive off their stock during the night of August 19, but was beaten back and fled. On the Little Sandy they "lay by" a day while the Indian wife of Henry the Hunter was "being delivered of a child." The men waited, played cards, hunted, and listened to the pitter-patter of a light rain. Field remarked sarcastically that it was "the first occasion ever known of a mountain journey being delayed one hour for such a reason."

At the end of the first week they were on the Sweetwater. The trail was clear, marked by innumerable wagon ruts and strewn with lost and discarded remnants from the Oregon parties. Some time was lost when carts accidentally overturned, and a few members of the party grew skeptical of the weather: frequent cold winds, thunderstorms, hail, rain, and threatening clouds. They all knew that an early winter was on its way. Some mornings they had to chop ice from cups and pans or were delayed by severe cold. They were thankful, however, for the numerous buffalo and at Independence Rock found that the cache, left there on their way west, was safe except for a few items.

They forded the north fork of the Platte on August 31, without the aid of rubber boats, and on the seventh of September encamped "at a large spring of warm water" within a few miles of Laramie Fork. The men at Fort Platte—the party was there by noon of the eighth—sold them supplies. Lieutenants Graham and Smith were treated with particular courtesy, since the men at the post had a large, hidden liquor supply and it was known that the two military observers opposed the illegal Indian liquor trade. For recreation nearly everyone attended a council with the local Indians, whose wives and children freely wandered about the expedition's camp. Stewart and Sublette planned to leave on September 13, but Christy was injured in a fall from a horse and was unable to travel until a day later.[22]

Their return trip down the Platte was slow—thirteen to fourteen miles a day—and exceedingly unpleasant. At Scott's Bluff they were caught in a cold rain which drenched them before they could seek shelter and left them soaked and shivering in their blankets. When they reached Ash Hollow and encamped for two days to prepare buffalo meat, a cold wind carrying a continuous heavy drizzle dampened all of them in body and spirit. Sublette, whose birthday fell while they were at the Hollow, "got half the camp drunk" on apple brandy and temporarily revived their lagging energies. Another cold rainstorm struck them on the north bank of the south Fork of the Platte, and they had to go hungry for the night while the rain continued.

They awoke on the twenty-ninth to find a cold, miserable morning and pushed ahead in the face of a "furious rain." When the storm reached its peak, the animals abruptly turned their tails to the rain and wind and refused to move another step. Sublette and Stewart ordered camp pitched and then waited out the all-night storm. The rain changed to snow, the smaller tents were blown down or leaned dangerously, and many men, soaked to the skin, took shelter in Stewart's large, crowded lodge. By morning the wind had diminished, but the camp lay under a heavy blanket of ice-encrusted early snow. Later in the day the men dried themselves as best they could, and four messes decided to push ahead to Westport, leaving the main party to wait another day for better weather. Some experienced mountaineers declared it was the most severe storm they had ever seen so early on the Platte.

By October 16, having had their fill of "the fun of a pleasure trip to the Rocky Mountains," the four messes—twenty-two men —reached Westport. There they boarded the steamer "Omega" and a week later were in St. Louis. Lieutenants Graham and Smith, included in the party, were anxious to reach Jefferson Barracks before they were court-martialed for desertion. They were nine

22 Andrew Drips to Maj. D. D. Mitchell, October 15, 1843, Drips Papers, 1832–60, MSS, MoSHi; Joseph Bissonett to Sibille and Adams, September 13, 1843, David Adams Family Papers, 1809–69, MSS, MoSHi.

days late as it was, but their excuses were accepted and they returned to active duty.[23]

Meanwhile, the main party under Stewart and Sublette continued down the Platte and by Friday, October 6, reached the Blue River. At Papin's Ferry they replenished their stores, and Sublette lost an "English Cow" in the crossing, but otherwise all was well, and they were out of danger of starvation. They jogged into Westport late in the afternoon of the twentieth and at Independence "were taken for Emigrants or a traveling menagerie." Field declared them the "fattest, greasiest set of truant rogues" imaginable. Many of the men immediately took the steamer "John Aull" for St. Louis, and Sublette shipped two carts loaded with peltries and harness aboard the "Nodaway." He and Stewart remained in western Missouri to settle accounts and then traveled overland. They were at Sulphur Springs by the first or second of November, pleased, as were most of their hardier companions, with the summer's tour to the Green.[24]

[23] Post Returns, Jefferson Barracks, October–November, 1843, Records of the Adjutant General's Office, Record Group No. 94, MSS, N. A.
[24] W. L. Sublette to Chouteau & Papin, April 27, 1844, Sublette MSS.

Politics and Property

SUBLETTE asked Dr. Beaumont to visit him at the farm, examine him, and tell him whether his health had been improved by his recent mountain excursion. The learned physician complied with his friend's request, but it seems that his report was not encouraging. Sublette's general health was not much better. In fact, he had signs of a dreaded disease—tuberculosis—far from uncommon in his family. But he was not in a critical condition, did not intend to withdraw from the world, and with care might live many more years. Instead of going into semiseclusion, he prepared for the future and drew up a new will on New Year's Day, 1844, in which he distributed his property amongst his close relatives and friends. Frances, his "estimed female friend" and future wife, received a life income from one hundred acres of Sulphur Springs. Whether or not she knew of his failing health is difficult to say, but it is likely that she did and planned to marry him with the mutual understanding that the marriage might not be a long one.[1]

Stewart lingered at the farm the entire month of November, 1843, before finally leaving for New Orleans. He remained at the Delta City until mid-March, 1844, and strongly hinted that he planned to return to the West, possibly with an expedition to

[1] Will of W. L. Sublette, January 1, 1844, Sublette MSS.

Santa Fé. He had become, however, by his brother's death in 1838, Sir William, nineteenth of Grandtully, and seventh baronet, and knew that he should first return to Scotland to oversee his estate. He traveled eastward from New Orleans and was in New York City by May, carrying with him "curiosities which for years he had been accumulating," and before sailing purchased "some south American terapin." Sublette had given him deer and antelope to take to Scotland, and as soon as Sir William arrived home, he renewed his correspondence with him. They exchanged agricultural news as they had in the past, and Stewart dispensed advice, such as that in a letter early in 1845, in which he said: "The whole farm [Sulphur Springs] should be in hay except what you put in garden grounds . . . hay is the surest commodity to fetch a price—in a dry season spread some nitrate of soda over the grass . . . & you will have the best crop in the state."[2]

Throughout the winter, Sublette busied himself with miscellaneous affairs: he paid his taxes, replenished his wardrobe, visited his neighbors, and received friends at the farm. Campbell, since October the proud father of a second son, told William of his previous summer's business trip and of future prospects for the remaining Sublette-Campbell accounts. Doubtless, Sublette was concerned about the debts, but not enough to allow them to interfere with his feelings for Robert. If William were the "unscrupulous money maker" some contended, he seldom allowed that trait to travel from his countinghouse to his farm. Hugh Campbell seems to have been correct years before when he said, "The attention—the downright brotherly friendship of Wm L Sublette is almost without a precedent. In this cold heartless world . . . it is like an *Oasis* in the desert to meet with such a man." Sublette's business success in the fur trade brought him into conflict with competitors who brought unfounded charges against him, but none of his close friends or loved ones ever found he was anything but friendly, companionable, generous, and accommo-

[2] *American & Commercial Daily Advertiser* (Baltimore), December 6, 1843; William Drummond Stewart to W. L. Sublette, January 14, March 23, July 3, 1844, March 1, 1845, Sublette MSS.

dating. He was not renowned for sparkling wit or the most graceful parlor manners—the metal of his life was tempered by years
of rough living—but he was fair and hard-working; admired most
by those who knew him best.[3]

He had decided in the autumn, despite his uncertain health,
that in 1844 he would re-enter the political arena. In the last
presidential race, of 1840, he and his friends campaigned at "the
old stand," only to be beaten by the Whigs, who sang and shouted
and swayed the masses. The Democrats had learned their lesson
and intended to fight fire with fire. Sublette had not been very
active politically for many months, but remained in close contact with the leaders of Missouri's democracy. Before leaving for
the mountains, he had written Benton to request a government
position for either Solomon or Andrew; the Senator advised him
to postpone his request until after the voters' verdict.

In November, 1843, Sublette and nine other pro-Van Buren
Democrats were appointed to attend the state party convention
scheduled for April. Not long after that, three of the delegation
resigned, and the remaining members were called together at
the office of the St. Louis *Missourian* to select substitutes. After
the meeting, held in early spring, Sublette and two other delegates, all eager to secure unity in their party's ranks, addressed
letters of inquiry to the Democratic Congressional and guberna-
torial hopefuls. The candidates were asked if they were willing
to abide by the decisions to be made at the coming Jefferson City
convention, and with one exception all those approached answered that they would. Since the death of Senator Lewis Linn,
in October, Missouri Democratic politics had been rent more
than ever before by the old Hard-Soft quarrel. Linn's successor
was David R. Atchison, a belligerent Soft, who would become
anathema to Benton. The growing split was certain to be carried
to the spring convention.[4]

3 Campbell Family Bible; Letter of September 27, 1835, Private Campbell
MSS.
4 *Missourian* (St. Louis), January 18, March 13, 21, 28, 1844; *Jefferson Inquirer* (Jefferson City), January 25, 1844; Watson, Sublette, and Tierman to
M. M. Marmaduke, March 1, 1844, Sappington Papers, 1810–65, MSS, MoSHi.

Sublette's plea for unity was only a small voice in the factional maze within the Democratic party—faction which would produce riotous local meetings. One such meeting, held on March 15, was planned as a large, yet peaceful assembly. Several party leaders petitioned the circuit court to use its quarters to celebrate former President Jackson's birthday. The court refused on the grounds that the gathering might be used to make "political capital," and the Democratic leaders, undismayed, received permission instead to use a new downtown warehouse belonging to Colonel J. B. Brant. Both Sublette and Campbell affixed their names to a list of seventy prominent men who called the meeting, and Sublette, in addition, was appointed to a twenty-man preparations committee. On Thursday, March 14, the committeemen met at the warehouse, decorated the premises, and decided to roast an ox on a vacant lot across the street. The following day at three o'clock, hundreds converged on the warehouse, and the meeting turned into a political rally. The milling throng, its spirits undampened by a pouring rain and muddy roads, listened to the music of a German brass band and enthusiastically voiced its Democratic sentiments.[5]

The chairman opened the meeting with remarks on party unity and a lengthy speech in praise of Jackson. It was a short-lived unity, however, since resolutions reported in by a committee of thirteen, one of whom was Sublette, were contested from the floor. There were shouts for changes and rejections of particular clauses, especially one in favor of Benton's re-election. A number of speakers immediately took the platform amidst a "most disgraceful turmoil and confusion," as the opposition press related, and spoke at length against the resolutions. Someone began to blow out the lights, and in the general din someone else screamed for adjournment, and the chairman willingly complied, yet the Softs were not finished for the day. One of their leaders held the rostrum and, given a "tremendous yell" of ap-

[5] *Missourian* (St. Louis), March 13, 21, 1844; *St. Louis Democrat*, March 12, 1844; *Daily Missouri Republican* (St. Louis), March 16, 1844; *Daily Peoples' Organ* (St. Louis), March 13, 1844.

proval, led his friends to vote down the pro-Benton resolution. By that time Colonel Brant demanded they vacate his warehouse, and they emptied the building quickly, leaving a basement full of uneaten food.[6]

That evening the Softs and a few Whigs met by candlelight in the courthouse, "declared war" on Benton, and roundly denounced Sublette and the other Hards for having "packed" the resolutions committee. The anti-Benton *Missouri Republican* sarcastically referred to the afternoon gathering as an event "never witnessed west of the Rubicon," and added that "Tammany Hall in its glory may have furnished something like it, but its equal was never seen here in St. Louis." The evening meeting was more to the *Republican's* liking.[7]

Both Hard and Soft delegations were sent from St. Louis County to the state convention, and Sublette's seat as a delegate was contested. He and his friends intended to support John C. Edwards for governor and oppose any vote of censure against Benton. When the convention opened on April 1, under the gavel of Sterling Price as temporary chairman, there was immediate confusion occasioned by a resolution pledging all delegates, for the sake of unity, to support all nominations. Heated debate did not settle the issue, and the convention adjourned until the following morning. When the body reassembled, a special credentials committee reported in favor of seating the powerful Hard delegation from St. Louis County. It was seated, and "the doom of the softs was sure." Before the convention adjourned for the night, Edwards was nominated for governor, and Sublette was jubilant.

The convention met again on Wednesday and Thursday and the Hards, with their dependable core of votes, swept their measures through the meeting. They carried their plan to redefine the state's Congressional districts, but postponed or defeated all resolutions which might split the party. After speeches on Thursday, April 4, the convention adjourned and the delegates returned

6 *St. Louis Democrat*, March 16, 1844; *Mill Boy* (St. Louis), March 23, 1844.
7 *Daily Missouri Republican* (St. Louis), March 16, 1844.

home. Sublette and his friends at least temporarily had won control of Missouri's Democratic party. Smarting from their defeat, the Softs met in St. Louis approximately a week later and resolved "to oppose the nominees of the convention." Sublette had worked for party unity, but, unity having failed, he worked even harder for Benton and the Hard ticket. A large gathering of Hards was held April 20, at the Concert Hall. He attended, accompanied by Campbell and brother Andrew, who served on the resolutions committee. They listened to speeches, selected one hundred persons to attend a meeting at Manchester, and completed their work to the tempo of a "fine band."[8]

At Baltimore the Democratic National Convention passed over Van Buren, Benton's choice, and nominated the expansionist James K. Polk and, for vice-president, George W. Dallas. Many St. Louis Democrats were surprised, but in a meeting held at the courthouse on Saturday evening, June 15, they accepted the Baltimore nominees. Although it was a rainy night, the room had "filled to overflowing," and the gathering was regarded by many as the "best meeting the democracy of St. Louis have held for many a day." One of Missouri's delegates at the national convention in Baltimore, Arthur L. Magenis of St. Louis, denounced the Polk-Dallas ticket. Magenis was also a Democratic elector for the seventh district of the state. Rumors circulated that he was mentally incompetent, and, despite Whig criticism, immediate steps were taken to replace him as an elector. At least two substitutes were suggested, one of whom declined the honor "on account of his professional engagements," before the Democrats of the seventh district decided to call a meeting of all delegates to the national convention to select a substitute for Magenis. Since two of the delegates were still in Baltimore, a bare quorum assembled early on Saturday morning, June 18, in Francis P. Blair's office. Sublette attended, but no decision was reached. Days passed; the Democratic leaders admitted they were at a loss for suggestions and finally asked Sublette if he would break

[8] *Jefferson Inquirer* (Jefferson City), April 8, 1844; *Missourian* (St. Louis), April 25, 1844; *Missouri Statesman* (Columbia), April 26, 1844.

his resolution not to hold office and serve as an elector. A week later William accepted and became Democratic elector for the seventh district.[9]

July to November, 1844, were intense campaign months. The Whigs vigorously protested that three of the Democratic electors were also state bank directors and that it was illegal for them to be both. The Democrats shrugged off the charge and ignored Magenis when he refused to resign as elector. Various men who wished to be chosen to carry the Democratic electoral votes to Washington in event of a Polk-Dallas victory solicited Sublette's support. Since some of the appeals were accompanied by references from his friends, they presented a problem requiring his best diplomacy. He was invited also to address political gatherings in scattered sections of Missouri, such as one at Hannibal on October 1, and another at Independence.[10] On September 14, he served as one of five vice-presidents of a nonpartisan citizens' meeting at the courthouse "in regard to the imprisonment of Thomas W. Dorr, the rightful governor of Rhode Island."[11] Dorr had been jailed as leader of an insurgent element in Rhode Island—an element that favored a much broader suffrage. To many Americans he was the hero of the hour, and to the thousands of Missourians who met on the fourteenth to defend him through resolutions, he was the very symbol of democracy in operation.

By mid-October, the presidential campaign had reached its last lap. On the nineteenth, there was a large meeting at Colonel Brant's warehouse, but this time there was more unity—the extreme Softs did not bother to appear. Benton delivered the principal address, Campbell was there and served on the resolutions

[9] St. Louis New Era, June 10, 14, 1844; Missourian (St. Louis), May 23, June 13, 20, 1844; Missouri Statesman (Columbia), May 10, 1844; Mill Boy (St. Louis), June 22, July 6, 13, 1844; Southern Advocate (Jackson, Missouri), July 13, 1844; F. Blair to W. L. Sublette, June 16, 1844; John Smith to W. L. Sublette, July 6, 1844, Sublette MSS.

[10] Peoples' Organ (St. Louis), August 19, 1844; Missourian (St. Louis), July 18, 1844; Memoirs of William A. Wilcox, 1844, St. Louis Reminiscences Envelope, MSS, MoSHi.

[11] Peoples' Organ (St. Louis) September 16, 1844.

committee, and Sublette may have been with him. The following week, Benton, in another speech, referred directly to Sublette as his lifelong friend and "one of St. Louis's most cherished citizens." Not to be outdone, the *Daily Missourian*, for the benefit of the voters, praised William as:

> ... *one of the oldest residents of St. Louis County, well known to us, as he is to nearly every man in it—who has been identified with her interests and those of the state from his boyhood, and enjoys, as he deserves to do, the respect, confidence, and esteem of the people in as high a degree as any other. Of a sound and discriminating mind, and devoted to the pursuit of agriculture, Col. Sublette is an admirable specimen of that class of her citizens who have done more than any and all others to stamp upon her the political character which she has obtained, and of whom she may well be proud her yeoman Democracy.*[12]

When the returns were counted, the Democratic ticket carried Missouri and the White House. On the twenty-fourth of November, Sublette reached Jefferson City to cast his vote for Polk and Dallas. He took a room at the Missouri House, hobnobbed with his political friends, and cast his ballot at the Capitol. He was on his way home within a few days, his political career essentially over, but while in Jefferson City he was re-elected a director of the state bank. The legislature, without a previous caucus, accepted him as a director by the top-heavy vote of 129 to 1. Campbell also was re-elected, and of the entire board only two were new men. Sublette's years of devoted service to the bank, his confidence in its stability, and his belief in its future were repaid by the legislature's reacceptance of him. He attended most meetings of the board during the winter and spring of 1845, and in May used his influence for a friend to fill the office of Notary of the Bank.[13]

[12] October 28, 1844.

Sublette's health did not improve during 1844, and it is possible that he was too active for his own good. Not only was he busy in politics, with his farm, and in the state bank, but he helped Campbell settle old business accounts. Since economic conditions were better and over one hundred individuals and firms still owed them money, Sublette made a collection trip to New Orleans. He left St. Louis probably in the first week of January, 1844; met an old political friend at Cairo on the way down-river; and remained in New Orleans at least a month, in quarters at the St. Charles Hotel. He visited and dined with friends after business hours, especially with Stewart, who had not left for Scotland as yet, and with Matt Field. William returned to St. Louis on or shortly before March 1, and learned that in his absence Campbell's four-month-old son had died.[14]

William had left Andrew in charge of the farm, and the younger Sublette had operated it in a fairly efficient manner; yet Andrew had a persistent cough and wanted to return to the mountains for his health. William regretted to see him go, but realized it would be best. In late April, Andrew left for Independence and Westport, where he gathered supplies and took charge of a company of twenty to twenty-five young men going to the mountains for their health. He led the invalid group as far as Fort Laramie. There he relinquished his command and moved down to Bent's Fort on the Arkansas. He met wandering brother Solomon at Bent's, and the two of them traveled to Taos for provisions. From Taos they returned to the Arkansas-Platte trading region, and by October, 1845, Andrew was back in Missouri much improved in general health.

13 *Daily Missouri Republican* (St. Louis), December 2, 6, 9, 1844; *Peoples' Organ* (St. Louis), December 7, 1844; *Journal of the Senate of the State of Missouri . . . One Thousand Eight Hundred and Forty-four*, 69–70, Appendices C, D, E, and H; *Journal of the House of Representatives of the State of Missouri . . . One Thousand Eight Hundred and Forty-Six*, Appendix F.

14 "Correspondence of Robert Campbell, 1834–1845," *loc. cit.*, 57; Robert Campbell to W. L. Sublette, January 6, 19, 1844; William Drummond Stewart to W. L. Sublette, January 14, 1844; Winston and Hermann to W. L. Sublette, February 2, 1844, Sublette MSS; *Daily Picayune* (New Orleans), February 6, 1844.

Before Andrew left for the West, Frances Hereford and William were married. Rev. William S. Potts, a prominent local clergyman and former president of Marion College, rode out to Sulphur Springs on March 31, and performed a simple evening marriage ceremony according "to the form prescribed by the General Assembly of the Presbyterian Church in the United States of America." Frances was fond of the country and of her husband's farm, and settled down with him to a rural life. Stewart wrote that he knew their marriage would be "a source of great comfort," yet some gossip surrounded the wedding, since it was said that Frances had "formed a prior attachment to Solomon." It is more than possible, however, that she scarcely knew him.[15]

In the spring Sublette was concerned for Frances, her mother, and Campbell—all were ill, but recovered—and was busy with many problems. His crops were "only tolerable" and had to be carefully nurtured until harvest, repairs had to be made on the house, the coal mines needed supervision, tools and equipment had to be repaired and replaced, and several Negroes had to be hired to supplement his labor force during the warmer months. Also, he retained his interest in the fur trade and from time to time until his death did what he could to aid friends in the West. Solomon thought William might go West again in 1844, and there seems to be some little evidence that he even considered an expedition in 1845. In January of that year Bernard Pratte asked him to join him in incorporating a western trading company, but William rejected the opportunity.[16]

His properties, widely scattered as they were, demanded much of his time. Recently, he had purchased four lots in Jefferson City and an additional 180 acres of land in Cole County. His old friend Bowlin was much involved in the property transfers and as a friendly gesture proudly named his new son "William Sublette Bowlin." While William added property in Cole County, he sold property in St. Louis County. In March, 1844, he sold

---

[15] W. L. Sublette's Marriage Certificate, March 21, 1844, Sublette MSS; Chittenden, *The American Fur Trade*, I, 225; Marriage Record 3, From January 4, 1843–February 18, 1848, p. 73, MS, St. Louis CRDO.

[16] Bernard Pratte to W. L. Sublette, January 15, 1845, Sublette MSS.

52 acres; in July, another 52 acres; and in March, 1845, sold 6 acres of his Sulphur Springs plot to his mother-in-law Mrs. Esther S. Hereford. He sold Campbell his interest in lot fourteen of Christy's Addition.[17]

His interest in the large tract of land he and his friends held at the site of Kansas City was uncertain. In the summer of 1844, Edmund Chouteau offered to buy one of his lots there, but he probably refused to sell. Shortly before Christmas an associate investor in the tract wrote Sublette that a warehouse and two stores were built and that they believed the Santa Fé trade would "go thear [sic] to Kansas City next Spring." He asked William to pressure the state legislature to license a ferry at Kansas City and personally to grant a power of attorney to "some one or two to make Deeds to Lots." Sublette was uninterested.[18]

Commercial life in St. Louis was brought to a standstill by the great flood of the summer of 1844. Refugees took shelter in county barns, but after the waters receded, business reopened and flourished. Variety shops, mercantile stores, and moneylenders did a thriving trade, and the city grew. Sublette, however, could find little in that world to interest him. Several of his friends believed he would make an ideal superintendent of Indian affairs at St. Louis and appealed to the President in his behalf. In December, 1844, his fellow Democratic electors wrote President-elect Polk: "We know of no man so well calculated from his thorough knowledge of Indian character . . . to preside over this department, and we cheerfully recommend him to you on the high ground that he has also been at all times, a warm and con sistent Democrat." William was pleased with the letter and on March 21 wrote Benton, mentioning the recommendation and asking the Senator to use his best offices to secure him the post.

[17] Deed Record E, pp. 551–52, F, pp. 224, 413, S, pp. 40–41, Cole CRDO; Original (Deed Record) G-3, pp. 301, 321, I-3, p. 227, R-3, p. 145, K, pp. 221–22, H-3, pp. 220–21; MSS, General Record (Deed Record) Q-3, p. 361, MSS, St. Louis CRDO.

[18] Edmund Chouteau to W. L. Sublette, August 9, 1844; O. Caldwell to W. L. Sublette, December 20, 1844; W. Gillis to W. L. Sublette, January 20, 1845[?], Sublette MSS.

Thomas A. Harvey, the acting superintendent in St. Louis, was a Tyler appointee, and Sublette believed he should be removed.[19]

Later in the spring additional pressure was brought to bear upon the President. Bowlin, W. P. Hale, and Edward Dobyns wrote the War Department to recommend Sublette, and on May 22, a committee of seventy-five well-known St. Louisans, Campbell included, sent the President a joint letter which said: "We have no hesitation in vouching for his character and qualifications; and asserting without the fear of successful contradiction that Col. Sublette's appointment . . . would be hailed with more joy in this state, than the appointment of any other man." Nevertheless, Polk refused to take any immediate action. Sublette and his wife, both in ill health and under Dr. Beaumont's care, waited at Sulphur Springs—waited for a message that did not come.[20]

He resolved finally to go East for his health. Perhaps he would spend most of the summer at Cape May, New Jersey, and at the opportune moment take a trip to Washington to see the President personally about the appointment. He knew that his recommendations were honest: few men in the West knew more about Indians. Had he not befriended them on many occasions? He could remember that in 1834 he and Campbell had gone to considerable trouble to rescue an Omaha Indian woman taken prisoner by the Iowa Indians. Also it seems he had allowed certain Indians to camp in the rear of his store in St. Louis, and tradition holds that he buried deceased Indian friends at his farm. He had once administered the estate of an Indian chief, bore at least three tribal names, and had both fought and lived with the red men.

On July 14, he, Frances, her sister Mary Hereford, Camp-

[19] The Democratic Electors of Missouri to James K. Polk, December 5, 1844; W. L. Sublette to Thomas H. Benton, March 21, 1845, Sublette MSS.

[20] W. P. Hale to the President of the United States, April 7, 1845, James B. Bowlin to the War Department, June 13, 1845, Edward Dobyns to the Indian Office, July 7, 1845, and President Polk to the War Department, June 30, 1845, Letters Received, 1845, Records of the Office of Indian Affairs, Record Group No. 75, MSS, N. A.; James B. Bowlin to the War Department, June 13, 1845, Thomas Hart Benton to the War Department, July 11, 1845, and W. P. Hale to the War Department, April 5, 1845, Letters Received, 1844-45, Records of the Office of the Secretary of War, Record Group No. 107, MSS, N. A.; Letter of St. Louis Businessmen's Committee to President Polk, May 22, 1845, Sublette MSS.

bell, and a Negro servant left St. Louis on the steamboat "Swift-sure, No. 3" bound for Cincinnati and Pittsburgh. The Hereford family agreed to care for the farm, and his business friend James W. Smoot consented to collect several notes which were due to expire in Sublette's absence. They passed Cairo on the fifteenth, made a short stop at Louisville, and reached Cincinnati the following day. Campbell's cousin Robert Buchanan greeted them at the wharf, and the next afternoon, Thursday, July 17, they boarded another steamer, the "Uncle Ben," and continued up the Ohio. According to Campbell, William was in "full health," although they had purchased "Sundries Ice & Medicines & C" in Cincinnati.[21]

Sublette was seriously ill by the eighteenth or nineteenth, when they reached Pittsburgh. On the twenty-second, while still aboard the boat, he drew up a new will in which Frances was given the bulk of his estate, including approximately one-half of Sulphur Springs. Andrew and Solomon were granted the remainder of the springs plus some minor land tracts and personal property. Theresa Cook was bequeathed a slave girl, another slave girl was to be freed within a year, and Campbell was to share with Frances any "surplus coming to my estate from the business of Sublette & Campbell." Andrew and Campbell were appointed executors, but nowhere in the document was there any hint, as has been charged, that Sublette, in order to prevent Frances from remarrying, "willed his property to his wife on condition that she should not change her name."[22]

As soon as quarters were available in Pittsburgh, the party moved into the city. A disastrous fire the previous April had burned over a large section of the metropolitan area, and hotel accommodations were at a premium. Sublette was moved into room No. 8 at the Exchange Hotel. Dr. William Addison, who resided nearby and was a well-known medical man, highly re-

21 "Correspondence of Robert Campbell, 1834–1845," *loc. cit.*, 65; *Daily Cincinnati Gazette*, July 17, 19, 1845; *Daily Missouri Republican* (St. Louis), July 12, 1845.

22 Deed Record U–3, p. 247, MSS, St. Louis CRDO; Record of Wills C, pp. 181–82, MSS, St. Louis PC.

spected as a local historian and naturalist as well as a physician, was consulted. Sublette failed rapidly; Dr. Addison could do little. The "taint of consumption" took its toll, and on Wednesday, July 23, William died, far from his beloved Sulphur Springs, farther from the mountains.[23]

Late in the afternoon or early on Thursday evening, Campbell took Frances and her sister to the levee and placed them aboard a steamer, probably the "North Bend," scheduled to leave for St. Louis in the morning. Hired servants carried William's remains aboard, but Campbell could not accompany them home, since he had "to proceed to Philadelphia" on emergency business and family affairs. He gave the two bereaved and lonely women a letter addressed to his cousin in Cincinnati, in the event they were delayed there on their way down-river. It took them thirteen days to reach St. Louis, possibly on account of inclement weather, a shallow channel, or stops in Cincinnati or Louisville. They were home by the seventh, and Sublette's remains were immediately taken to the farm to be prepared for burial in the family plot. The *Daily Missouri Republican*, his political adversary in life, commented, "His death is as unexpected as it will be sincerely deplored by numerous friends all over the state."[24]

Carriages gathered at the corner of Fourth and Chestnut early in the morning on a cloudy August 8, a short distance from the old Sublette-Campbell store. All "friends of the deceased" were invited to join the funeral procession to the farm, where services were to be held. The mourners slowly moved out the Old Manchester Road through a slight shower, and at Sulphur Springs, with the Herefords, neighbors, friends, and slaves in attendance, William was buried near his great stone house.[25]

[23] *Daily Morning Post* (Pittsburgh), July 25, 1845. The *Post* gave July 24 as the date of death. Campbell, in a letter to Robert Buchanan, stated that it was July 23, and the *Daily Missouri Republican* (St. Louis), August 1, 1845, accepted that date.

[24] "Correspondence of Robert Campbell, 1834–1845," *loc. cit.*, 65; *Pittsburgh Morning Chronicle*, July 25, 1845; *Daily Missouri Republican* (St. Louis), August 8, 1845; *Boonville Observer*, August 12, 1845; *Saint Louis American*, August 1, 1845; *Lexington Weekly Express*, August 12, 1845.

[25] *Daily Missouri Republican* (St. Louis), August 1, 8, 1845.

Frances was consoled by her brothers and sisters "to ask the Almighty for solace and to rely upon her many relatives around her." Since Andrew was still in the West, Campbell, aided by Micijah Tarver as counsel, began to settle the estate. By September 15, Sublette's will was recorded, and two weeks later his personal estate was appraised at slightly over $7,500. Campbell then proceeded to carry out the bequests of the will, but would not complete his duties until 1857, since there were difficulties over remaining partnership accounts, suits in debt, and the Kansas City lands. At times he had sharp differences of opinion with Frances because she was a competent manager of her share of Sulphur Springs and resented Campbell's knowledge of her affairs.[26]

Andrew, having reached Missouri in early autumn, 1845, aided Campbell whenever possible with the estate. Andrew, however, was not content to become a farmer—no more content than he had been five years before—and after a short visit to the Whitleys in Kentucky the next year, looked around for a new occupation. Since the Mexican War was under way, he offered his services to the Missouri Mounted Volunteers for the duration; was accepted as a captain in charge of Company A, Oregon Battalion; and on September 22, 1847, was ordered "to proceed to Grand Island on the Platte River . . . as escort to Lieutenant D. P. Woodbury." Andrew was mustered out November 6, 1848, at Fort Leavenworth and the following June accompanied navy Lieutenant Edward Fitzgerald Beale from St. Louis overland with messages to California. In California he worked in the gold fields for a time, but the work was detrimental to his precarious health and he fell ill. Grove Cook took him into his home and nursed him back to health. In 1851 or 1852, Andrew was in Los Angeles, where he formed a partnership with James Thompson to supply wheat to the superintendent of Indian affairs in California. Before the contract could be fulfilled, however, he died as the result of an encounter with a grizzly bear while hunting in the hills

26 Record of Wills C, p. 183, MSS; File of Estate of William L. Sublette, File 2052, MSS, St. Louis PC.

near his home. Some of the Herefords who had by then settled at Los Angeles arranged for his burial on December 20, 1853.[27]

Thomas Hereford, after Thompson, Andrew's business partner, resigned the position, served as administrator of the estate. Thompson had estimated that Andrew's property was worth approximately $5,000, but Hereford estimated that after he had paid all Andrew's debts scarcely $2,000 would remain, since, as he said in a letter to Solomon, "As long as he [Andrew] had money every one that wanted any of it got it as you well knew his propensities for cards." When a final settlement was made early in 1857, Hereford informed Solomon that property valued at only $200 remained.[28]

Solomon did not return to St. Louis until early September, 1846, after an absence of three years in the West. During those years he engaged in the Indian trade, found his way to California, and kept up an intermittent correspondence with his family. After parting with William at Laramie Fork in the summer of 1843, Solomon traveled south to the Platte-Arkansas River area, where he met Andrew in 1844 at Bent's Fort. They were at Taos in October, then back on the Arkansas, and in the spring of 1845, he was in Taos once again. During the summer of that year, Andrew set out for St. Louis, but Solomon turned west, joined a small group of fifteen adventurers, and on October 5, reached Sutter's Fort in California. He spent the next seven months on the Pacific Coast between Sutter's domain and Los Angeles, saw Grove Cook, traded in land and animals, and made a name for himself on Christmas Eve, 1845, when at Yerba Buena (San Francisco) he and a group of celebrants awakened a local merchant and abused him "shamefully." In May, 1846, he started for St. Louis by a circuitous route—happy to be on his way home.[29]

[27] File of Andrew W. Sublette, Capt. U. S. A., 1846–48, Records of the Adjutant General's Office, Record Group No. 94, MSS, N. A.; *Sacramento Daily Union*, December 29, 1853; File of Estate of Andrew W. Sublette, No. 43¼, MSS, Los Angeles CPC; A. W. Sublette to S. P. Sublette, March 20, 1850, Sublette MSS; *San Francisco Herald*, June 8, 1853; *St. Louis Globe Democrat*, April 30, 1899.

[28] *Los Angeles Star*, December 31, 1853, April 22, 1854; Thomas Hereford to Solomon P. Sublette, September 18, 1854, January 20, 1857, Sublette MSS.

He petitioned Benton for a job in the Indian Service, particularly to fill any vacancy which might occur in the Missouri Agency. Benton promised help, although he could not secure an immediate appointment. Meanwhile, Solomon waited and, while waiting, carried a mail express shipment from St. Louis to Santa Fé. Upon his return he was commissioned, October 21, 1847, "agent for the United tribe of Sacs & Foxes of the Mississippi." The *Jefferson Inquirer*, more out of faith than knowledge of the man involved, predicted he would fill the job efficiently, but he held it scarcely six months, then resigned in April, 1848, because of "continuous sickness."[30]

Frances, who had been ill and despondent during the winter of 1847–48, planned to accompany her brother Thomas to the West to seek better health. She met Solomon at Independence— he had proposed—and in something of a surprise ceremony in May, 1848, they were married. They remained in Independence several months. Frances returned to the farm in the spring of 1849, although Solomon did not return until the late autumn or early winter. That year Theresa Cook died in the cholera epidemic in St. Louis, and on May 17, the old Sublette-Campbell store was swept away in a great business-district fire. Fortunately, the insurance on the building was enough to cover the loss and to settle once and for all the last debts of the old partnership.

After 1849, Solomon and Frances spent most of their time in St. Louis County at the Sublette farm. They learned that crop raising was a difficult, many times a costly, business. Their family obligations gradually increased. Frances had given birth to her first child, a son, Solomon Perry, Jr., in December, 1849. A daughter, Esther Frances, followed in October, 1853; then another son, William Hugh, in June, 1856. Both sons died before the age of

[29] *Daily Missouri Republican* (St. Louis), September 11, 1846; S. P. Sublette to W. L. Sublette, February 2, April 18, May 5, 1844; S. P. Sublette to A. W. Sublette, May 5, June 6, October 20, 1844; J. A. Sutter to S. P. Sublette, December 22, 1845, Sublette MSS; Vol. III, Part 4 (315) and Vol. IV, Part 1 (6), 1845–46, Larkin MSS; *New Helvetia Diary . . .* , 5–6.

[30] Solomon P. Sublette to Thomas H. Benton, December 11, 16, 1846; United States War Department to Solomon P. Sublette, October 21, 1847, Sublette MSS; *Jefferson Inquirer* (Jefferson City), November 6, 1847.

two and the sorrow of their deaths seriously affected their mother's health. In August, 1855, she made a will in which she left all her property to Solomon, except for one hundred acres to go to her daughter. Solomon died first, on August 31, 1857, but Frances quickly followed, on September 28 of the same year. The Herefords at the farm took charge of young Esther Frances (Fannie), who was also in poor health and survived only until May 6, 1861, when she died and was buried in the family plot. The Herefords considered themselves legitimate heirs to Sulphur Springs, since Fannie was the last of her line—the last of an entire branch of the Sublette family.[31]

Solomon and Frances, after their marriage, had moved into new quarters on the farm—probably into the house occupied by the Herefords near the southeast corner of the tract, facing what is now Shaw Avenue. In the same year, 1848, lawyers representing Solomon, Frances, and Andrew sold 388 acres of the springs tract, including resort facilities and the stone house, to David W. Graham. Two years later Graham resold 29.99 acres of that tract—acres containing the house and resort—to Thomas Allen. Much of the remaining land Graham subdivided. Allen, who was a leading St. Louis businessman and a power in the Missouri Pacific Railroad, offered in November, 1853, to sell or lease the resort and house either as a private estate or as "a suitable place for a public resort, or for a water cure." The railroad which he represented had opened a station at Cheltenham quite close to the resort, and visitors could commute easily to St. Louis. He was unsuccessful, however, and two years later was still advertising the resort.[32]

Finally, he found a buyer. On February 1, 1858, for the

[31] *In the Supreme Court of Missouri, October Term, 1902,* pp. 159–60; File of Estate of Solomon P. Sublette, File 5072, MSS; File of Estate of Frances S. Sublette, File 5073, MS, St. Louis PC; Church Record (Baptized Children), entry of May 8, 1859, MS, Central Presbyterian Church, Clayton, Missouri; Notes on the Sublette Burial Ground, Bellefontaine Cemetery Records, 1868, MS, Bellefontaine Cemetery, St. Louis.

[32] General Records Z–4, pp. 273–74, and W–5, pp. 388–89, MSS, St. Louis CRDO; *Saint Louis Daily Evening News,* November 9, 1853; *Daily Missouri Republican* (St. Louis), February 13, 1855.

sum of $25,000—$8,000 in cash—he conveyed the entire tract and all its buildings to two men who were spokesmen for a small, local French Icarian community. The Icarians, devoted followers of Étienne Cabet, a utopian-communist who had died in St. Louis two years before, established themselves at the resort and discovered that Sublette's stone house was large enough to shelter nearly the entire brotherhood. Yet they could not meet the payments on the property, disbanded in 1864, and returned the entire tract to Allen. The following year he sold it for $18,000 to Samuel Humbleton and James Green of St. Louis, who in turn transferred it to Theodore Kock. By 1870, the resort was in near ruin, and the River des Peres had turned into a typhoid- and malaria-ridden sewer. The Icarians had suffered from the pestilential waters, and the *St. Louis Times* related in 1872 that "the cottage [resort] and spring have both fallen into bad repute and the odor of one is nearly as bad as that of the other." The Sublette mansion, according to the Icarian reports, was destroyed by fire three years later.[33]

That portion of Sulphur Springs not sold by Solomon, Frances, and Andrew in 1848 was the tract engrossed by the Herefords after little Fannie's death. Five years later they subdivided the tract and in June, 1869, began to sell one-acre building lots in the "Fairmount" portion of the estate. Mary C. Hereford participated in the dedication, at which refreshments were served to omnibus-loads of prospective buyers from the city. The previous year she had arranged for the bodies of the Sublette family, Micijah Tarver, and several slaves to be moved from the burial ground at the farm to a large lot in Bellefontaine Cemetery, where a sizable granite shaft was erected to mark their final resting place.[34]

The last valuable tracts of Sublette's landed empire were being distributed when the question of legal title to the property was raised. In the spring of 1895, a few descendants of the Whitley

33 General Records, Book 196, p. 392 Book 313, p. 115–16, Book 336, pp. 321–22, MSS, St. Louis CRDO; *St. Louis Times*, August 4, 1872; Jules Prud-hommeaux, *Icarie et son Fondateur Étienne Cabet*, 440.

34 *Saint Louis Dispatch*, June 9, 1869.

family met in St. Louis and organized as heirs of the Sublette estate "that they might all act in unison." A leading St. Louis lawyer, Judge Thomas B. Crews, who had been asked to handle their case and had opened a special estate office in downtown St. Louis, explained that by law they were entitled to one-fifth of Solomon's and one-half of Andrew's share in the tract of about 250 acres taken in by the Herefords. The property was valued by the *St. Louis Chronicle* at $27,000,000—a great overestimate.[35]

One intriguing aspect of the case soon presented itself and brought heirs from the Sublette family tree into the legal picture. Word had been received earlier that Pinckney W. Sublette had not been killed in the mountains in 1828, and was known to be alive in Civil War times. Shortly after receipt of that news, a will was produced which Solomon Sublette supposedly made in 1856—a will stating that if his daughter Fannie should die without issue, as she did, then all his property was to go "to my brother Pinckney W. Sublette if living and at his death if single . . . and without issue . . . to my next of kin on my fathers side."[36]

In the spring of 1896, a group of Sublette heirs presented the will for probate, but the court refused to honor it "upon the ground of the insufficiency of the evidence." The Whitley heirs thought best not to join forces with the Sublette heirs, but hoped the will would be accepted, since it would "have the effect of strengthening the evidence for all concerned." Judge Crews personally traveled west to Wyoming to view the reported remains of Pinckney, took depositions that convinced him of their authenticity, and had the bones and tombstone marked, "P. W. S. 1864," removed to St. Louis as evidence.[37]

The Whitley heirs had some difficulty raising the funds necessary to prepare their case for court, and the Sublette heirs

[35] *St. Louis Chronicle*, September 12, 1895; *St. Louis Post Dispatch*, October 26, 1923; Notes on Meeting of Whitley heirs, May 1, 1895; Letter of April 26, 1895, Whitley MSS.

[36] Photostat of Will of Solomon P. Sublette, April 15, 1856, Sublette MSS.

[37] Circular to the Whitley heirs, 1897[?]; Letter of October 13, 1898, Whitley MSS; *St. Louis Globe Democrat*, May 20, 1906; *St. Louis Post Dispatch*, January 28, 1926.

had even less success. By February, 1900, however, the Whitley heirs had arranged for court hearings, which opened before the St. Louis Circuit Court that year. The defendants were the numerous individuals and business firms who had secured titles from the Herefords to portions of the Sublette land. Some of the defendants already had acquired clear title through operation of Missouri's statute of limitations (ten years), and many others soon would have unencumbered title. Time was at a premium for the plaintiffs.[38]

The court refused to accept Pinckney's remains as evidence—if they were his remains—and decided in favor of the many defendants. Immediately the plaintiffs moved for a new trial, the motion was denied, and they appealed to the Missouri Supreme Court. In 1911 it upheld the lower court's decision, but as late as 1926 some heirs tried to revive the case in the St. Louis Circuit Court. It refused to reconsider, and two years later the Supreme Court, on appeal, refused to reopen litigation. The rapid westward growth of St. Louis had by then transformed Sulphur Springs into an industrial and residential area.[39]

"Pinckney's" bones were still in the St. Louis courthouse. In 1935, upon petition to the court by Perry Jenkins of Wyoming, a dust-covered box was returned to that state and there in July its contents "re-interred . . . at a celebration of the 100th anniversary of the grand rendezvous of 1835." The reburial of the remains was most appropriate, since they were placed in Sublette County, formed in 1921 through Jenkins' efforts in the Wyoming Legislature. To many westerners the remains now at rest beneath a stone monument on a bluff overlooking the upper Green River Valley certainly are those of Pinckney W. Sublette.[40]

38 Circular to the Whitley heirs, July, 1897; Letter of October 25, 1895, Whitley MSS.

39 Perry S. Rader (reporter), *Reports of Cases Determined by the Supreme Court of the State of Missouri Between February 18, 1928, and May 18, 1928*, 128.

40 Charles Kelly to Edna Martin, August 12, 1935, Bancroft Library Correspondence File, MSS, Bancroft Library. The quotation is from a newspaper clipping (no title or date) in possession of the University of Wyoming Division of Archives, Laramie.

The Sublettes—William, Milton, Andrew, Pinckney, and Solomon—were part of the solid foundation placed beneath American westward expansion. Their lives extended from Kentucky, where they were born—not with the proverbial silver spoon, but with one of better than average metal—to the mountains. The fur trade was the key to their careers. Each exploited the West's resources and learned the West's secrets; yet only William took the first wagons to the Popo Agie; only he divided the fur empire with the Astor interests; only he built a landed estate from his western profits; and only he was the West's ardent spokesman. Of the five, he knew best what he wanted and believed he knew what the nation needed: an agrarian commonwealth. His was the dream of Arcadia.

The Ancestry
of Phillip A. Sublette

GENEALOGISTS INTERESTED in the Sublette family have formulated rather divers interpretations of Phillip A. Sublette's line of descent from the original Abraham and Susanne Sublette (sometimes spelled Soblet, Soublett, or Soublette), who reached Virginia fifteen years after the revocation of the Edict of Nantes. A careful examination of the available records has suggested principally one line of descent which, until contrary evidence is produced, may be given serious consideration.

When the first Abraham Sublette died in 1716, he left either four or five children. Most likely there were five: Pierre Louis, Abraham, Jr., Jacques, Ann, and Littleberry. Pierre Louis married Marte (Martha) Martain in 1723, and had four to six children, definite lines of descent being traceable through at least three: William, Benjamin, and Louis. Until the early 1780's no Sublettes had entered Kentucky, but remained concentrated in Chesterfield and Powhatan counties, Virginia. Beginning in 1780 with Lewis Sublette, several received land grants in Kentucky, and after 1820 the grants were numerous.

Louis Sublette, son of Pierre Louis and Martha, married Frances McGruder in Virginia about 1745. Of their numerous progeny (perhaps seven), one son, Abraham, saw service in the

Virginia militia and moved to Lincoln County, Kentucky, in 1798 or 1799. Later, in 1810, records reveal that he had moved with his family to Green County, Kentucky. One of his sons, a younger Abraham, was the same year a resident of Pulaski County, Kentucky.

Lewis Sublette, another son of Louis and Frances, although having received a military land grant in Kentucky in 1780, was a resident of Chesterfield County, Virginia, as late as 1783. In that year or early in 1784, however, he took his wife, Mary Trabue Sublette, and large family to Kentucky to settle on Greer Creek in Fayette (later Woodford) County and operated a ferry across the Kentucky River. Mary Trabue Sublette died in the 1790's, and her husband subsequently married Sarah Samuels. He died in 1827, leaving his widow in possession of his home. His children were Lewis, Jr., John T., Frances, James, and William.

Littleberry Sublette, Sr., whom we may regard as the father of Phillip A. Sublette, probably was a brother to Lewis Sublette, Sr., of Woodford County. There is adequate proof in the records of Green County, Kentucky, that Littleberry, Sr., left at least five sons: Littleberry, Jr., Joseph Burton, Lenious Bolin, Hill (Hilly), and Samuel (see footnote 8, Chapter I). Other children, including Phillip A. Sublette, either appear in earlier Virginia records (Chesterfield County) or may be presumed through later family testimony to have been of that particular branch. A complete check of all extant Kentucky county tax lists failed to produce the name of Phillip A. Sublette before his marriage to Isabella Whitley in 1797. It is reasonably certain that he reached Kentucky with Littleberry, Sr., and the others in 1796, and, leaving them in Woodford County, went on to Lincoln County.

Two other Sublettes, William and Benjamin, Sr., both brothers of Louis Sublette and uncles of Littleberry, Sr., left large families, many members of whom settled in Kentucky in Warren, Lincoln, Adair, and Green counties. By the 1820's there were scores of Sublettes in Kentucky, living in widely scattered areas.

SOURCES: Willard R. Jillson, *The Kentucky Land Grants* ("Filson

Club Publications," No. 33 [Louisville, 1925]), 124, 241, 418, 738; Willard R. Jillson, *Old Kentucky Entries and Deeds* ("Filson Club Publications," No. 34 [Louisville, 1926]), 65, 292, 363, 532. Annie W. Burns, Abstracts of Pension Papers of Soldiers in the Revolutionary War, War of 1812 and Indian Wars, Who Settled in Lincoln County Kentucky, 34, MSS, State Historical Society of Missouri, Columbia, Missouri; Third Census of the United States (1810), Kentucky Population Schedules, Record Group No. 29, MSS, N. A.; First Census of the United States (1790), Virginia Population Schedules, Record Group No. 29, MSS, N. A.; Deed Record D, p. 278, MSS, Woodford CC, Versailles, Kentucky; File of Estate of John T. Sublette, File Box 30–31, MSS, Woodford CC; Huntley Dupre, "The French in Early Kentucky," *Filson Club History Quarterly*, XV, (April, 1941), 91; File of Estate of Lewis Sublette, File Box 32–33, MSS, Woodford CC; Will Book I, pp. 71–72, MSS, Woodford CC; Woodford County Tax Lists, 1791–97, MSS, Kentucky Historical Society.

The Brothers
of Phillip A. Sublette

Two BROTHERS of Phillip A. Sublette had settled in Missouri by 1823. Lenious Bolin (sometimes spelled "Bolon" or "Bowling") was in St. Clair County, Illinois, in November, 1819, on his way to Cape Girardeau County, Missouri, where he made his home after 1820 in Randal Township. There, in all probability, he ran a ferry at Cape Girardeau. When he died late in 1849, he left a wife and five children: James G., John A., Robert L. B., Mary Anne, and H. Clara Sublette.

Littleberry Sublette, the second brother, married in Green County, Kentucky, in 1814, but did not reach Missouri until over ten years later, when he settled on a 160-acre tract two and one-half miles east of Liberty in Clay County. He and his wife remained there and reared a large family.

Another of Phillip's brothers, Joseph Burton, also may have moved to Missouri as early as 1820, but there is so little information that a definite statement may not be made. Two others, Hill (Hilly) and Maston Sublette, apparently Phillip's brothers, may have joined Joseph Burton in Missouri. Other Sublettes, either closely or distantly related to Phillip's family, were in the Missouri-Illinois region. Thomas Sublette was in St. Louis by 1818, and eventually settled in the Cape Girardeau area. There was a letter in the St. Louis Post Office in 1820 for either Samuel or Abraham Sublette, and two years later a Samuel Sublette was listed as a tax delinquent in Cape Girardeau County. In 1825 another letter was being held in the Edwardsville, Illinois, Post Office for George A. Sublette. There was at least one William Sublette in western Illinois. Such a person, with a wife Nancy, lived at Lebanon in 1821–22. He or another William was engaged in a slave transaction at the same time in Cape Girardeau County, and it is probable that this William is the same one who operated Brown's Tavern at the sign of General Jackson on Main Street in Jackson, Missouri, during 1820–21.

SOURCES: *In the Supreme Court of Missouri, October Term 1902*, 67, 69, 70; *Missouri Herald* (Jackson), April 1, 8, 1820; *Independent Patriot* (Jackson), April 7, May 26, December 22, 1821, January 9, March 9, May 4, July 27, 1822, April 19, 1823; January 10, July 10, October 9, 1824, October 7, December 6, 1826; *St. Louis Enquirer*, April 8, 1820; *Missouri Advocate and St. Louis Enquirer*, May 6, 1826; *Missouri Intelligencer* (Franklin), September 20, 1820; *Missouri Gazette & Public Advertiser* (St. Louis), October 9, 1818; *Edwardsville Spectator*, October 8, 1825; Circuit Court Record B, pp. 65, 195, 213, MSS, Cape Girardeau CCC, Jackson, Missouri; Will of Lenious B. Sublette, December 4, 1849, Original Wills S, MSS, Cape Girardeau CPC; Deed Record F, pp. 29, 88, 274–75, MSS, Cape Girardeau CCC; Deed Record G, pp. 380–81, 451–52, 467–68, MSS, Cape Girardeau CCC; Deed Record B, pp. 65–66, MSS, Clay CRDO, Liberty, Missouri; Deed Record E, pp. 263–64, MSS, Clay CRDO; Annie W. Burns, Marriages and Wills Green County Kentucky (1800–40), MSS, Filson Club Library; The Little (Marriage) Book, 1793–1819, pp. 109, 112, MSS, Green CC; File of *Thomas Peniston et al. v. Summons Henry A. Steppe*, File 8027, MSS, St. Louis CCC; Sublette MSS. The archives of St. Clair County, Illinois, carry numerous references to William and Nancy Sublette as well as to other Sublettes such as Abraham and August B.

Articles of Agreement

ARTICLES OF AGREEMENT made and entered in to this 18th day of July 1826 by and between William H Ashley of the first part and Jedediah S Smith David E Jackson and Wm L. Sublette trading under the firm Smith Jackson & Sublette of the second part witnesseth that whereas the said party of the second part are now engaged in the fur trade and contemplate renewing their stock of merchandise for the ensuing year for the purpose of continuing their said business should their prospects of success Justify their doing so now Therefore the said party of the first part promises and hereby obliges himself to furnish such an assortment of merchandise as said party of the second part may require according with an Invoice hereunto annexed reference thereunto will more fully show and for the prices mentioned to wit Gunpowder of the first and second quality at one dollar fifty per pound Lead one dollar per pound Shot at one dollar twenty five cents per pound Three point blankets at nine dollars each Green ditto at eleven dollars each Scarlet cloth at six dollars per yard Blue ditto common quality from four to five dollars per yard Butcher knives at seventy cents each two and a half point blankets at seven dollars each North West Fuzils at twenty four dollars each Tin kettles different sizes at two dollars per pound Sheet iron kettles at two dollars twenty five cents per pound Squaw axes at two dollars fifty cents each. Beaver traps at nine dollars each Sugar at one dollar per pound Coffee at one dollar twenty five cents per pound flour at one dollar per pound Alspice at one dollar fifty cents per pound Raisins at one dollar fifty cents per pound Grey cloth at common quality at five dollars per yard flannel common quality at one dollar fifty cents per yard Callicoes assorted at one dollar per yard domestic cotton at one dollar twenty five cents per yard Thread assorted at three dollars per pound Worsted [?] binding at fifteen dollars per —— finger rings at five dollars per gross Beads assorted at two fifty cents per pound Vermillion at three dollars per pound fills [files?] assorted at two dollars fifty cents per pound fourth proof rum reduced at thirteen dollars fifty cents per gallon Bridles assorted seven dollars each Spurs at two dollars per pair Horse shoes and nails at two dollars per pound Tin pans assorted at two dollars per pound handkerchiefs assorted at one dollar fifty cents each. Ribbons assorted at three dollars per bolt Buttons at five dollars per gross Looking glasses at fifty cents each flints at fifty cents per dozen Mockacine [?] alls at twenty five cents per dozen Tobacco at one dollar twenty five cents per pound copper kettles at three dollars per pound Iron buckles assorted at two dollars fifty cents per pound finc Steele at two dollars per pound Dried fruit at one dollar fifty cents per pound Washing soap at one dollar twenty five cents per pound Shaving soap at two dollars per pound first quality James River Tobacco at one dollar seventy five cents per pound Steel bracelets at one dollar fifty cents per pair Large brass wire at two dollars per pound which merchandise is to be by said Ashley or his agent delivered to said Smith Jackson & Sublette or to their agent at or near the west end of the little lake of Bear river a water of the Pacific Ocean on or before the first day of July 1827 without some unavoidable occurrence should prevent. but as it is uncertain whether the situation of said Smith Jackson & Sublettes business will justify the proposed purchase of merchandise as aforesaid it is understood and agreed between the said parties that the said party of the second part shall send an express to said

Ashley to reach him in St. Louis on or before the first day of March next with orders to forward the merchandise as aforesaid, and on its arrival at its place of destination, that they the said Smith Jackson & Sublette will pay him the said Ashley the amount for merchandise sold them on this day for which the said Ashley holds their notes payable the first day of July 1827 for. and it is further understood that the amount of merchandise to be delivered as aforesaid on or before the first of July 1827 shall not be less than seven thousand dollars nor more than fifteen thousand and [?] it [?] is [?] in [?] the power of said party of the second part to make further payment in part or in whole for the merchandise there [?] to be delivered that they will do so if not that they will pay the amount at St. Louis on or before the first day of October in the year 1828 but if the said party of the first part receive no order from said party of the second part to forward said merchandise as aforesaid or direction not to forward it by or before the time before mentioned then this article of agreement to be null and void and it is understood and agreed between the two said parties that so long as the said Ashley continues to furnish said Smith Jackson & Sublette with merchandise as aforesaid That he will furnish no other company or individuals with merchandise other than those who may be in his immediate service.

John Sublette

FREQUENTLY, in Western Americana, historians are obliged to give their opinions, individually or collectively, upon the claims raised by a particular person that he was the descendant of some eminent mountaineer. Such a work as this on William L. Sublette and his family would be incomplete without at least one such contention. The claim here referred to is that of John Sublette of Carbon County, Wyoming, a widower, who died on October 3, 1928, at the age of eighty-eight, leaving three surviving sons and four daughters.[1] In 1913, fifteen years prior to his death, he was interviewed by Professor Grace Hebard of the University of Wyoming. At that time he stated that he was born March 5, 1840, in Platte County, Missouri, and that his parents were John Sublette, Sr., and Millie Donnel Sublette. He also stated that his father was originally from Kane Valley, Kentucky, and was "a brother to Milton, William, Solomon and Pinckney Sublette."[2]

Coutant located a transcript of the story and stated in his

---

[1] This information is from a newspaper clipping from the *Wyoming Tribune & Cheyenne State Leader* (November 19, 1928), now at the University of Wyoming.

[2] Statement of John Sublette to Grace Hebard, December 7, 1913, Hebard Collection, 1833–1935, MSS, University of Wyoming Division of Archives, Laramie.

History of Wyoming that John was the son of Andrew W. Sublette, no doubt believing that Andrew was synonymous with John Sublette, Sr. When the Federal Writers' Project *Guide to the Oregon Trail* was prepared, the story was included, and the location of John Sublette's small cabin, at Elk Mountain, Wyoming, was designated. Unfortunately his claim to fame was unknown until after the decision of the Supreme Court of Missouri regarding the Sublette lands, and it was not until 1925 that Judge Crews, who had been so active in the case, learned of John Sublette's existence.[3]

The author has investigated the claims of John Sublette as far as time and circumstances would permit. John Sublette's photographs reveal no striking family resemblance with those photographs available of Solomon and Andrew Sublette. Investigation into the circuit court and recorder's records of Platte County, Missouri, did not reveal the marriage of John Sublette, Sr., and Millie Donnel; nor did they reveal their presence in that county at any time. Kane Valley, Kentucky, however, was one of the regions in which the Sublettes of Kentucky settled at an early date. In addition, there was at least one John Sublette, and possibly more, among the nephews and grandnephews of Phillip A. Sublette, some of whom, as has been said, settled in Missouri.

The author has tentatively concluded, on the basis of his investigations and genealogical knowledge of the Sublette family, that John Sublette, of Elk Mountain, Wyoming, if closely related to William Sublette, was probably a second cousin, possibly the grandson of Littleberry Sublette of Clay County, Missouri.

[3] T. B. Crews to Dr. G. H. Hebard, March 20, 1925, Hebard Collection, 1833–1935, MSS, University of Wyoming Division of Archives, Laramie.

Bibliography

I. MANUSCRIPTS

A. *Collections*

Adams (David) Family Papers, 1809–69, MoSHi.

Ashley, William Henry, Papers, 1811–40, MoSHi.

Bellefontaine Cemetery Records, 1868, Bellefontaine Cemetery, St. Louis.

Campbell, Robert, Papers, 1825–79, MoSHi; Papers, 1832–42, William H. Semsrott, St. Louis; Papers, In Private hands, St. Louis.

Chouteau-Maffitt Collection, 1828–54, MoSHi.

Chouteau-Papin Collection, 1753–1872, MoSHi.

Chouteau-Walsh Collection, 1794–1869, MoSHi.

Clark, William, Papers, 1766–1899, MoSHi; Papers, 1825–32, KHi.

Dobyns Family Papers, 1867–76, MoSHi.

Documents on Microfilm from the Records of the Department of the Interior now in the National Archives Relating to the Fur Trade of the Missouri River Area, 1823–40, MoSHi.

Draper Collection of Kentucky Manuscripts (Microfilms of the Draper Collection in the State Historical Society of Wisconsin), 1775–1845, Filson Club, Louisville.

Drips, Andrew, Papers, 1832–60, MoSHi.

Emmons, Benjamin, Collection, 1768–1942, MoSHi.

Englemann, George, Letter Book G, 1843, Missouri Botanical Library, St. Louis.

Ermatinger, Edward, Letters, 1828–56, Provincial Historical Society, Victoria, B. C.

Field, Matthew and Cornelia, Letters (Harvard Microfilm Collection), 1843, MoSHi.

Field (Ludlow-Field), Collection, 1842–44, MoSHi.

Flint, Timothy and Abel, Letters, 1817–18, MoSHi.

Hebard, Grace, Collection, 1833–1935, University of Wyoming Division of Archives, Laramie.

Kingsbury, J. W., Collection, 1791–1911, MoSHi.

Larkin, Thomas O., Documents for the History of California. Papers of the Consul of the U. S. in California before the Conquest, Vols. III and IV, 1845–46, Bancroft Library, Berkeley.

Leonard, Abiel, Collection, 1786–1933, State Historical Society of Missouri, Columbia; Papers, 1769–1928, UMWMC, Columbia.

McLeod, John, Correspondence, 1812–44, Provincial Historical Society, Victoria, B. C.

Sappington Family Papers, 1810–65, MoSHi.

Sibley Family Papers, 1803–53, Lindenwood College, St. Charles, Missouri.

Smith, Jedediah S., Letters, 1827–31, KHi.

Sublette Family Papers, 1819–60, MoSHi.

U. M. O., Letter Book B (P. Chouteau Collection), 1823–35, MoSHi.

Vasquez Family Papers, 1797–1860, MoSHi.

Whitley Heirs (Sublette Estate), Papers, 1895–1907, John E. Sunder, Austin, Texas.

B. *Individual Items*

Alexander Ross' Journal of the Snake Country Expedition of 1824, Oregon Historical Society, Portland.

American Fur Company Account Books, 1822–60, MoSHi; Letter Books III and V, 1833–1836, New York Historical Society, New York City.

Applegate, J. Views of Oregon History, 1878, Bancroft Library.

Aull, James and Robert, Account Books, 1828–37; Aull Brothers Journal; Aull Brothers Letter Book III, Commercial Bank of Lexington, Missouri.

Baptisms, 1835–44, Old (Roman Catholic) Cathedral, St. Louis.

Burns, Annie Walker. Abstracts of Pension Papers of Soldiers in the Revolutionary War, War of 1812 and Indian Wars, Who

Settled in Lincoln County Kentucky, State Historical Society of Missouri; Marriages and Wills, Green County Kentucky (1800–40), Filson Club.

Church Record (Baptized Children), 1850–60, Central Presbyterian Church, Clayton, Missouri.

Diary (author unknown), May 14–July 13, 1835, Oregon Historical Society.

Ebbert, G. W. A Trapper's Life in the Rocky Mountains and Oregon from 1829 to 1839, Bancroft Library.

Farrar and Walker. Day Book, 1832–36, MoSHi.

Field, M. C. Diary of 1843, MoSHi.

Glauert, Ralph E. The Life and Activities of William Henry Ashley and His Associates, 1822–1826, A. M. thesis, Washington University, 1950.

Hunt, Wilson Price. Fur Account Book, 1840–41, MoSHi.

Inventory of the Trade Goods of Jedediah S. Smith, July 11, 1831, Museum and Historical Society of New Mexico, Santa Fé.

Kearny, S. W. Diary, September 17, 1824–May 10, 1826. MoSHi.

Kennerly, W. Clark. Diary, August 17–October 13, 1843, MoSHi.

Letters of A. Richey to A. D. Borradaile, February 26, 1832, Missouri History Envelope, MoSHi; Alma O. Tibbals to author, January 11, 1953; Charles Kelly to Edna Martin, August 12, 1935, Bancroft Library Correspondence File; David L. Hieb to author, October 1, 1951; Frederick Graff to Charles Graff, June 29, 1838, St. Louis Miscellaneous Envelope, MoSHi; Henry L. Ellsworth to E. Herring, November 8, 1833, Indians Envelope, MoSHi; J. W. Taylor to Jane Taylor, December 31, 1828, University of Washington Library, Seattle; James R. McDearmon to Martha A. McDearmon, December 6, 1830, and January 22, 1831; UMWMC; Jedediah Smith to Joel Poinsette, December 16, 1826, Pennsylvania Historical Society, Philadelphia; LeRoy Hafen to author, October 26, 1951; Mary H. Bruere to Mary D. Bruere, June 4, 1837, St. Louis Early Days No. 1 Envelope, MoSHi (on loan from C. Corwith Wagner, St. Louis); Perry W. Jenkins to author, September 26, 1951; Richard Rowland to his Sister, January 9, 1844, Oregon Historical Society; T. H. Benton to Governor Reynolds, November 10, 1842, Benton Family Papers, MoSHi; Tucker and Williams to Wyeth, December 22, 1932, Oregon Historical Society; W. H. Ashley to

Charles Macatester and Company, January 17, 1831, Simon Gratz Collection, Pennsylvania Historical Society.

Memoranda on the Road, 1836, Illinois Historical Society, Springfield.

Murphy, Joseph. Account Books, 1825–40, MoSHi.

Newell, Robert. Diary, 1829–43, University of Oregon Division of Archives, Eugene.

Nidever, George. Life and Adventures of George Nidever a Pioneer of California Since 1834, Bancroft Library.

Ogden, Peter Skene. Journal of Proceedings in the Snake Country Commencing in August, 1827, Oregon Historical Society.

Schell, H. S. Memoranda Forts Laramie and Kearny, 1870, Bancroft Library.

Shepard, Cyrus. Journal, 1834 (Spring–Summer), Coe Collection, Yale University Library, New Haven.

Spaulding, H. H. Narrative of an Overland Journey to Fort Vancouver and Lapwai in 1836 Together with an Account of the Beginning of the American Protestant Missions Beyond the Rockies, Oregon Historical Society.

Van Tassel, David D. A Study of the Influence of the Frontier on a Wisconsin Mining Town, M. S. Thesis, The University of Wisconsin, 1951.

White, James Haley. Reminiscences, 1822–23, St. Louis Reminiscences Envelope, MoSHi.

Wilcox, William Allen. Memoirs, 1830–45, St. Louis Reminiscences Envelope, MoSHi.

Work, John. Journal, July 5–September 15, 1826, University of Washington Library, Seattle.

II. PUBLIC RECORDS

A. *United States Government Records (National Archives)*

1. CENSUS BUREAU—RECORD GROUP NO. 29

First Census of the United States (1790), Virginia Population Schedules.

Third Census of the United States (1810), Kentucky Population Schedules.

2. DEPARTMENT OF STATE—RECORD GROUP NO. 59

Letter of William H. Ashley to the Secretary of State, March 23, 1831, Passport Applications.

3. GENERAL LAND OEEICE—RECORD GROUP NO. 49

Fayette Cash Entry No. 19935, November 10, 1841, Cash Entries for Fayette Land Office.

Lexington Cash Entries Nos. 5571 and 5573, September 7, 1838, Nos. 16564 and 16580, May 1, 1843, Cash Entries for Lexington Land Office.

4. OFFICE OF INDIAN AFFAIRS—RECORD GROUP NO. 75

Letters Received, 1824–41.

5. UNITED STATES ARMY—RECORD GROUP NO. 27

Weather Reports for Jefferson Barracks and the St. Louis Arsenal, Surgeon General's Office, 1830 and 1845, Meteorological Records of the Surgeon General's Office.

6. UNITED STATES ARMY (ADJUTANT GENERAL'S OFFICE)— RECORD GROUP NO. 94

Files of B. L. E. Bonneville, Capt. U. S. A., 1831–35, and Andrew W. Sublette, Capt. U. S. A., 1846–48.

Letters Received, 1843.

Post Returns, Jefferson Barracks, 1843.

Special Orders, 1840–51.

7. UNITED STATES ARMY (RECORDS OF THE OFFICE OF THE SECRETARY OF WAR)—RECORD GROUP NO. 107

Letters Received, 1836 and 1844.

Letters Sent, 1836.

Unregistered Letters Received, May, 1829.

B. *State of Missouri Records*

1. OFFICE OF THE SECRETARY OF STATE

Missouri Contracts, 1815–43.

Record and Index of U. S. Lands Sales, 10(B), 1831–34.

Records of Sale U. S. Land V (1836–39), and VI (1839–40).

2. OFFICE OF THE CLERK OF THE SUPREME COURT

Files of *Jos. W. Cunningham adms. David Cunningham* v. *Wm. L. Sublette*, Case No. 642, and *The State of Missouri to use of Sublette and Campbell* v. *Melton et al.*, Case No. 1387.

C. *County Records*

1. CALIFORNIA

File of Estate of Andrew W. Sublette, No. 43¼, 1853-57, Los Angeles CPC.

2. ILLINOIS

Common Law Chancery & Peo. Record, 1837-39, Adams CCC.
Deed Books 1, M, 1837-50, Adams CRDO.
Deed Record F, 1838, McLean CRDO.
Deed Records A, B, D, E, G, 1838-51, Jefferson CRDO.
Deed Records L, M, 1850-51, Macon CRDO.
Files of *Sublette and Campbell* v. *Benjamin R. Austin et al.*, Case No. A 918; v. *E. M. McClellan et al.*, Case No. A 499; v. *William Warwick*, Case No. A 558.

3. KENTUCKY

Deed Book A, Adair CC.
Deed Books 4, 6, 7, and 8, Green CC.
Deed Record 1, 1801-1805, and Deeds 2, 7-Part 2, 1811, 1826-32, Pulaski CC.
Deed Records I, 1817-19, K, 1819-22, and Recorded Deeds, 1817-19, Lincoln CC.
Files of Estates of John T. Sublette, 1812, File Box 30-31, and Lewis Sublette, 1827, File Box 32-33, Woodford CC.
Index to Marriages No. 1, 1784-1818, Marriage Certificates, 1784-1836, and Marriage Licenses, 1797-1800, Lincoln CC.
Lincoln County Tax Lists, 1799, 1800, 1804-1805, 1809-15, 1817, and 1819, Kentucky Historical Society, Frankfort.
Ordinary, 1811-12, and Ordinary, 1815, Lincoln CCC.
Order Book No. 7, 1809-19, and Order Books, 1812-20, Lincoln CC.
Order Books No. 1-6, 1799-1827, Pulaski CCC.
Orders No. 1-2, 1799-1815, Pulaski CC.
Pulaski County Tax Lists, 1801-1804, 1806-1808, Kentucky Historical Society.
Surveys-Green County, No. 662, Green CC.
Tavern Bonds, 1810-17, Lincoln CC.
The Little (Marriage) Book, 1793-1819, Green CC.
Will Book I, 1830, Woodford CC.
Woodford County Tax Lists, 1791-97, Kentucky Historical Society.

4. MISSOURI

Administrators Bonds, 1827–35, St. Charles CPC.

Callaway County Tax Lists, 1823 and 1835, MoSHi.

Chancery Record No. 2, 1838–45, St. Louis CCC.

Circuit Court Record A, 1839, Gasconade CCC.

Circuit Court Record A–2, 1844, Chariton CCC.

Circuit Court Record B, 1815–25, Cape Girardeau CCC.

Circuit Court Record B, 1842, Ste Genevieve CCC.

Circuit Court Record Vol. 2, 1835–38, Marion CCC.

Circuit Court Record 4, 1840, Lafayette CCC.

Circuit Court Records A and B, 1837–40, Ray CCC.

Circuit Court Records A and B, 1836–48, Saline CCC.

Circuit Court Record B, Cole CCC.

County Court Record, 1821–37, St. Charles CC.

Deed Record I, Jackson CRDO.

Deed Records E, F, and G, 1818[?]–28, St. Charles CRDO.

Deed Records B and E, Clay CRDO.

Deed Records C, D, and F, Ray CRDO.

Deed Records D, E, F, and S, 1841–45, Cole CRDO.

Deed Records F and G, 1820–31, Cape Girardeau CCC.

Executions, 1819–39, St. Charles CCC.

Executions, 1837–42, St. Louis CCC.

File of *Sublette* v. *Burgess and Miller*, File Box 10, Lafayette CCC.

File of *Sublette and Campbell* v. *Detchemendy*, File No. 24, Ste Genevieve CCC.

File of *Sublette and Campbell* v. *Tompkins Smollett*, Case No. 708, Marion CCC.

File of *Sublette and Campbell* v. *Williams*, File Box 2, Gasconade CCC.

File of *Wm. L. Sublette* v. *T. S. Barkley and H. A. Barkley*, Case No. 1036, Ralls CCC.

Files of *Austin Shelton admr. of John Gaither decd.* v. *Wm. L. Sublette*, File 3; *John R. White* v. *Milton Sublette*, File 75; *Jos. Cunningham admr. of David Cunningham decd.* v. *Wm. L. Sublette*, File 52; *St. Louis Gas Light Co.* v. *Wm. L. Sublette*, File 222; *Sublette and Campbell* v. *Charles Keneday*, File 187; v. *Cyrus Harper*, File 147; v. *Hannah Fletcher*, File 236; v. *Henry Fraeb*, File 43; v. *Jeremiah DeGroff Manny & Violet Primrose*, File 138; v. *John A. N. Ebbets*, File 513; v. *Joseph G. Laveille*, File 100;

v. *Lilburn W. Boggs and Angus S. Boggs,* File 16; v. *Louis Vasquez and Andrew W. Sublette,* File 288; v. *Perpetual Insurance Company,* File 372; v. *Peter and Joseph Powell,* File 88; v. *Robert W. Taylor,* File 633; v. *The Mineral Point Bank,* File 192; v. *Wm. H. Bleaker,* File 529; *Thomas G. Berry* v. *Wm. L. Sublette,* File 90; *Thomas Peniston et al.* v. *Summons Henry A. Steppe,* File 8027; *William Hannah admr. of John Hannah decd.* v. *Wm. L. Sublette,* File 2; *Wm. L. Sublette* v. *John Forstaken,* File 113; v. *Owen W. Grimes,* File 35; *Wm. L. Sublette for John F. Darby* v. *Hiram Darby,* File 529(2); St. Louis CCC.

Files of *Daniel Griffith* v. *P. A. Sublette and John Richards,* Court Files March Term 1820 to July Term 1820; *Sublette and Campbell* v. *Benjamin and Joseph Orrick,* File 9753; *The State of Missouri* v. *P. A. Sublette and Morgan Swope,* Court Files November Term 1819 to February Term 1821; and *The State of Missouri* v. *Solomon Whitley and William L. Sublette,* Court Files March Term 1823 to November Term 1823, St. Charles CCC.

Files of Estates of Frances S. Sublette, File 5073; Jedediah S. Smith, File 930; Solomon P. Sublette, File 5072; William H. Ashley, File 1377; William L. Sublette, File 2052, St. Louis PC.

Files of Estates of Isabella Sublette, No. 3419, and Phillip A. Sublette, No. 3420, St. Charles CPC.

Files of *Jacob Stollings* v. *Sublette and Campbell,* File No. 563, and *Sublette and Campbell* v. *J. Stollings,* File No. 561, Ray CCC.

Files of *L. W. Boggs et al.* v. *Sublette and Campbell,* Case No. 586; *Robert Campbell* v. *A. L. Boggs et al.,* Case No. 518; *State ex Rel. Sublette and Campbell* v. *N. Melton et al.,* Case No. 660; *Wm. L. Sublette et al.* v. *A. Kennedy,* Case No. 476; v. *James A. Crump,* Case No. 647; v. *John C. Gorden et al.,* Cases No. 811, 866, and 938; v. *Wm. H. Dyer et al.,* Case No. 473, Cole CCC.

Files of Recommendation of J. S. Besser for Constable, File Box 3-2-2; and Road Petition of July, 1820, Road Papers 1820–29, St. Charles CC.

Files of *Sublette and Campbell* v. *H. C. Miller and Others,* Case No. 10; and v. *Thos. L. Price,* Case No. 12, Saline CCC.

Letters, 1815–28, Probate Record I, 1827–36, and Wills & Letters of Administration & Letters Testamentary I and II, 1822–52, St. Charles CPC.

Marriage Record, 1807–26, St. Charles CRDO.

Marriage Record A, 1821–36, Callaway CRDO.

Marriage Records 3 From January 4, 1843 to February 18, 1848, St. Louis CRDO.

Minute Book, June 9, 1835–September 29, 1838, and Record Books A–2, B, and D, 1816–40, St. Charles CCC.

Original Wills S, 1849, Cape Girardeau CPC.

Originals K, Q, R, T, U, V, X, Z, C–2, D–2, E–2, F–2, I–2, K–2, M–2, S–2, T–2, X–2, E–3, G–3, H–3, I–3, R–3, U–3, and General Records A–2, F–2, K–2, Q–3, T–3, G–4, G–6, P–4, Z, W, Book 196, Book 313, and Book 336, St. Louis CRDO.

Record (3) Court of Common Pleas, 1842, St. Louis CCC.

Record of Land Owners St. Louis County, 1841, St. Louis CCC.

Record of Wills C, 1840–50, and Records L, M, 1846–50, St. Louis PC.

Records C and E, Civil Cases, 1839–43, and Record F, Jackson CCC.

Records of St. Louis County Court Nos. 1–3, 1824–44, Register's Office, City Hall, St. Louis.

St. Charles County Census Records, 1817 and 1819, and St. Charles County Tax Lists, 1818–19, St. Charles CC.

Township Plats I, St. Charles CRDO.

D. *Municipal Records*

1. MISSOURI

P. A. Sublette Account Book and Legal Record, 1818–21, and Record Book A, 1820–35, City Hall, St. Charles.

Register of Water Licenses, 1835–39, Office of the Comptroller of the City of St. Louis, City Hall, St. Louis.

III. GOVERNMENT PUBLICATIONS

A. *United States Congress*

House Executive Documents. 19 Cong., 1 sess., *No.117;* 21 Cong., 2 sess., *No. 41;* 23 Cong., 1 sess., *No. 45.*

Senate Documents. 18 Cong., 1 sess., *No. 1;* 20 Cong., 1 sess., *No. 96;* 23 Cong., 2 sess., *No. 69.*

B. *State of Missouri Records*

Acts of the First General Assembly of the State of Missouri . . . 1820. St. Louis, 1820.

Bay, S. M. (reporter). *Reports of Cases Argued and Decided in the Supreme Court of the State of Missouri, From 1839 to 1840.* Jefferson City, 1841.

Geyer, Henry S. (reporter). *A Digest of the Laws of Missouri Territory.* St. Louis, 1818.

In the Supreme Court of Missouri, October Term 1902, Division No. 1.

Journal of the House of Representatives of the State of Missouri . . . (1836), Bowling Green, 1837; (1840), Jackson, 1841; (1842), Jefferson City, 1843; (1846), Jefferson City, 1847.

Journal of the Senate of the State of Missouri . . . (1836), Bowling Green, 1837; (1842), Jefferson City, 1843; (1844), Jefferson City, 1845.

Laws of the State of Missouri . . . (1836), St. Louis, 1841.

Rader, Perry S. (reporter). *Reports of Cases Determined by the Supreme Court of the State of Missouri Between February 18, 1928, and May 18, 1928.* Columbia, 1929.

C. *City of St. Louis*

City Ordinances 301–800, 1835–41.

IV. NEWSPAPERS

Arkansas: *Arkansas Gazette* (Little Rock), 1826–27, 1831, 1836, 1839.

California: *Alta California* (San Francisco), February 21, 1852; *Los Angeles Star*, December 31, 1853, April 22, 1854; *Sacramento Daily Union*, December 29, 1853; *San Francisco Herald*, June 8, 1853.

District of Columbia: *Daily National Intelligencer*, April 22, 1829; *Globe*, December 14, 1832.

Georgia: *Savannah Daily Republican*, May 27, August 19, 1843.

Illinois: *Edwardsville Spectator*, 1819–22; *Pioneer of the Valley of the Mississippi* (Rock-Spring), April 24, 1829; *Western (or Illinois) Intelligencer* (Kaskaskia), 1816–19.

Indiana: *Wabash Express* (Terre Haute), March 29, 1843.

Kentucky: *Kentucky Gazette* (Lexington), 1787–1800; *Louisville Public Advertiser*, August 6, 1823; *Reporter*, or *Kentucky Reporter* (Lexington), 1812–17; *Western Citizen* (Paris), December 30, 1817.

Louisiana: *Daily Picayune* (New Orleans), 1843–44; *Weekly Picayune* (New Orleans), 1843.

Maryland: *American and Commercial Daily Advertiser* (Baltimore), April 17, December 6, 1843; *Baltimore Republican & Commercial Advertiser*, December 13, 1832; *Niles' Weekly* (or *National*) *Register* (Baltimore), 1827, 1834–35, 1843.

Missouri: *Boonville Observer*, 1845; *Daily Evening Gazette* (St. Louis), 1838–44; *Daily Evening Herald and Commercial Advertiser* (St. Louis), 1835; *Daily Peoples' Organ*, or *Peoples' Organ* (St. Louis), 1844–45; *Independent Patriot*, or *Southern Advocate* (Jackson), 1821–24, 1838, 1844; *Jefferson Inquirer* (Jefferson City), 1842–44, November 6, 1847; *Lexington Weekly Express*, August 12, 1845; *Mill Boy* (St. Louis), 1844; *Missouri Advocate and St. Louis Enquirer*, 1825–26; *Missouri Argus* (St. Louis), 1836–41; *Missouri Gazette*, or *Missouri Gazette & Illinois Advertiser*, or *Missouri Gazette & Public Advertiser*, or *Missouri Republican*, or *Daily Missouri Republican* (St. Louis), 1816–55, October 17, 1879; *Missouri Herald* (Jackson), 1819–20; *Missouri Intelligencer*, or *Missouri Intelligencer and Boon's Lick Advertiser* (Franklin, Fayette, and Columbia), 1819–35; *Missouri Saturday News* (St. Louis), 1838–40; *Missouri Statesman* (Columbia), 1844; *Missourian* (St. Charles), 1820–22; *Missourian* (St. Louis), 1844; *Old School Democrat and St. Louis Herald*, 1843; *The Radical* (Bowling Green), April 15, 1843; *Saint Louis American*, August 1, 1845; *St. Louis Beacon*, 1830–32; *St. Louis Chronicle*, September 12, 1895; *St. Louis Commercial Bulletin and Missouri Literary Register*, or *Daily Commercial Bulletin*, 1835, May 4, 1840; *Saint Louis Daily Evening News*, November 9, 1853; *St. Louis Democrat*, March 16, 1844; *Saint Louis Dispatch*, June 9, 1869; *St. Louis Enquirer*, 1819–20, 1823; *St. Louis Globe Democrat*, April 30, 1899, May 20, 1906; *St. Louis New Era*, 1843–44; *St. Louis Post Dispatch*, October 26, 1923, January 28, 1926; *St. Louis Times*, March 2, 1833, August 4, 1872; *Weekly Reveille* (St. Louis), March 1, 1847; *Western Atlas and Evening Gazette* (St. Louis), 1842; *Western Pioneer* (Liberty), November 1, 1844.

Ohio: *Cincinnati Advertiser & Ohio Phoenix*, May 19, 1830; *Daily Cincinnati Gazette*, July 17, 19, 1845.

Oregon: *Oregon Spectator* (Oregon City), December 24, 1853.

Pennsylvania: *Daily Morning Post* (Pittsburgh), July 25, 1845; *Pittsburgh Morning Chronicle*, July 25, 1845.

V. BOOKS AND PAMPHLETS

Abel, Annie H. (ed.). *Chardon's Journal at Fort Clark, 1834–1839.* Pierre, 1932.

Alter, J. Cecil. *James Bridger, Trapper, Frontiersman, Scout, and Guide.* Salt Lake City, 1925.

Anderson, William Marshall. *Adventures in the Rocky Mountains in 1834.* Reprinted from the *American Turf Register* of 1837. New York, 1951.

Ashton, John. *History of Shorthorns in Missouri Prior to the Civil War,* in *Monthly Bulletin* (Missouri State Board of Agriculture), Vol. XXI (Jefferson City, 1923).

Audubon, John James. *Audubon and His Journals.* Ed. by Maria R. Audubon and Elliott Coues. 2 vols. London, 1898.

Beckwourth, James P. *The Life and Adventures of James P. Beckwourth, Mountaineer, Scout, Pioneer, and Chief of the Crow Nation of Indians.* Ed. by C. G. Leland. London, 1892.

Bidwell, Percy W., and John I. Falconer. *History of Agriculture in the Northern United States 1620–1860.* Washington, D. C., 1925.

Boyer, Mary Joan. *The Old Gravois Coal Diggings.* Festus, Mo., 1954.

Bruff, J. Goldsborough. *Gold Rush: The Journals, Drawings, and Other Papers of J. Goldsborough Bruff.* Ed. by Georgia W. Read and Ruth Gaines. 2 vols. New York, 1944.

Bryan, W. S., and Robert Rose. *A History of the Pioneer Families of Missouri.* . . . St. Louis, 1876.

Buel, Leopard, and Floyd C. Shoemaker (eds.). *The Messages and Proclamations of the Governors of the State of Missouri,* I. Columbia, Mo., 1922.

Burnett, Peter H. *Recollections and Opinions of an Old Pioneer.* New York, 1880.

Cable, John Ray. *The Bank of the State of Missouri* (*Columbia University Studies in History, Economics and Public Law,* Vol. CII, No. 2). New York, 1923.

Campbell, Robert. *The Rocky Mountain Letters of Robert Campbell.* Printed for Frederick W. Beinecke. New York, 1955.

Catlin, George. *Illustrations of the Manners, Customs, and Condition of the North American Indians.* 2 vols. London, 1850.

Chambers, W. N. *Old Bullion Benton: Senator from the New West; Thomas Hart Benton, 1782–1858.* Boston, 1956.

Chittenden, Hiram Martin. *History of Early Steamboat Navigation on the Missouri River.* 2 vols. New York, 1903.

———. *The American Fur Trade of the Far West.* 2 vols. New York, 1935.

Clyman, James. *James Clyman, American Frontiersman, 1792–1881.* Ed. by Charles L. Camp. San Francisco, 1928.

Coleman, J. Winston, Jr. *Stage-Coach Days in the Bluegrass.* Louisville, 1936.

Collins, Lewis. *History of Kentucky.* 2 vols. Covington, Ky., 1882.

Coman, Katharine. *Economic Beginnings of the Far West: How We Won the Land Beyond the Mississippi.* 2 vols. New York, 1912.

Coutant, C. G. *The History of Wyoming from the Earliest Known Discoveries.* Laramie, 1899.

Cowan, B. O., and W. L. Nelson. *Shorthorn Cattle in Missouri,* in *Monthly Bulletin* (Missouri State Board of Agriculture), Vol. XII (Jefferson City, 1914).

Dale, Harrison C. *The Ashley-Smith Explorations and the Discovery of a Central Route to the Pacific, 1822–1829.* Glendale, Calif., 1941.

Dana, Edmund E. *Geographical Sketches of the Western Country.* Cincinnati, 1819.

Dawson, Nicholas Cheyenne. *Narrative of Nicholas Cheyenne Dawson: Overland to California in '41 & '49, and Texas in '51.* Ed. by Charles L. Camp. San Francisco, 1933.

De Smet, Father Pierre-Jean, S. J. *Life, Letters, and Travels of Father Pierre-Jean De Smet, S. J. 1801–1873.* Ed. by H. M. Chittenden and A. I. Richardson. 4 vols. New York, 1905.

De Voto, Bernard. *Across the Wide Missouri.* Boston, 1947.

Dick, Everett. *The Sod-House Frontier, 1854–1890.* Lincoln, 1954.

Emigrant's Guide, or Pocket Geography of the Western States and Territories, The. Cincinnati, 1818.

Flint, Timothy. *Recollections of the Last Ten Years.* Boston, 1826.

Gray, Lewis Cecil. *History of Agriculture in the Southern United States to 1860.* 2 vols. Washington, D. C., 1933.

Gregg, Josiah. *Commerce of the Prairies.* 2 vols. New York, 1844.

Harper, Frank B. *Fort Union and Its Neighbors.* N. p., n. d.

Hoffman, Charles F. *A Winter in the West.* New York, 1835.

Hulbert, Archer B., and Dorothy P. (eds.). *The Oregon Crusade.* Denver, 1935.

Ingraham, Prentiss (ed.). *Seventy Years on the Frontier*. Chicago and New York, 1893.

Irving, Washington. *The Adventures of Captain Bonneville, U. S. A.* New York, 1859.

Jillson, Willard R. *The Kentucky Land Grants*. Louisville, 1925.

———. *Old Kentucky Entries and Deeds*. Louisville, 1926.

John Fletcher Darby of Missouri. N. p., n. d.

Larpenteur, Charles. *Forty Years a Fur Trader on the Upper Missouri: The Personal Narrative of Charles Larpenteur, 1833–1872*. Ed. by Elliott Coues. 2 vols. New York, 1898.

Lavender, David. *Bent's Fort*. Garden City, 1954.

Leonard, Zenas. *Adventures of Zenas Leonard, Fur Trader and Trapper, 1831–1836*. Ed. by W. F. Wagner. Cleveland, 1904.

Lucas, J. B. C. *Letters of Hon. J. B. C. Lucas from 1815 to 1836*. Ed. by B. C. Lucas. St. Louis, 1905.

Ludlow, N. M. *Dramatic Life as I Found It*. St. Louis, 1880.

Lyman, George D. *John Marsh, Pioneer: The Life Story of a Trail-Blazer on Six Frontiers*. New York, 1931.

McAdams, Ednah. *Kentucky Pioneer and Court Records*. Lexington, 1929.

McCoy, Alexander, and others. *Pioneering on the Plains*. Kaukauna, Wis., 1924.

McLoughlin, John. *The Letters of John McLoughlin from Fort Vancouver to the Governor and Committee: First Series, 1825–38*. Ed. by E. E. Rich. (*Publications of the Champlain Society, Hudson's Bay Company*, Vol. IV). Toronto, 1941.

Marsh, James B. *Four Years in the Rockies; or, The Adventures of Isaac P. Rose*. New Castle and Columbus, 1884.

Michaux, François André. *Travels to the West of the Alleghany Mountains*. Vol. II of Thwaites' *Early Western Travels, q.v.*

Miller, Alfred Jacob. *The West of Alfred Jacob Miller*. Ed. by Marvin C. Ross. Norman, 1951.

Minutes of the South District Association of Baptists, Met at M'Cormacks Meeting House, in Lincoln County, on the Third Saturday in August, 1812. Lexington, Ky., n. d.

Morgan, Dale. *Jedediah Smith*. New York and Indianapolis, 1953.

Murray, Charles A. *Travels in North America During the Years 1834, 1835 & 1836*. 2 vols. London, 1839.

Neihardt, John G. *Collected Poems of John G. Neihardt.* New York, 1926.

Nevins, Allan. *Frémont, the West's Great Adventurer.* 2 vols. New York and London, 1928.

New Helvetia Diary of Events from 1845-48. San Francisco, 1939.

Parker, Samuel. *Journal of an Exploring Tour Beyond the Rocky Mountains . . . in the Years 1835, '36, and '37.* Ithaca, N. Y., 1838.

Phillips, Paul C. (ed.). *Life in the Rocky Mountains.* Denver, 1940.

Porter, Kenneth W. *John Jacob Astor, Business Man.* 2 vols. Cambridge, Mass., 1931.

Primm, James Neal. *Economic Policy in the Development of a Western State: Missouri 1820-1860.* Cambridge, Mass., 1954.

Prudhommeaux, Jules. *Icarie et son Fondateur Étienne Cabet.* Paris, 1907.

Rogin, Leo. *The Introduction of Farm Machinery in Its Relation to the Productivity of Labor in the Agriculture of the United States During the Nineteenth Century (University of California Publications in Economics,* Vol. IX). Berkeley, 1931.

Rollins, Philip Ashton. *The Cowboy.* New York, 1936.

Sheldon, Addison E. (ed.). *Records of Fort Atkinson 1819—1827,* IV–VI. Lincoln, 1915.

Simpson, George. *Part of Dispatch from George Simpson, Esqr, Governor of Ruperts Land to the Governor and Committee of the Hudson's Bay Company, London, March 1, 1829, Continued and Completed March 24 and June 5, 1829.* Ed. by E. E. Rich. *(Publications of the Champlain Society, Hudson's Bay Company,* Vol. X). Toronto, 1947.

Steele, John. *The Traveler's Companion Through the Great Interior.* Galena, Ill., 1854.

Sullivan, Maurice S. *The Travels of Jedediah Smith: A Documentary Outline Including the Journal of the Great American Pathfinder.* Santa Ana, Calif., 1934.

Talbot, Theodore. *The Journals of Theodore Talbot, 1843 and 1849-52.* Ed. by Charles H. Carey. Portland, Ore., 1931.

Thwaites, Reuben Gold (ed.). *Early Western Travels.* 32 vols. Cleveland, 1904-1907.

Tibbals, Alma O. *A History of Pulaski County, Kentucky.* Louisville, 1952.

Triplett, Frank. *Conquering the Wilderness.* Chicago, 1895.

Upham, Charles W. *Life, Explorations, and Public Services of John Charles Frémont.* Boston, 1856.

Vandiveer, Clarence A. *The Fur Trade and Early Western Exploration.* Cleveland, 1929.

Victor, (Mrs.) F. Fuller. *The River of the West.* Hartford, Toledo, Newark, and San Francisco, 1870.

Ware, Joseph E. *The Emigrants' Guide to California.* St. Louis, 1849.

Wetmore, Alphonso. *Gazetteer of the State of Missouri.* St. Louis, 1837.

Williams, Joseph. *Narrative of a Tour from the State of Indiana to the Oregon Territory in the Years 1841–2.* New York, 1921.

Wood, Dean E. *The Old Santa Fé Trail from the Missouri River.* Kansas City, 1951.

Wyeth, John B. *Oregon.* Cambridge, Mass., 1833.

VI. ARTICLES

Anderson, William Marshall. "Anderson's Narrative of a Ride to the Rocky Mountains in 1834" (ed. by Albert J. Partoll), *Frontier and Midland*, Vol. XIX (1938), 54–63.

Atherton, Lewis E. "Western Mercantile Participation in the Indian Trade," *Pacific Historical Review*, Vol. IX (September, 1940), 281–95.

Aull, James and Robert. "Letters of James and Robert Aull" (ed. by Ralph P. Bieber), *Missouri Historical Society Collections*, Vol. V (June, 1928), 267–310.

Belden, Josiah. "The First Overland Emigrant Train to New California," *Touring Topics* (June, 1930), 14–18.

Bingham, Henry Vest. "The Road West in 1818: The Diary of Henry Vest Bingham" (ed. by Marie Windell), *Missouri Historical Review*, Vol. XL (January, 1946), 174–204.

Bott, E. A. O'Neil. "Joseph Murphy's Contribution to the Development of the West," *Missouri Historical Review*, Vol. XLVII (October, 1952), 18–28.

"Bradley Manuscript–Book II," *Contributions to the Historical Society of Montana*, Vol. VIII (1917), 127–96.

Campbell, Robert. "Correspondence of Robert Campbell, 1834–1845" (ed. by Stella M. Drumm and Isaac H. Lionberger), *Glimpses of the Past*, Vol. VII (January–June, 1941), 3–65.

Carey, Charles Henry. "The Mission Record Book of the Methodist

Episcopal Church, Willamette Station, Oregon Territory, North America, Commenced 1834," *Quarterly of the Oregon Historical Society*, Vol. XXIII (September, 1922), 230–66.

Day, (Mrs.) F. H. "Sketches of the Early Settlers of California Isaac J. Sparks," *The Hesperian*, Vol. II (July, 1859), 193–200.

DeLand, C. E., and D. Robinson. "Fort Tecumseh and Fort Pierre Letter Books," *South Dakota Historical Collections*, Vol. IX (1918), 69–240.

Dorsey, Dorothy B. "The Panic and Depression of 1837–43 in Missouri," *Missouri Historical Review*, Vol. XXX (January, 1936), 132–61.

Drumm, Stella M. "William Lewis Sublette," in Dumas Malone (ed.), *Dictionary of American Biography*, XVIII, 189.

Dupre, Huntley. "The French in Early Kentucky," *Filson Club History Quarterly*, Vol. XV (April, 1941), 78–104.

Eaton, W. Clement. "Nathaniel Wyeth's Oregon Expedition," *Pacific Historical Review*, Vol. IV (June, 1935), 100–13.

Fisher, Rev. Ezra. "Correspondence of the Reverend Ezra Fisher" (ed. by Sarah F. Henderson and Nellie E. and Kenneth S. Latourette), *Quarterly of the Oregon Historical Society*, Vol. XVI (September, 1915), 278–311.

Genealogy and History, Vol. VIII, No. 1 (February 15, 1947), 4.

Geyer, Charles A. "Notes on the Vegetation and General Character of the Missouri and Oregon Territories . . . During the years 1843 and 1844," *London Journal of Botany*, Vol. IV (1845), 479–92, 653–62.

Gronert, Theodore G. "Trade in the Blue-Grass Region, 1810–1820," *Mississippi Valley Historical Review*, Vol. V (December, 1918), 313–23.

Guthrie, Chester L., and Leo L. Gerald. "Upper Missouri Agency: An Account of the Indian Administration on the Frontier," *Pacific Historical Review*, Vol. X (March, 1941), 47–56.

Hafen, LeRoy R. "Mountain Men—Andrew W. Sublette," *Colorado Magazine*, Vol. X (September, 1933), 179–84.

"Jedediah Strong Smith," *Illinois Monthly Magazine*, Vol. XXI (June, 1832), 383–98.

Kennerly, James. "Diary of James Kennerly 1823–1826" (ed. by Edgar B. Wesley), *Missouri Historical Society Collections*, Vol. VI (October, 1928), 41–97.

Lane, William Carr. "Letters of William Carr Lane 1819–1831," *Glimpses of the Past*, Vol. VII (July–September, 1940), 56–114.

Lee, Rev. Jason. "Diary of Rev. Jason Lee—Part I," *Quarterly of the Oregon Historical Society*, Vol. XVII (June, 1916), 116–46.

Mattes, Merrill J. "Hiram Scott, Fur Trader," *Nebraska History*, Vol. XXVI (July–September, 1945), 127–162.

———. "Jackson Hole, Crossroads of the Western Fur Trade, 1807–1840," *Pacific Northwest Quarterly*, Vol. XXXVII (April, 1946), 87–108.

Mayo, Bernard, "Lexington: Frontier Metropolis," in Eric F. Goldman (ed.), *Historiography and Urbanization Essays in American History in Honor of W. Stull Holt*. Baltimore, 1941.

Merk, Frederick (ed.). "The snake Country Expedition Correspondence 1824–1825," *Mississippi Valley Historical Review*, Vol. XXI (June, 1934–March, 1935), 63–67.

Miller, Henry B. "The Journal of Henry B. Miller" (ed. by Thomas M. Marshall), *Missouri Historical Society Collections*, Vol. VI (June, 1931), 213–87.

Ogden, Peter Skene. "The Peter Skene Ogden Journals" (ed. by T. C. Elliott), *Quarterly of the Oregon Historical Society*, Vol. X (December, 1909), 331–65; Vol. XI (March, 1910), 355–99.

Powers, Kate N. B. "Across the Continent Seventy Years Ago," *Quarterly of the Oregon Historical Society*, Vol. II (March, 1902), 82–106.

Reading, Pierson Barton. "Journal of Pierson Barton Reading" (ed. by Philip B. Bekeart), *Quarterly of the Society of California Pioneers*, Vol. VII (September, 1930), 148–98.

Reid, Russell, and Clell G. Gannon (eds.). "Journal of the Atkinson-O'Fallon Expedition," *North Dakota Historical Quarterly*, Vol. IV (1929), 5–56.

Ross, Alexander. "Journal of Alexander Ross—Snake Country Expedition, 1824" (ed. by T. C. Elliott), *Quarterly of the Oregon Historical Society*, Vol. XIV (December, 1913), 366–88.

Russell, Bessie K. "My Hunting Trip to the Rockies in 1843," *Colorado Magazine*, Vol. XXII (January, 1945), 23–38.

Russell, (Mrs.) Daniel R. "Early Days in St. Louis from the Memoirs of an Old Citizen," *Missouri Historical Society Collections*, Vol. III (1911), 407–22.

Stephens, F. F. "Banking and Finance in Missouri in the Thirties,"

Proceedings of the Mississippi Valley Historical Association, Vol. X (1918–21), 122–34.

Talbert, Charles G. "William Whitley, 1749–1813," *Filson Club History Quarterly*, Vol. XXV (April, 1951), 101–21.

Tobie, E. H. "Joseph L. Meek, a Conspicuous Personality, I, 1829–1834," *Oregon Historical Quarterly*, Vol. XXXIX (June, 1938), 123–46.

Viles, Jonas. "Old Franklin: A Frontier Town of the Twenties," *Mississippi Valley Historical Review*, Vol. IX (March, 1923), 269–82.

Waldo, William. "Recollections of a Septuagenarian," *Glimpses of the Past*, Vol. V (April–June, 1938), 59–94.

Warner, J. J. "Reminiscences of Early California from 1831 to 1846," *Annual Publications of the Historical Society of Southern California*, Vol. VII, Parts 2–3 (1907–1908), 176–93.

Wilhelm, Paul. "First Journey to North America in the Years 1822 to 1824," *South Dakota Historical Collections*, Vol. XIX (1938), 7–474.

Work, John. "The Journal of John Work; July 5–September 15, 1826" (ed. by T. C. Elliott), *Washington Historical Quarterly*, Vol. VI (January, 1915), 26–49.

VII. INTERVIEWS

Esther W. Burch, June 23, 1951, Stanford, Ky.; W. N. Craig, June 23, 1951, Stanford, Ky.; Mrs. E. B. Federa, June 19, 1951, Louisville, Ky.

Index

Bill Sublette: Mountain Man is set in 11-point Janson, leaded two points. Janson is one of the best types produced during the period when Dutch type founders and printers were in the ascendance, in the last half of the seventeenth century. It is one of the most popular faces for fine bookwork in this country. The title page drawing is by Joe Beeler.

University of Oklahoma Press: Norman